HISTORY OF THE RENAISSANCE
1350–1550

BOOK V – POLITICS and POLITICAL THEORY

by
EMIL LUCKI

University of Utah Press

Library of Congress Catalog Card 64-1883

Table of Contents

List of Maps

Editor's Note

D R. EMIL LUCKI's *History of the Renaissance* is the product of many years of study and teaching in the field and of his conviction that in the past some important phases of Renaissance civilization were not given sufficient emphasis in the general histories of the Renaissance. The result quite naturally turned out to be a thorough and a comprehensive manuscript, but too large to be published at today's costs as a single volume; and since printing it in two volumes was precluded by the organization of the work in five parts, the decision was therefore made to conform to the organization of the manuscript and to print it in five quality, but modestly priced, paperbacks. This latter project is now under way with the present Book V being the fourth of the series to be printed.

Aside from the obvious virtues of a small and inexpensive book, two other important considerations dictated the decision.

While the series on the Renaissance is labeled "history," the subject matter of each book is of such a nature that the individual books in the series should appeal not only to students of history but also to students in the various other disciplines that are concerned with the study of Western culture. Thus, students of economics and business should find Book I, *Economy and Society*, of much value; and students of religion will discover Book II, *Church and Religion*, equally useful. Book III, *Education, Learning and Thought*, may be expected to appeal to students interested in education, philosophy, and science; while Book IV, *Literature and Art*, may serve the needs of those majoring in these fields. Finally, the present book on politics and political theory should be welcome to students interested in political history. Thus, while the series as a whole can be used as a history textbook on the Renaissance, individual books can be used as collateral and enrichment reading in other courses.

Another reason for publishing the manuscript in several volumes is to make it easily available to the general public. The message and the style of the work are of such a nature that the work should be made available to as wide an audience as possible; and publishing it in one expensive volume or even in two would have defeated the purpose — hence the decision to print it in five handy books.

The University of Utah Press is indeed pleased to have a part in publishing Professor Lucki's *History of the Renaissance*. We believe it is a work which both in its entirety and severally through its parts will leave its mark in the academic world and among the reading public at large.

A. R. MORTENSEN

Preface to the Series

O NE WAY to ascertain the character of a society at a given epoch is to study its economy, religion and church, education and thought, literature and art, and its politics. If the purpose of the inquiry is also to discover in what ways this society differs from that of the preceding age, then a similar examination of the civilization of the earlier period becomes a necessity.

Such are the purposes and nature of this series of five small books on the Renaissance. They will attempt to describe Renaissance civilization and at the same time to discover in what ways this civilization was new and to what extent it was an outgrowth of the Middle Ages.

The purposes of the work naturally determine the chronological limits of the period to be studied. In general, scholars who write about the Renaissance date it approximately from 1350 to 1550. However, while the span of these two centuries may be accepted as the core of the Renaissance period, the dates 1350 and 1550 cannot possibly be regarded as fixed termini. In connection with the history of the church, for example, the date 1517, the year when Luther posted his ninety-five theses, has far more significance as a dividing date than the year 1550. It would be more meaningful, therefore, to stop the survey of church history at 1517 than at 1550. On the other hand, to terminate the survey of astronomy at 1550 would be unjustified, for the Copernican revolution, although made public in 1543, did not gain acceptance until at least a century had elapsed. Similarly, the logical beginning of the study of Renaissance Papacy is not with the events of the year 1350 but with the clash between Boniface VIII and Philip IV of France which occurred some fifty years earlier; and the study of Italian Renaissance painting, not with the works of some painter or painters of the year 1350, but with those of Giotto, whose dates are 1276–1336, or with those of Cimabue who lived even earlier, from about 1240 to 1301. It is clear, therefore, that in any survey of the Renaissance age the beginning and the terminal dates will vary with each aspect of the Renaissance civilization. Dates which may be appropriate for literature may not be appropriate for science, and dates which may hold true for Italy may not apply to Germany.

Aside from the matter of dating the Renaissance, three other factors have influenced the nature and the organization of this work.

One of these additional factors is the secondary purpose of the work, namely, the attempt to discover how the Renaissance civilization was influenced by the preceding age. To answer this crucial question it is necessary to look at the pre-Renaissance century; and so, in general, each phase of the civilization is treated in two stages, the late medieval stage and the Renaissance stage.

A very strong second factor is the desire to provide the reader with an adequate cross-sectional view of each phase of the civilization as well as with its historical, developmental process. If the focus were on the latter alone, then the work would result in a survey of the new developments, in an account, for example, of the growth of a capitalistic economy and not in a picture of the entire economy, or of the decline of the church and not in a view of the church as a whole. Such a treatment would simply reinforce the traditional notion that the Renaissance was a period of innovations, which, while true in part, is certainly in need of revision.

The third factor is the desire to show the several sides to the Renaissance civilization. To accomplish this task, clearly all the major aspects of the civilization need to be examined, and the examination must be comprehensive. Accordingly, some aspects, such as agriculture, economic theory, church organization, educational system, historiography, and diplomacy, are studied at length because to date they have been slighted in histories on the Renaissance; while others, even those which are usually emphasized, such as humanism and art, are treated in considerable detail in order to bring out clearly their dependence on, and deviation from, the medieval civilization.

If this comprehensiveness has resulted, in some places, in a wealth of factual information, the reader is assured that the facts are presented not as ends in themselves, to be learned, but as guides to interpretation. With too few facts at his disposal the reader would have insufficient information upon which to base his judgments, and he would have to depend upon the author's interpretations. While some dependence on the writer is inescapable, it should be reduced to the minimum, as the purpose of any academic discipline is to encourage independence of mind but dependence on evidence. The facts in these books are intended to serve just such a purpose. EMIL LUCKI

Preface to Book V

I T WOULD be the height of optimism to believe that one could add much to the knowledge of Europe's political history during the Renaissance period. Here and there some particulars discovered by recent research might be added or used to correct some old facts, but generally the additions or the revisions would not be substantial. Hence, if a work on this subject might be justified it would be on the grounds either of wider coverage or of difference in emphasis. This volume attempts to do both.

As to wider coverage, this book gives somewhat more attention to central-eastern Europe than most general histories on the Renaissance are wont to do. And the reason for looking beyond western Europe is the fact that the first century of the Renaissance, 1350 to about 1450, is exactly the period when Hungary and Poland-Lithuania came of age politically and internationally. Indeed, for a while they actually became a second focus of European power politics; for while Italy and Byzantium were losing to the Turks, and Spain was suffering from the "Century of Troubles," and England and France were tearing each other apart in the Hundred Years' War, these two countries were consolidating, conducting a crusade against the Ottomans, and, in the case of Poland-Lithuania, reducing the Teutonic Knights. This was tantamount to the addition of a second locus of political power, and so the area deserves more attention than it has received in past histories of the Renaissance.

As to the difference in emphasis it is in keeping with the plan of this entire series of books on the Renaissance. Instead of focusing on the political changes and innovations of the Renaissance period, an appoach which inevitably leads to an exaggerated view of the Renaissance as a "new" age, the book examines both the continuations and the changes in order to discover whether the "new monarchies" were as "new" as the title implies. The book, therefore, is primarily a comparative study of the politics of the late Middle Ages and of the Renaissance period.

If this comparison is to be brought out effectively, it is necessary to approach the subject topically as well as chronologically. Accordingly, the book examines the internal and international developments separately for each period while observing chronology within each topic.

In writing such a comparative history there is always the danger that the simple narrative may be slighted and that the student who is not familiar with the political story of the area and the period concerned may find himself at a loss here and there. If so, the student can do a little preliminary reading of survey histories. It is easier for him to get the necessary narrative than to work out the comparisons which are often, too often, missing in general histories and which require somewhat deeper knowledge than is provided in simple surveys. It is the hope, however, that the emphasis on the comparative will more than compensate for any thinness of the chronological narrative.

EMIL LUCKI

CHAPTER **I**

Internal Political
Developments on the Eve
of the Renaissance

THE RENAISSANCE period in European political history is generally associated with such monarchs as Louis XI and Francis I of France, Henry VIII and Elizabeth of England, Ferdinand and Isabella of Spain, Matthias Corvinus of Hungary, Gustavus Vasa of Sweden, and Suleiman the Magnificent of Turkey, and, on the strength of their accomplishments, the period is characterized as one of powerful, centralizing monarchies and of rising national states. This characterization has considerable truth in it, but it is obviously one-sided, as the political history of two entire centuries cannot be judged by the deeds of the great rulers alone. The appraisal should be made on a more comprehensive basis, and it should include consideration of the political trends on the eve of the Renaissance. The resulting picture may well require a revision of the popular view.

Political Physiognomy

An examination of a political map of pre-Renaissance Europe shortly before 1350 will reveal a political physiognomy which both resembles that of modern Europe and differs from it. In the Iberian Peninsula there is a recognizable Portugal, but the remainder of the peninsula is constituted not of a united Spain, but of four smaller states, the three Christian states of Castile, Navarre, and Aragon and, in the south, the Moorish principality of Granada. France is there, but it is not modern France; for, in the west, Aquitaine is in the hands of the English, although only as a fief of the French kings; and in the east, Provence, Burgundy, and a strip of territory north to Flanders are not yet part of the kingdom. England is not yet Great Britain, as Wales is only nominally part of it and Scotland is independent and hostile. There is no Germany, but a congeries of princely and ecclesiastical states and free towns, loosely bound in the Holy Roman Empire. Nor is there a political Italy. Instead, there are within the peninsula a number of small states: some merchant republics — Genoa, Venice, Florence, Siena; some princely despotisms — Milan, Ferrara, Verona; some feudal principalities — Savoy, Montferrat; the monarchies of Naples and of Sicily; and the papal states. In the Scandinavian peninsula, Denmark, Norway, and Sweden are extant already. But along the Baltic are to be found the cities of the Hanseatic League and the territories carved out by the two crusading orders, Livonian Brothers of the Sword and the Teutonic Knights. In central Europe, Poland is in existence, but it is not as extensive as pre-World War II Poland; Lithuania is there, extending farther south, all the way to the Black Sea, but it is a tribal rather than a modern state despite its size; and Hungary is recognizable. But in the Balkans the situation is quite different. Serbia and Bulgaria occupy most of the region. There is no Romania, but there is a Byzantine Empire, much smaller than in the early Middle Ages and confined to the southeast angle of the peninsula. In place of Greece there are a number of Venetian outposts and several principalities held by princes of western origin, the result primarily of the conquest of Byzantium by the Fourth Crusade. Farther to the east, in what today is Russia, there are some strangely named principalities, among which is Muscovy, the heart of future Russia, and a number of ill-defined Mongol territories. In sum, without paying attention to exact boundary delineations, the map shows some features that are recognizably modern and some that are quite different.

Spain — Divided and Turbulent but Showing Signs of Consolidation

In the four Christian principalities in the Iberian Peninsula the political situation on the eve of the Renaissance may appear to be one of endless civil war and turmoil. Successions are contested between nephews and uncles; regencies are fought over by relatives and other aspirants to political power; nobility is turbulent; and towns seem to be defiant of royal authority and clamoring for more autonomy. However, all is not meaningless chaos, for there is a noticeable pattern: these numerous discords are but rounds in a protracted bout between localism and centralization and between privilege and allegiance, with fortunes fluctuating, to be sure, but with some prospect that ultimate victory will fall on the side of central authorities. A glance at the developments in the two principal states, Castile and Aragon, will disclose the pattern.

In Castile we might begin our survey with the reign of the celebrated Alfonso X (1252–1285). A promoter of culture and so known as the "Learned" or "Wise," Alfonso also sought to establish primogeniture as the rule for succession to the throne. The innovation provoked a series of civil wars between the partisans of the children of his oldest son Ferdinand (d. 1275), who predeceased him, and his younger son Sancho, and between Sancho and his younger brothers. Sancho won in the end, but in turn he left a minor — Ferdinand IV (1295–1312) — as heir, which provoked another contest. This was repeated when Ferdinand left a year-old infant (Alfonso XI) as his successor, and the strife continued until Alfonso reached his majority and for some five more years when he finally restored order. All this turmoil lasted some fifty years; but it did not result in powerlessness of the rulers, for every victory over the opposition, whether nobiliary or urban, entailed punishment of the vanquished and some curtailment of their independence, and in each case the victor was the sovereign. Even if some compensation had to be made to the royal supporters, the net result was really the strengthening of the monarchy, as is manifested in the centralizing program of Alfonso XI. He was able to impose his officers, *corregidores,* on the towns to stand watch over the interests of the crown. In 1342 he succeeded in introducing a new permanent tax (*alcabala*) on all sales and thereby increased the royal resources and independence. In 1348 by the *Ordenamiento de Alcalá* he made the *Siete Partidas* of his namesake, Alfonso the Wise, a national law, at least where it did not conflict with the extant common law, the municipal charters (*fueros*) of the towns, or the privileges of the nobility. Together these amounted to a noticeable assertion of monarchic power in Castile.[1]

In Aragon the turbulence was equally chronic, but here much of the strife stemmed from the complications which the conquest of Sicily in 1283 by Peter III (1276–1285) injected into the dynastic politics. The conquest not only caused two decades of war with the Angevins, the papacy, and the French, but also provoked disputes between Peter's sons and their successors as to the division of the patrimony. This naturally played into the hands of the nobles and towns who were indisposed to support the kings in what appeared to them to be personal foreign ventures. To conciliate these opponents the crown found it necessary to reaffirm their principal privileges. In 1283 Peter issued the *Privilegio general* which conceded to the united nobles and towns, called the Union, four privileges: (1) annual parliaments, (2) exemption from military service outside the kingdom, (3) no imposition of new taxes without the approval of the cortes, and (4) elimination of arbitrary punishment. His successor, Alfonso III, extended the concessions by the promulgation of the *Privilegio de la Union* in 1287. Henceforth the king's councillors were to be elected by the cortes; no proceedings could be taken against any member of the Union without the consent of the cortes; and the right of deposing the king in the event he failed to comply with the terms of the *Privilegios*. These were stringent limitations on the monarchy, and the monarchs naturally endeavored to nullify them. James II did so in 1301, but his repudiation lasted only a short time. The real reaction started with Peter IV (1336–1387) whose provision to leave the throne to his daughter Constanza — he had no sons — provoked opposition on the part of his brother Jaimie and Jaimie's supporters, the Union. In the conflict Peter won decisively, destroyed the Union, revenged himself cruelly on the leaders, and revoked all the extraordinary concessions granted by the *Privilegios*. This was accomplished in 1348. Here also, then, the crown was asserting itself and initiating a program of centralization.[2]

Portugal — Some Monarchic Gains

Carved out of reconquered Moorish territory by Ferdinand the Great of Castile in the second half of the eleventh century, Portugal remained a dependency of Castile until 1143 when, by the Treaty of Zamara, it gained its independence and acquired the overlordship of the papacy. Thereafter, while extending its territory southward with the help of a series of crusades, it ran into conflict with the local church in consequence of the latter's accumulation of vast land holdings. Although repeatedly humbled in the 1200's, the monarchy by the end of the thirteenth century began to assert its authority. In the reign of

Dinis the Husbandman (1279–1325), in 1286, a law was passed which banned further purchase of land by corporations and required that all such purchases since the beginning of the king's reign be disposed of within a year. Another law five years later prohibited the religious novices from granting their lands to the orders they were joining. The successor of Dinis, Alfonso IV (1325–1357), despite the uprising he provoked when he had his son's mistress murdered, was apparently able to retain the gains which had been made at the expense of the church.

England — The Rise of National Monarchy

If the rise of strong monarchy in Spain had scarcely begun on the eve of the Renaissance, in England the advance was already substantial. Here, however, it was national monarchy which advanced, that is, monarchy which found respect and strength through the promotion and the use of such national institutions as parliament and common law.

This progress started in the reigns of Henry I and Henry II, who inaugurated the system of royal courts. It was interrupted by the weak reign of Henry III but resumed its advance in the reigns of Edward I (1272–1307), Edward II (1307–1327), and Edward III (1327–1377).[3]

Edward I succeeded to the throne of his father Henry III after the baronial opposition to an executive independent of the baronage had been suppressed. His domestic program was therefore bound to be directed toward the further strengthening of the monarchy. His general popularity, his successful suppression of the Welsh bid for independence, and his several victories over obdurate Scotland favored such a program, and much was therefore accomplished.

In regard to the nobles, Edward sought to protect the royal rights and to recover any that may have been infringed upon. By the Statute of Gloucester (1278) the nobles were required to show by what right they were exercising their franchises and to surrender those to which they could not establish valid claims. Even if Edward did not deprive many nobles of their unlicensed franchises, it was enough to put them on notice that they could no longer arrogate privileges to themselves without royal approval. By the clause *de donis conditionalibus* in the

Second Statute of Westminster (1285) he prohibited alienation at will of infeudated lands with entail. If the prohibition protected the feudatories, it also advantaged the king who was the principal suzerain. Five years later, by the Third Statute of Westminster, the royal rights were protected by a ban on new subinfeudation. The restriction had the double effect of assuring the king that the fief holder would be able to meet his obligations to the crown, and of preventing his feudatories from acquiring more vassals for themselves. Thus, without depriving the nobles of what was rightfully theirs, Edward safeguarded the rights of the crown. If at the time the gains profited the nobility as well as the crown, eventually the crown became the real beneficiary.

With reference to the church, Edward followed a similar policy of preserving monarchic interests. We have shown in Book II of this series how Edward dealt with the English church during the clash with Boniface VIII, that he compelled the clergy to shoulder their share of national burdens as subjects of the state, as the rest of the nationals did. Here we may add two other measures of his which enhanced this policy. He supported parliament's protests against papal provisions, and in 1279, by the statute *De religionis*, he banned the granting of lands to the church without royal approval on the ground that the lands which passed into the "dead hand" of the church deprived the state of its potential feudal resources.

While protecting the rights of the monarchy by such statutes as listed above, Edward also strove to make the administrative machinery more effective. In general, this promotion consisted of increased professionalization and departmentalization of the royal administration. Thus it was in his reign that the several common–law courts took their shape: the Court of King's Bench, the Court of Exchequer, the Court of Common Pleas, and the Court of Equity. With the appearance of each court, additional cases came under the purview of the king's justices, and in that way the king was able to fulfill his function as the fountain of justice. To serve in that capacity was to add to the strength of the monarchy.

Finally, Edward increased the potential of the crown by promoting the growth of towns. Any increase in the number and the size of the towns had the effect of countering the feudatories and the church, and to the extent that the prestige of the latter declined that of the monarchy increased.

Yet, while monarchy was thus strengthened, it was not arbitrary and personal monarchy which grew, but "national" monarchy. All the important measures — only a few were specified — were enacted by the king in parliament, so that they were the expression of the national will, as it were. Parliament itself was formalized by the composition of the famous Model Parliaments of 1295 and 1296 at which were present not only the nobles and prelates but also two knights from each shire, two burgesses from each borough, and two proctors from each religious chapter. Although the clergy subsequently met separately in what is known as the convocation, the principle was established that "What touches all should be considered by all." Then it was parliament that required Edward to confirm the charters, of which the Magna Carta was the core, and bound the king to respect the national rights enshrined therein. Finally, the king was limited by the very laws which he got his parliaments to enact. These enactments and the judicial decisions arising out of their implementation became the common law of the land, and it was not easy for the king to disregard them. All the foregoing may look like limitations on the king, and indeed they were limitations, but only on his arbitrariness. If he ruled the nation in accordance with the law and through the parliament — which, incidentally, he could summon and dismiss at will — his position as monarch remained unassailable. Thus, by "nationalizing" the office of the monarch, the rulers were actually gaining in power.

The system which Edward I cultivated so steadily came under fire in the reign of his son Edward II (1307–1327). By surrounding himself with favorites in whom the magnates had no confidence, that is, by trying to operate personally rather than through the recognized national leaders, and by failing in his international ventures, Edward provoked violent opposition to his regime. In the conflict that ensued each side had its innings. In 1311 Edward was compelled to accept a very important limitation on the power of the crown. The magnates, referred to as the Lords Ordainers, compelled him to agree to the principle that the councillors of the king, namely, the policy-making body, must be the nominees of the parliament. In 1322 Edward had his turn. At the

Parliament of York the Ordainers were denounced and some were later executed, while Edward resumed government through his personal appointees. But not for long, for the failure of Edward's Scottish expedition (1322–1325), followed by harsh conscription demands to raise a new force to ward off a threatened French invasion, cost him the nation's favor.[4] His newly acquired supporters aligned with the opposition and with Edward's estranged wife, and together they forced his abdication at the Parliament of Westminster (1327); and several months later he was murdered. The reign was a test whether "national" monarchy was to remain "national," namely, "limited," and the principle was preserved. Henceforth, parliament was to be the principal instrument of government, and whoever controlled parliament controlled the nation.

Once the parliament discovered that it was the key to the government of the nation, it strove to acquire even greater rights. This it was able to do in the reign of Edward III (1327–1377) whose wars on the continent obliged him to heed its demands. By declining to provide the necessary funds for prosecuting the war, parliament won the principles that parliamentary approval was necessary for taxation, for recruitment of nonfeudal levies, and for the appointment of royal councillors; that money was to be appropriated for specific items; and that the expenditure of it was to be checked annually by parliamentary auditors. Having discovered the power of the purse, parliament used it to extend its controls over the monarchy, and in doing so furthered the transformation of the latter from a personal to a national institution. However, if the monarchy retained the support of the parliament, its position remained one of strength.

But nationalization of the monarchy was not the only development in Edward's reign. One measure was taken which extended the arm of the monarchy even deeper into the reaches of the nation. By two statutes Edward established the institution of the Justices of the Peace, the "work horses" of the crown as they are sometimes called. In 1327 the conservators of peace, which were established in the reign of Henry III, were required to receive indictments for trials before the itinerant justices, and in 1332 they were empowered to try cases of felony and trespass. Since they were crown appointees, the judicial arm of the crown was thereby extended to cover an ever-increasing number of the king's subjects.

Thus, by 1350, the trend of a strong if "limited" monarchy was firmly established in England. Future years were merely to build on the foundations laid in the late Middle Ages.

France — Inception of Monarchic Centralization

In France, also, the principal internal political development on the eve of the Renaissance was the rise of the monarchy. From the time of the first Capetian, Hugh (987–996), the institution of the monarchy made progress, at first imperceptibly, and then, under Philip II (1180–1223) and Saint Louis (1223–1270), more rapidly. The main pattern established then, extension of royal territory by any means possible — marriage, purchase, escheat, conquest — enforcement of the king's feudal rights, establishment of nonfeudal taxes, and development of nonfeudal administrative offices, both at the court and in the royal territory, to perform the duties of government, continued in the late Middle Ages.[5] To these some new measures were added in the early fourteenth century. The result was a significant increase in the position of the monarchy on the eve of the Renaissance.

The main advance was made in the reign of Philip IV (1285–1314). As a result of his clash with pope Boniface VIII over the issue of the crown's right of taxing the clergy without papal approval and over the question of immunity of criminous clerics from royal justice, he asserted the position of the monarchy against the church — henceforth the clergy could neither evade their responsibility to the state nor shield themselves from the law of the land by hiding behind their priestly robes.[6] And by forcing Pope Clement V to liquidate the Knights Templar, he both increased and dramatized the supremacy of the state.[7] Moreover, to carry his fight against the church, Philip had recourse to a new measure which still further reinforced the crown. He called the first Estates General, the equivalent of the English parliament, once in 1302 and again in 1308 and secured from them support for his policy. By identifying his subjects with his cause he naturally strengthened his position and that of the monarchy as well.

In addition to encroaching on the church and exploiting the
national voice for royal purposes, Philip IV advanced the cause of the
monarchy by promoting the departmentalization of the court official-
dom.[8] The *Parlement* of Paris, with its three bureaus, *chambre des
plaids, chambre des requêtes, chambre des enquêtes*; the treasury,
separated into a *chambre des comptes* for public accounts and a *chambre
aux deniers* for the king's personal accounts; the Chancery, that is,
the secretariat of the state, headed by such energetic royalist spokesmen
as Pierre Flotte, Guillaume de Nogaret, and Enguerrand de Marigny;
and the *Chambre* under a chamberlain looking after the king's personal interests — all were incepted in his day and all were becoming
so many instruments for carrying out the king's will smoothly and
effectively. On the local level the royal *baillis* — called *sénéschaux*
south of the Loire — with their numerous *serjeants* served to extend
the royal arm into the heart of the nation, and at times indeed too
vigorously for the good of the king's reputation.

Finally, like many kings before him and after him, Philip tried to
extend the royal domain. He succeeded in acquiring the city of Lyon
in 1307 and in arranging for his son's marriage to the heiress of Franche-
Comté. But his efforts to obtain Flanders and Gascony were frustrated.
Despite much expenditure of blood and money all he won in Flanders
was an uncertain possession of the towns of Lille and Douai, while his
clash with the papacy made it necessary for him to give up Gascony
which he had temporarily occupied by subterfuge.

Philip IV's vigorous monarchic program was relaxed by his son
and successor, Louis X (1314–1316), due to the strong demands of the
local Estates for guarantees against violation of rights, but the relaxa-
tion was more formal than real.[9] Under Louis' brother, Philip V
(1316–1322), the policy, if not its harshness, was resumed. Numerous
ordinances made the administration more penetrating and effective,
while frequent meetings with the Estates and other types of assemblies
made the policy more acceptable. During the next two reigns, that of
Charles IV (1322–1328), the last of the Capetians, and of Philip VI
(1328–1350), the first of the Valois, the program was continued, although both men are often considered as reactionary because of their
cultivation of chivalry. However the kings may have been inclined

personally, the established machinery of government continued to carry on the monarchic program, grinding away at independent jurisdictions and collecting the king's dues and often more than his rightful share. Besides, both kings pursued the standing policy of expanding the royal domain. Charles, for example, detached Agenais from the English-held Guienne; while Philip purchased Montpellier from King James of Majorca (1349) and the right of succession to Dauphiné for the heir apparent of the French crown (1343–1344, 1349). Indeed, it was their policy of encroaching on Guienne that led to the outbreak of the Hundred Years' War with England. Thus, at the beginning of the Renaissance period, a strong French monarchy was definitely on the rise.

This monarchy, however, was assuming a character different from that of English monarchy. Both, of course, were becoming effective feudal monarchies, with the kings acquiring the power to enforce their feudal rights on their vassals; both were also supplementing this gain by the cultivation of the office of kingship as the preserver of peace and order in the land and as the guardian of the nation's welfare. But whereas English monarchy as described above assumed a national character, French monarchy was developing into a personal authority. There was no French nation as yet, although the extension of the royal domain and authority stimulated some nationalistic sentiment, and the consequence was the lack of a single national will to impose limitations on the rising monarchy. Hence its personal though still feudal character.

The Holy Roman Empire — Decline and Transformation

The internal political developments in the Holy Roman Empire reveal several recognizable trends, all of them adverse to a strong monarchy.[10]

One was the chronic contention over the emperorship. In 1250, when Frederick II died without victory over the papacy and his Italian opponents, the office was claimed by his son Conrad IV and the papal candidate William of Holland. On the death of these two in 1254 and 1256, respectively, again two candidates were elected, Alfonso X of

Castile and Richard, Earl of Cornwall, brother of Henry III of England. Although the two did not engage in war over the office — Alfonso did not even visit Germany — they competed with each other by bidding for the favor of the princes and the towns. This continued until 1272 when Richard died. In 1273, the first Habsburg, Rudolf, was elected. Alfonso was induced to renounce his claims, but on the other hand the King of Bohemia, Ottokar, opposed Rudolf's election and warred on him until he was himself killed in 1278. Rudolf's successor, Adolf of Nassau (1292–1298), had no competitor at the outset, but in 1298, after he had unexpectedly grown stronger by the acquisition of some territory in Meissen and Thuringia, he provoked the opposition of the electors and Albert I of Austria and was deposed. Albert and Henry VII (1308–1313) had no opponents, but Louis (Lewis) IV (1314–1347) was opposed until 1325 by Frederick the Handsome of Austria, and at the end of his reign, by Charles of Bohemia, the future Charles IV. From these repeated clashes over the emperorship, the imperial office naturally lost prestige while those who jockeyed the office, the princes, nobles, and towns, were the gainers. They wrested privileges or arrogated to themselves rights and powers that belonged to the central government.

Another trend was the result of the relative weakness of the candidates who were chosen. Fearing to elect princes who were strong in their private resources, the electors preferred candidates who were too weak to threaten their interests. Every emperor duly elected in this century belonged to this category except Albert of Austria, and then he was chosen only because the electors needed his help to resist the anti-emperor Adolf of Nassau. The result of this weakness of the incumbents was their exploitation of the emperorship to enhance their familial rather than imperial interests. Practically every candidate pursued this policy of family aggrandizement. Rudolf of Habsburg invested his two sons with Austria, Styria, and Carniola, which he confiscated from Ottokar of Bohemia. Adolf of Nassau encroached upon Thuringia and Meissen. Albert of Habsburg fought to acquire the same two territories and succeeded in having his son Rudolf elected as King of Bohemia. Henry of Luxemburg married his son John to the daughter of the last Premysled king of Bohemia and secured that country for his family. Lewis of Bavaria sought to take possession of Tyrol and Carinthia. This trend is significant, for it pointed to the eventuality when the Empire would lose its independent status and become an adjunct of some princely state.

A third trend, actually a result of the two foregoing tendencies, was the readiness of the emperors to forego their imperial rights in Italy. Rudolf, for example, renounced the claims to Naples and to the Romagna. Charles IV, quite a *politique*, actually agreed to stay in Rome for one day, the day of his coronation, and then to depart from Italy. Only Henry of Luxemburg tried to reassert his rights, but then it was with the approval of the pope who hoped to use him to prevent the dismemberment of the papal territory among the host of grasping despots. However, when Henry's movements revealed his intention of restoring imperial authority in Lombardy and Tuscany and of reviving the imperial claims to Naples, and when the initial success of his invasion made the various Italian princes and cities apprehensive for their future independence, both the pope and the Italians beset him with rebellions and thwarted his program.[11] Louis IV led an expedition to Italy and even received the imperial crown (January 1328) — from the officials at Rome — but this invasion appears to have been motivated less by any intent to revive the Empire in Italy than by the hope that it might force the pope to recognize Louis as Emperor.[12] Besides, like most of the former imperial expeditions into that peninsula, it ended in utter failure. On the whole, then, it was quite clear that the age of imperial control of Italy was over; and without Italy the Empire could hardly be a true Holy Roman Empire. It was bound to be Germanic.

The fourth trend was actually this process of Germanization, to which there were two phases. One was the progressive severance of non-Germanic speaking territories from the Empire. Italy, as pointed out above, was as good as lost. Franche-Comté, although officially still a fief of the Empire, was passing under French influence as a result of its acquisition for the French Dauphin. The formation of Switzerland belongs to this phase also, although some of its constituent members were German speaking. In 1291 three districts, the future cantons of Uri, Schwyz, and Unterwalden, entered into a permanent alliance to protect themselves against the attempts of the Habsburgs to impose their feudal lordship on them, and subsequently, taking advantage of the imperial contests and of their own victory over Leopold of Austria in 1315 at Morgarten, they obtained recognition as a quasi-independent federation. Shortly thereafter other communities joined the alliance, Lucerne in 1332, Zurich in 1352, Bern in 1353, and so Switzerland was becoming a separate state. The second phase was the rejection of the papal claims to make emperors. Since Italy was practically lost and since the popes were residing in Avignon and conducting their foreign policy allegedly at the behest of the French kings, it was natural that papal participation in the making of emperors should be opposed. The major step came when Pope John XXII insisted on Louis IV's unconditional surrender and when, due to French intrigue, he failed to reach an understanding with the German princes who were working for a reconciliation between the two heads. Six of the German electors met and issued the famous Declaration of Rense (1338) which proclaimed that the Empire was held from God, that the act of election duly invested the emperor with the powers of his office, and that papal confirmation was therefore unnecessary. The declaration was confirmed at the Diet of Frankfurt held the same year and became the law of the Empire. All that was left to the pope was the rite of coronation; henceforth the Germans would make their emperors themselves.

But here, a word of caution. Although we have been treating this exclusion of the papacy from the process of emperor-making as a new trend, it really was not entirely novel. One but needs to recall the pronouncements of the earlier emperors, Henry IV and Fredericks I and II, who clashed with the papacy, to realize how ancient was the claim that imperial authority is not mediated through the head of the church but is derived directly from God — *a Deo solo per electionem principum.*[13] Still, there was a difference between the claims of old and their restatement at Rense and Frankfurt. Whereas formerly the claims were asserted by the emperors during conflicts with the popes but were allowed to lapse upon restoration of peace, now the emperor was joined by the nation, as it were, in making the claim and the claim was perpetuated, for within two decades it was made a cardinal principle of the constitution.

Closely related to this matter of imperial election was the fifth trend, namely, the determination of the electors. In the more glorious days of the Empire, the emperor was elected by all the nobility and the prelates. Naturally the great princes and the archbishops exerted more influence than the lesser magnates. With time this pre-eminence hardened into a recognized right, and by the middle of the thirteenth century custom accepted six or seven of the chief princes as the rightful electors.

Three of these were ecclesiastics, the archbishops of Mainz, Treves, and Cologne. The lay electors were not quite so fixed, but they were customarily drawn from the rulers of Saxony, Bavaria, Bohemia, Rhenish-Palatinate, and Brandenburg. So well established was this practice that in 1356, when Charles IV promulgated the famous Golden Bull as the constitution of the Holy Roman Empire, he defined the electors as seven, retaining the three archbishops, eliminating Bavaria — it was excluded presumably as reprisal for the troubles that Louis IV's bid for the emperorship brought upon the Empire and because it belonged to the same family as the house of the Rhenish-Palatinate — and assigning the Saxon electoral vote to Saxe-Wittenberg.

Like the matter of the electors, so most of the other trends described above found expression, directly or implicitly, in the Golden Bull. Although the Bull fixed the constitution for the future, it really was a summation of the developments of the preceding century and may properly be considered here.

The Bull was the work of Charles IV, the candidate whom the electors — only five participated in the election — and the pope (Clement VI) selected as the one most likely to bring the conflict between the papacy and Emperor Louis IV to an end. As King of Bohemia Charles commanded considerable power; his recognition by most of the princes provided him legal sanction and added prestige; and his practical good sense enabled him to gauge the political winds expertly.

His motive was dual: promotion of peace and order in the Empire, and the preservation of Bohemia as an independent state within the Empire. To achieve this it was necessary to win the leading princes to his side, and to do so he had to offer them a stake in the proposed program. Hence the constitutional definition of the electors; hence the provision that the electoral office was attached to the lands and that the states of the lay electors should descend by primogeniture; and hence the concession of such sovereign prerogatives as the right of coinage and of final justice to the electors and absolute autonomy to the Kingdom of Bohemia. To preserve these privileges it was expected that the electors would work together, and this cooperation in turn, it was hoped, would contribute to the preservation of peace and order. To promote this further, the Bull provided for election by simple majority vote, declared that election and coronation at Aix-la-Chapelle was all that was required to make an emperor, and ignored the papal claim. Regency was provided for, and an annual meeting stipulated.

The obvious fact about the constitution provided by the Golden Bull is that it fixed the Holy Roman Empire as a kind of trust of the big princes. Instead of strengthening the central government, it strengthened the local governments of the princes, the very opposite of what was happening in France and England.

Italy — Crystallization of States and Despotisms

PRINCIPAL STATES IN ITALY Italy at the outset of the Renaissance period was only a "geographical expression." In the south were the two kingdoms of Sicily and Naples. Originally they were one, the domain of Charles of Anjou, who conquered them from the Hohenstaufen, but in 1282 the Sicilians revolted against Charles and put themselves under the protection of Peter III of Aragon, husband of Constance, daughter of former King Manfred and the rightful heiress to Sicily. In the ensuing war, which closed in 1302 with the treaty of Caltabellota, the Aragonese clung to their acquisitions, and thereafter Sicily and Naples remained separate. North of the Angevin kingdom of Naples and stretching in the form of an elbow from the mouth of the Tiber River to that of the Reno, a little south of the Po, were the papal states; and the plural designation is quite proper, for the territory was a complex of feudal fiefs, communes, and despotisms, all nominally subject to the papacy, and all seeking independence now that the popes resided in Avignon. Indeed, the movement grew so threatening that to check it the papacy was obliged, first, to dispatch Cardinal Albornoz to suppress the rebels and, then, to return itself to Rome. Esconced within the elbow of the papal territory were the rival city states of Siena, Florence, Pisa, and Lucca, and a number of smaller communities still clinging to their independence. Along the north, stretching from Genoa to Venice, were a variety of units. Genoa and Venice were maritime, merchant republics; Milan, Mantua, Verona, Padua, and Ferrara were despotisms in the process of consolidation and expansion; while the March of Montferrat and the County of Savoy were feudal lordships.

TERRITORIAL CONSOLIDATION Variant as these states were, they exhibited at least two political developments in common at this time. One was their progressive territorial crystallization. Completed in Sicily and Naples by the beginning of the fourteenth century, this process was growing in territories north of the papal states and was at its optimum in Tuscany and Lombardy. Eager to secure wide metropolitan areas as markets for the products of their shops and as sources of food for their increasing populations, the cities resorted to expansion in their immediate vicinities. In this race the lesser towns were absorbed by the larger, and the larger towns fought each other for the contested areas. Out of this process boundary delimitations emerged and the respective units began to take their shape.

THE RISE OF AUTHORITATIVE GOVERNMENTS The second political development was the trend toward authoritative government in most of the states named. Since a correct appraisal of this second movement is essential to a proper appraisal of the Renaissance, it will merit more than a passing mention.

Leaving aside the two monarchic and the papal states, we can discern a general pattern of development in the other units irrespective of whether they ended in personal despotism, as in Milan, or class despotism" as in Florence. All these communities started out as communes or municipalities, with elected senators, usually twelve, to serve as an executive body, and a popular assembly, often called *parlemento*, to elect and to legislate. In due time, most of them began to have recourse to *signorias* (that is, governments), usually of one man, invested with extraordinary powers. These were instituted in time of crises, when the communes found it difficult to suppress the neighboring lords, or when their wars against their neighbors took turns for the worse, or when civil wars

broke out within the communities — Italian town life was full of contention between capitalists and the poorer craftsmen, between Ghibelline (nominally pro-imperial) and Guelf (nominally pro-papal) parties,
and between feuding families — and the victorious party wished to
protect its gains. At first, these *signorias* were authorized for a limited
time, but toward the end of the thirteenth century and thereafter they
tended to root themselves for longer periods. When they became permanent, they became despotisms, the last stage in this trend toward
authoritarianism.

As illustrations of this development three cases might be examined,
those of Milan, Venice, and Florence.

In Milan the first step occurred when the citizens invested a local
nobleman, Pagano della Torre, with the office of Captain of the People
out of gratitude for having rallied them after the disastrous defeat at
Cortenuovo (1237) at the hands of Frederick II, the Holy Roman
Emperor. Defending the city against the emperor's vicar in northern
Italy, the cruel Ezzelino da Romano, and against other dangers, the
family continued to hold the government of the city under varying
titles — *podestá, signor,* "Perpetual Ancient" —for the next forty years,
until 1277 when they were ousted by a revolution led by Ottone Visconti, a member of an opposing faction, who was denied admission to
the city when he was appointed archbishop. The victorious party proclaimed Ottone *signore* for life. In 1287 he arranged for his grandnephew Matteo to be Captain of the People, and in 1294 Matteo negotiated with Emperor Adolf for the title of Vicar of the Empire. In 1302
the Visconti were driven out by the ousted Torriani, but they returned
in 1310 with the help of Emperor Henry VII, and in 1311 their vicariate
was restored to them. From then on, with only one or two short
interruptions, the family held the *signoria* until 1447 when the male
line expired. Thus an office which began as an appointive office and
nominally remained such became for all practical purposes a family
perquisite. Indeed, in 1350, it was officially recognized as hereditary.
In the meantime, of course, it became personal and authoritative.[14]

In Venice the development consisted of progressive limitations of
the power of the doge and a corresponding acquisition of political
power by the capitalist class. From the first the dogeship was an elec-

tive office, but it tended to become hereditary and princely as indicated by the fact that during 225 years before the year 1033 it was held by three families only, Badoer, Sanudo, Orseolo, and that the Orseoli married into the Byzantine and Hungarian royal families. These tendencies alarmed the citizens and they proceeded to impose curbs on the ducal office in a series of *coup d'états*. In 1033 occurred the first of these. It forbade co-optation and so prohibited the doges from inducting their sons into the ducal office. It provided for two councillors whose concurrence was necessary for all measures; and for a *guinta*, an assembly of notables, to be consulted on all important matters of state. In 1172 occurred the second *coup d'état*, provoked by loss of war with Constantinople and the ensuing economic and fiscal dislocation. This time a new institution was created, one which represented the wealthier classes who feared a possible alliance between the doge and the proletariate. It was the *Gran Consiglio*. The city was divided into six districts each of which elected two representatives who in turn nominated forty representatives, making a total of 480 members. To this body were transferred the rights of legislating and of electing the doge, rights which theretofore belonged to the *arengo*, that is the whole citizen body as an assembly. This presumably was to make the highest executive office and legislative authority secure in the hands of responsible republican families who, incidentally, were the wealthy families. The third step occurred in 1297 and was also precipitated by failure in foreign policy. It is referred to as the "Closing of the Council," as it defined strictly who could sit in the Council, and was designed largely to make it next to impossible for "new men," that is, men who never sat in the Council and whose ancestors never enjoyed this privilege, to be elected to office. In this way the Council was held captive by a relatively small percentage of the citizens, principally by families who were reputed to be "safe," that is, loyal to the republican regime and to the merchant class to which they invariably belonged. Since the government was "captive" of the Council, it meant that the government of Venice was the will of organized capitalism. In 1310 a further step was taken in the creation of *Dieci* (the Ten) which may be defined as the Committee of Public Safety. The committee was elected by the Council and was empowered to take all measures necessary to preserve the state and the constitution. Occasioned by a conspiracy on the part of a doge, its tenure was limited to two months (the presumed duration of the crisis), twice extended for additional two-month periods, then for five years, and finally, in 1335, it was declared to be a permanent body of the government. Since its authority was absolute, its deliberations secret, and its power unlimited, it became the main organ of the administration, and since it was elected annually by the Grand Council, it was the sleepless watchdog of the republic and of the business interests. Few changes were made in the constitution after that date — in 1423 the *arengo*, which had ceased to exist long before, was formally abolished — so that the development of Venetian authoritative government was completed at the very outset of the Renaissance period.

Unlike the case in Venice and Milan, authoritative government in Florence did not become a reality until about the middle of the Renaissance age. Nevertheless, the trend away from citizen democracy and toward monopoly of government by the rising capitalist class was well established. Until 1162, Florence, like most of the other towns, was a commune headed by popularly elected consuls, but after that date the first step was taken which advanced the influence of the capitalist class, namely, the creation of the office of the *podesta*, or city manager as it might be called today.

There were two kinds of *podestas*, imperial appointees thrust upon a subdued city to attend to the emperor's interests therein and those engaged by the cities themselves. Florence had both kinds, but only the second type concerns us here.

Because partisan rivalries threatened the unity of the city, and unity was needed to stave off the revived imperial threats, an outsider was chosen to manage the affairs of the city. To prevent him from transforming his office into a personal despotism, he was limited to a short tenure, usually one year, subjected to an audit, and saddled with assistants who were drawn from the *rectores* (heads) of the *arti* (gilds). If all three checks were instituted in the name of freedom, the last was more than that. Actually, by having gild representatives serve as assistants to the highest executive organ, the business interests insinuated themselves into power.

Once the shift toward control by the business elements started, there was no holding them back, particularly after 1250 when the great opponent to urban self-government, Frederick II, died. Measure followed measure, all in the name of democracy but generally to the political advantage of the business interests.[15] In 1250, to protect itself against expected resumption of imperial intervention, the city organized the *Primo Popolo* (First Democracy). This was the creation of a citizen militia of twenty companies headed by a *capitano del popolo* who was to associate with the *podesta* in the government of the community. The *capitano* was provided with a council of twelve who in turn were advised by an extraconstitutional body of thirty-six *Sapientes* ("wise men") who were really "experienced" spokesmen of commerce and industry. Temporarily interrupted by the victory of the imperialist party (battle of Montaperti, 1260) and by a *signoria* of Charles of Anjou whose help was needed to counter the imperialists in Tuscany, the trend was resumed by the organization of the *Parte Guelfa* (1267), and the establishment of the priorate (1282). The *Parte* was organized to keep watch against possible resurgence of the defeated and condemned imperialists, the Ghibellines, many of whom belonged to the noble class, and to supervise the confiscation of their property; and its operations naturally strengthened the influence of the capitalists on the administration. The priorate was an executive committee of six, one from each of the six divisions into which the city was organized, chosen by the seven greater gilds — judges and notaries, money changers, clothmakers, silk weavers, doctors and druggists, furriers, and dealers in cloth. The priors were to belong to the Guelf party and to be active members in the higher gilds. They were to reside in the town hall for the two-month term of their office and to guide the administration, the former executive bodies — captain of the people, *podesta*, and the original council of twelve — being subordinated to them. To strengthen their authority they secured the promulgation in 1293 of the famous Ordinances of Justice. These ordinances defined the functions of the various executive organs, assigning the principal role to the priors; established a separate militia of 1,000 men headed by a seventh prior, the *gonfalonier* (standard bearer), who was to be elected by the six priors and whose duty it was to implement the orders of the priorate and to execute the sentences pronounced in the court of the *podesta* against the magnates; and drew up a list of about 150 families of magnates who were barred from government office and who were required to provide 2,000 lire as bond for their good behavior. These regulations hardened the control of the government in the hands of the capitalist class, and until 1313, largely because of the economic prosperity of the town, there were no serious threats to this control.

From 1313 on, however, as a result of a number of difficulties which beset the town, this class government gradually lost public support, and in 1343 it was actually overthrown.[16] There were long and costly wars with Pisa and Lucca which generally went against Florence and so provoked open criticism of the government and incited intraparty disputes and divisions. Family feuds, always chronic, became even more numerous and violent and weakened the party still more. And finally, by 1343, there were a number of bank failures — the collapse was triggered by Edward III's default of his huge debts to the Bardi and Peruzzi — which created a financial panic dislocating business in general, closing numerous craftshops, and throwing people out of work.[17] To bail itself out of these several crises, the government had recourse to *signorias*, first (1313–1322) to Robert, King of Naples; then (1325–1330) to his son and heir, Charles of Calabria, and finally (1342–1343) to the latter's vicar, Walter of Brienne, duke of Athens. But while the first two *signorias* may be said to have rescued Florence from impending military disasters and to have pulled the party out of its difficulties, the last one backfired. Some Florentines began to suspect Walter of Brienne of being a tool of big business; others saw him as currying favor of the lesser gilds and of the proletariate; and still others looked upon him as a satellite of the French and the papacy. And when his remedial actions failed to stem the impending financial collapse, a coalition of disenchanted capitalists, of antiparty businessmen — many of them were newly risen and so were not admitted to the inner circle of the party — and lesser gilds succeeded in ousting him. Of course the populace was incited to rise against tyranny! The rebellion naturally restored the republic but, as might be expected, with a somewhat revised constitution.

The revision of 1343 is usually regarded as a step in the liberalization of the government, as the beginning of the "democratic interlude."
To some extent this is true, for the new constitution provided for a
priorate of nine members: two to represent the seven greater gilds;
three, the five middle gilds; and three, the nine lesser gilds. But while
the base of the priorate was broadened, the fact that a majority of its
members came from the top twelve gilds meant, of course, that the
business elements still retained control of the government. Moreover,
the revision also provided for the re-enfranchisement of many of the
magnates who were proscribed by the Ordinances of Justice, and this
reinforced the preponderance of the top class. Since this revised government persisted without any important constitutional changes until 1383,
when the next rebellion took place, it is clear that by the beginning of
the Renaissance period Florence, although still calling itself a democracy, was really a republic of the more substantial business elements.
Its political base may have been broader than that of Venice, but it remained nevertheless a capitalist preserve.

Although only three states were selected to illustrate the rise of
authoritative governments in Italy before the Renaissance, it would be
easy to establish this same fact for several other towns. Thus, for
example, Verona evolved into a personal despotism of the Della Scala
family from the year 1259 on. Thus Ferrara accepted a member of the
ancient noble family of Este as "hereditary ruler" from 1264 on. Thus
Rimini, a town in the papal territory, gave itself up to the Malatesta
and in 1334 voted them *plenitudo potestatis* (unlimited power), although it was not until 1355 that the Malatesta formalized their "usurpation" by recognizing papal suzerainty and receiving in return the
vicariate of the city.[18] Thus even little Orvieto, after duplicating the
course taken in Florence, finally, in 1334, appointed Manno Monaldes-
chi as *signor* under the titles of *Gonfaloniere del Popolo* and *Gonfaloniere della Guistizia* for life.[19] If Siena, like Florence, had not yet
succumbed to princely despotism before the opening of the Renaissance,
it had already an established oligarchy,[20] for the most part representing
business, which managed to maintain its preponderance throughout
the Renaissance period in spite of the changes in its formal constitution
from 1355 on. In sum, then, it is clear that the development of despot-

isms in Italy, whatever their nature, was actually completed or well advanced by the time the Renaissance began.

Scandinavian Countries — Monarchies Limited and Impotent

Whereas most of Europe, the Holy Roman Empire excepted, saw the development of strong central governments by the end of the Middle Ages, Denmark, Norway, and Sweden witnessed the reverse. There the monarchies, lacking a substantial native middle class — most of the business was in the hands of the Hansa merchants whose only interest was to exploit the economic resources therein — to counterbalance the nobility, steadily yielded before the selfish interests of the latter. Moreover, monarchy was elective and this enabled the nobility as well as prelates to insist on guarantees of their privileges and thus to preserve and expand their jurisdictions. Finally, primogeniture was not in force, and the provisions that the monarchs made for their sons frequently led to intrafamily disputes which further played into the hands of the nobility. The cumulative effect of all this was the reduction of the monarchy to a shadow power, as even a cursory review of the political situation in each of the countries in the first half of the fourteenth century will confirm.

DENMARK We may begin the survey of the situation in Denmark with the death of King Eric VI in 1319. Eric had no male heir, so a contest arose over succession. His brother Christopher was elected, but only after he had signed a capitulation promising to govern under the supervision of the parliament of nobles and of high clergy and to make no wars and demand no taxes without their consent. Powerless and without resources, he was unable to check the feudality who found a leader in his son's tutor, the ambitious Gerhard, Count of Holstein; and so when he died in 1332, he left the monarchy weaker than it was at his accession. For the next eight years Denmark had no king and was ruled by Gerhard as regent. Then, upon Gerhard's murder, Christopher's son Waldemar was elected. He made an attempt to strengthen the monarchy by bidding for the support of the lesser nobility and the church and by recovering the lost royal domains. But the effort was without avail, for he soon discovered that he could retain the throne only if he ruled through the nobility, and accordingly, in 1360, he confirmed them in all their rights. Hence, if he restored the monarchy and some of its lands, he did not really strengthen the central government noticeably.[21]

NORWAY In Norway the century opened with Haakon V (1299–1319) on the throne. Having the church as an ally, he tried to reduce feudalism by resuming all fiefs and abolishing feudal rights — ordinance of 1308 — but without success. He was followed by his grandson, Magnus II Smek (1319–1363), whom the nobility preferred in place of his (Haakon V's) daughter — for whom he had sought to obtain the throne — and the preference, it is suggested, was prompted by the fact that Magnus was still an infant. This choice naturally secured the nobles in their powers. Moreover, Magnus was also elected King of Sweden and generally neglected Norway, which further advantaged the nobility. Nor was there any strengthening of the monarchy when in 1343 on the demand of the Norwegian magnates Norway was provided with its own sovereign in the person of Magnus' younger son Haakon VI. The incumbent was only three years old at the time and the government naturally remained in the hands of the nobles.[22]

SWEDEN The situation in Sweden was equally sorry.[23] The reign of King Birger Magnusson (1290–1319) opened with an eight-year regency under Torgils Knutsson, Lord High Constable; it was then beset by civil discord, first, between the king's brothers and Knutsson, then, after 1305, when Knutsson was executed, between the king and his brothers; and it ended with the king dying in exile. The reign of his nephew Magnus Eriksson (1319–1363), whom we have already met as King in Norway, was not much better. The first thirteen years of his rule were a period of regency when the power of the nobility naturally throve. Subsequently, after first showing some promise of national consolidation through such measures as the compilation of common law and of a general municipal law, the reign encountered trouble when in furtherance of this program Magnus tried to reduce the amount of tax-free land held by the nobility and to abolish the old privileges of the church. The nobles rose in revolt, his son Eric rebelled, and the famous St. Bridget stirred a verbal crusade against him. Thus the year 1350 came to Sweden amid monarchic wreckage.

Poland — Revival of Monarchy

The internal political developments in Poland on the eve of the Renaissance were in favor of the monarchy. From the time when Boleslaw III (1102–1138) had divided the kingdom into five autonomous principalities, one for each of his five sons, in the hope of eliminating fratricidal wars, monarchic authority steadily declined until Poland ceased to exist as a kingdom. Then, repeated partitions of the principalities weakened the authority of the princes themselves and feudalism set in. This state of affairs continued until the end of the 1200's when the restoration of the monarchy was undertaken.[24]

Behind this move there were several forces. Perhaps the most compelling one was the growing danger from the raids of the Lithuanians, Russians, and Tartars on the east, and from the aggression of Bohemia on the southwest. Another factor was the concern of the church for its rights. Having secured its freedom from the monarchy at the time of the Gregorian reform, the church missed the protecting hand of the monarchy when the disintegration set in and the local princes began to encroach on its lands and its rights. Hence the prelates, while mindful of their privileges, began to work for the restoration of the monarchy. Finally, a new social element, the knightly class, had risen in sufficient numbers to become a factor in politics, and it seems that many of its members preferred to establish bonds with more distant powers than with the local lords who could keep them under closer surveillance. With these forces inviting the restoration of the monarchy, an unsuccessful attempt was presently made by a Piast prince of the province of Great Poland (1295) and a successful one by Ladislas Lokietek IV (the Dwarf), a Piast prince of the province of Kujavia.

Without detailing the complicated political machinations and the several wars by which Ladislas IV finally secured the national crown in January 1320, we need only recognize the fact that he recovered some of the provinces for the monarchy and that in winning the crown he transformed the old concept of the state as a dynastic territory to that of "the Crown of the Kingdom of Poland," that is, he changed it from a private territory to an institution.

What Ladislas IV started, his son Casimir III, the Great (1333–1370), continued. Abandoning Silesia to the Bohemians and temporarily yielding Pomerania to the Teutonic Knights, he concentrated on strengthening the position of the state. He recovered for the crown additional Piast provinces or parts thereof, created permanent central offices, appointed royal supervisors (*storostas*) in regional districts to look after the interests of the crown, established a uniform code of laws for two of the larger provinces, and suppressed a union of the nobles in the province of Great Poland who attempted to oppose his program of recovering alienated crown lands. In addition, he encouraged the growth of towns, founded the University of Cracow, and protected the peasantry from oppression by the lords. All these measures strengthened the monarchy at home. In addition, he oriented Polish expansion southward into Galicia and Volyhnia with notable success and thereby enhanced Poland's prestige internationally. This success naturally increased his popularity with his people. The net result of Casimir's labors was that the Renaissance period opened in Poland with a revived and a glorious monarchy, as his title "the Great" clearly implies.

Lithuania — From Tribe to State

Poland's eastern neighbor, Lithuania, also saw the development of a monarchic state.[25] Until about the middle of the thirteenth century there was no Lithuanian state but a series of tribes. Then, after 1240, one of the tribal chieftains, Mindaugas, began uniting the tribes into a single nation, mostly because of the pressure of the crusading order, the Livonian Brothers of the Sword. To remove the order's justification for invading the lands of the Lithuanians, Mindaugas accepted Christianity and in 1253 was crowned king with a crown provided by Innocent IV. But when this conversion failed to stem the attacks of the crusading knights, Mindaugas apostasized and his unifying program came temporarily to an end.

Half a century later the work of unification was resumed by the great Prince Gediminas (1315–1341). As in the case of Mindaugas, the constant danger from the crusaders was an impelling reason for the consolidation, but an equally effective factor was the success with which he led his warriors eastward into White Russia and southward into the regions once held by the great Kievan state. The annexation of these territories raised his prestige and redounded to his strength among the Lithuanian people. When he died in 1341 he left a united state, ready for its most glorious period in history.

Hungary — Establishment of a Western Type of Feudal Monarchy

The fourteenth century opened in Hungary with the demise of its founding dynasty (Arpad) when Andrew III died in 1301 and with the elevation of the famous Angevin dynasty in 1308. The founder of the new line was Charles Robert, great-grandson of Charles of Anjou (brother of Louis IX of France) and grandson of Mary, daughter of Stephen of Hungary (1270–1272). His reign lasted from 1308–1342 and was marked by the revival of monarchy and the rapid infiltration of western culture.[26]

When Charles ascended the throne, he found Hungary in the grip of local princes and the power of the monarchy at the vanishing point. In 1222, only seven years after the English magnates had forced John I to sign the Magna Carta, the Hungarian nobility had wrested similar guarantees from King Andrew II. They and the prelates compelled him to sign the Golden Bull, and by it they secured exemption from taxation, freedom from arbitrary imprisonment and confiscation of property, the right to dispose of their lands at pleasure, and, most significantly, the right to assemble annually to present their grievances. Thereafter they obtained repeated confirmations of these privileges, with the result that their position was steadily strengthened and that of the monarchy was steadily weakened. This was especially true of the magnates who held the clan chieftanships, for they added constitutional rights, so to speak, to their office as clan leaders and so became doubly strong.

Charles, therefore, had his work cut out for him if he was to rehabilitate the monarchy at all. As it happened, he had the necessary drive and perseverance to tackle the difficult problem. By unremitting war he dissolved the clans, reduced the dynasts, and recovered much of the crown land they had occupied. He organized a central administration after the pattern of the western states, appointed local supervisors, and established royal courts. To increase the revenue of the crown he promoted exploitation of wasteland belonging to the crown, abolished internal toll stations and replaced them by customs stations on the frontiers, negotiated trade treaties, and stabilized the currency. He even appropriated a third of the papal tithe. By the time of his death Hungarian monarchy was a respectable power.

Yet if Charles accomplished all this, it is obvious that he could not have done the job alone and that he must have had support. The support came from the church and from his partisans, and these naturally had to be rewarded. Since the paritsans were the nobility, not the mighty dynasts who were suppressed, but the lesser feudatories, the price of their support was their admission as partners in the state. This he paid, for it was the only valuable prize he had at his disposal. The result was that the monarchy which he revived did not become personal nor authoritative but a feudal monarchy.

This fact is important, since it laid the foundation of Hungary's monarchy as one limited by its colleagueship with the nobility. But it also pointed to the past when due to the weakness of the Arpads the nobility had secured extensive privileges.

Balkan States — Revival and Decline of Byzantium and Consolidation of Slavic States

The internal political conditions in the several states in the Balkan and Greek peninsulas depended largely on the fluctuation of power politics in that area, especially as they affected the Byzantine empire. In general, a state in formation saw the strengthening of its monarchy, while a state in decline saw its central authority weakened.

BYZANTIUM In Byzantium both trends took shape.[27] In the first two decades after the reconquest of Constantinople from the western powers (1261), the authority of the central government grew with the success that the emperors had in recovering the lands lost during the Latin occupation. Thus, for example, the rulers of autonomous Salonika and Epirus accepted the suzerainty of Michael VIII Palaeologus (1261–1283); thus also the Genoese, who had helped in the re-establishment of the empire and had become unbearable in their conduct, were driven out of Constantinople and lodged in Nicaea. But from that time on, the imperial authority began to decline. The reign of Andronicus II (1282–1328) was torn by civil war twice, once between his son and co-emperor, Michael IX, and the Catalan Company,[28] a band of mercenaries brought from Sicily to oppose the Turks; and a second time, between his grandson Andronicus III and the emperor himself when the latter attempted to exclude him from the throne on the grounds of immoral conduct. The reign of Andronicus III (1328–1341) escaped this plague, but that of his son John V (1341–1376, 1379–1391), who was only nine years old at his accession, suffered immeasurably from partisan civil war between his father's main supporter, John Cantacuzenus, and his mother and other chiefs of state who were jealous of Cantacuzenus' prominence. These dynastic and palace conflicts aggravated the state of affairs in the country by attracting to them certain religious and social tensions. From the time that Michael VIII had entered into negotiations with the papacy for the reunion of the churches, the nation was split between those who were prepared to accept reconciliation and those who remained adamantly orthodox, and the opposition was fanned into white heat by the way the differences were exploited for partisan advantages. At the same time frictions between the rising feudal aristocracy and the oppressed commoners were exploited and fanned into uprisings by one party against the other. Under these circumstances, therefore, the authority of the emperor deteriorated steadily. Moreover, these wars devastated the land and naturally reduced the fiscal and military resources of the government and ultimately its power also.

Contributing to this decline of the central government was the rise of two decentralizing forces new to the Byzantine world. One was the practice of providing appanages for the sons of the emperor; and the other was the introduction of feudalism. Both were the heritage of the occupation by the Latins, and both naturally contributed to the weakening of central authority.[29] In fact, according to the Venetian ambassador at Constantinople, the imperial situation was truly hopeless. In 1355 he reported to his government that

> This Empire is in a bad state, even, to be truthful, in a desperate one, as much because of the Turks who molest it sorely on all sides, as because of the Prince and his government with which there is general discontent; the people would prefer the rule of the Latins, mentioning as their first choice our seigniory and commune, if they could obtain it. For in truth they cannot remain as they are for anything in the world.[30]

BULGARIA Bulgaria, having regained its independence from Byzantium in 1186 and having profited from the fall of Byzantium to the Latins in the Fourth Crusade, established itself as the major power in the Balkans in the first half of the thirteenth century. But thereafter, due to the dynastic rivalry and particularly to the repeated inroads of the Tartars, it declined. In 1330 at the battle of Velbuzhd it was badly defeated by the rising Serb state and reduced to dependence.[31] Under these conditions the authority of its czars naturally declined.[32]

SERBIA In the case of Serbia the reverse held true. Established as a nation by Stephen Nemania (1165–1196), advanced by the wars and diplomacy of another Stephen (1196–1228) who secured the kingship for himself and a primatial status for the church, Serbia continued to grow as a nation and its monarchy with it. Checked for a while by the Bulgar expansion, it resumed its territorial growth both at the expense of Bulgaria and the Byzantine empire until in 1330 its victory at Velbuzhd made it the predominant power in the Balkans.

The victorious King Stephen Urosh III was succeeded by even a greater ruler, his son Stephen Urosh IV (1331–1355) known as Dushan, who murdered him in 1331. Dushan extended Serbian frontiers into Macedonia, Thessaly, and Epirus, and planned an attack on Constantinople. At the same time he began to organize the territory for more effective government. Having himself crowned "Emperor of the Serbs and Greeks" (1346), he tried to give meaning to the title by strengthening the central authority. He was the commander-in-chief of the army and supreme judge. At the court, under him, were a number of administrative officers, and locally he was represented by his appointees, the *zupans*. The law was of his making but he recognized old customs, as manifest by the code (*Zakonik*) which he promulgated for the whole land. In theory and in practice, therefore, the Serbian monarchy on the eve of the Renaissance was authoritative.

It was, however, subject to the limitations that plagued most European lands, namely, the power of organized nobility. Since the thirteenth century the nobles met as an assembly (*sbor*) which had the right to participate in the elevation of the czars, in promulgation of law, and in deliberations on matters of peace and war. In Dushan's reign, however, the assembly proved to be his mouthpiece, as he succeeded in suppressing all nobiliary opposition. Only in the event of disputed successions or of weak and militarily unsuccessful kings could the assembly become a threat to personal rule.

WALLACHIA AND MOLDAVIA North of the Danube River, as part of the complex of Balkan states, were two small principalities of Wallachia and Moldavia. Without attempting to reconstruct their history, we need only mention that as the Renaissance approached these two principalities came into being. They are therefore part of the phenomena of rising states before the advent of Renaissance.

Ottoman Turkey — Establishment in Asia Minor

Although the Ottoman Turks did not secure a foothold in Europe until 1354, they had already occupied the Byzantine territory in Asia Minor and organized a state.[33] Since later they merely built on the foundations they laid before the Renaissance, we are justified in considering these early developments here.

Successful conquerors that the Ottomans were, their state was a product of their military enterprise. Starting as mercenaries of the Seljuk Turks, the Ottomans gained their independence when the Seljuks disintegrated and readily conquered both the lands of their former paymasters and of their weak neighbors, the Byzantines. By 1333 they were at the Dardanelles, masters of Asia Minor, and looking hopefully to the day when they could set foot in Europe. Carved by the sword, the state was to be held by the sword. Accordingly a permanent army was created. Its core was the corps of Janissaries (*yeni cheri*), new soldiers, raised from young captive Christians or, when these were not sufficient, from Christian youths taken as tribute. They were brought up in Mohammedan faith and raised to be extra loyal to the Sultan. Ottomans were also organized into a cavalry force; they were to serve on call and were provided with military fiefs as compensation. However, these fiefs were not hereditary but revocable, so that their holders had to remain loyal at all times. Over these forces the sultan was the final commander-in-chief and with them he not only made conquests and guarded his lands but also made his word the law of the land. Since there was no limit to the sultan's authority, all of the soldiers and the administrators being considered his "slaves," the Ottoman state was an unlimited autocracy.

Russia — Emergence of Muscovy

East of the states studied so far were the lands of present-day Russia. No great state was there as yet, for the south was occupied by the Tartars (Golden Horde) who moved about and raided at will, and the north was divided among several Russian principalities, such as Novgorod, Rostov-Suzdal (sometimes called Vladimir), Tver, and Moscow — all subject to the Tartars, all held by descendants of the founder of medieval Russia, Rurik, but in bitter rivalry with each other. Yet signs of the future were becoming manifest. One of the principalities, off the beaten track of Tartar raiders, was that of Moscow. Its relative security from these raids attracted to it inhabitants from the more exposed regions, and its population grew while that of the others declined. Included in this transfer was the head of the church of the Russians. Abandoning the former capital of the church, Kiev, by then a ghost town, the Metropolitan moved first to Vladimir (1300) and then, after 1325, when Vladimir lost its power, to Moscow, and the presence of the church head there naturally added prestige to the town and to its princes and strengthened their claims to lordship over all Russian principalities. At the same time the princes avoided Tartar raids by ingratiating themselves with their khans, and in the end their skillful servility won them recognition as the Grand Princes of Russia (1328). This occurred in the reign of Ivan I (1328–1340), nicknamed Kalita (moneybag), when he was deputized by the khan to collect the Russian tribute for him and was awarded the title of Grand Duke of Vladimir. The two offices enabled the Muscovite prince to interfere "legitimately" in neighboring principalities, and although it was done in the name of the Tartar masters, the practice nevertheless strengthened his position in relation to the other princes. This position was actually formalized in the reign of Ivan's son Simeon (1340–1353), "in whose hands," it is reported, the khan "put all the other princes." Simultaneously with the exercise of these rights, the new Grand Dukes began to make annexations to their principality at the expense of the neighboring princes of Tver and Rostov. Thus by 1350 Moscow had entered upon its role as *sobiratel* (gatherer) of the Russian people into one.[34]

Summary

From this rapid survey of the political developments in the various European countries on the eve of the Renaissance, it is clear that the general trend was the steady consolidation of the state both in territory and authority. To be sure there were exceptions to the trend, as in the case of the Holy Roman Empire and Scandinavia, where the reverse was true. But on the other hand, in Venice, Milan, and several other Italian towns, centralization of government had actually attained its maximum. It seems proper therefore to maintain that the national state, which is often regarded as a product of the Renaissance age, was well on its way before the Renaissance began.

1. A fuller statement may be found in R. Bigelow Merriman, *The Rise of the Spanish Empire in the Old World and in the New*, vol. I, *The Middle Ages* (New York: Cooper Square Publishers, Inc., 1962 [reprint of 1918 ed. by Macmillan]), 94–141, 194–7, 206–65. For a recent condensed account see H. V. Livermore, *A History of Spain* (London: George Allen and Unwin Ltd., 1958), 132–47.

2. Merriman, *op. cit.*, I, 311–62, 383–99, 428–49; Livermore, *op. cit.*, 147–56.

3. A good recent study of the period is May McKisack's *The Fourteenth Century, 1307–1399,* vol. V of *The Oxford History of England* (Oxford: Clarendon Press, 1959).

4. On this reversal and its constitutional implications see Michael R. Powicke, "The English Commons in Scotland in 1322 and the Deposition of Edward II," *Speculum,* XXXV (1960), 556–62.

5. For a rapid survey of this growth see Robert Fawtier, *The Capetian Kings of France. Monarchy and Nation (978–1328),* trans. Lionel Butler and R. J. Adam (London: Macmillan and Co., Ltd., 1960).

6. A short account of this clash may be found in *ibid.*, 90–95 and in my *History of the Renaissance*, Book II, *Church and Religion* (Salt Lake City: University of Utah Press, 1964), 115–8.

7. For Philip's motivation see Fawtier, *op. cit.*, 38–39.

8. A comprehensive study of the royal administration at this time is provided in Ferdinand Lot and Robert Fawtier, *Histoire des institutions françaises au moyen âge*, tome II of *Institutions royales* (Paris: Presses universitaires de France, 1958), 48–99, 140–59, 239–56, 332–48.

9. *Ibid.*, 558–9.

10. An excellent short treatment of the subject in English is available in C. W. Previté-Orton, *History of Europe from 1198 to 1378* (New York: G. P. Putnam's Sons, 1937), 138–51, 299–324. Of course, J. V. Bryce's classic work, *The Holy Roman Empire,* dated though it is, should be read by all.

11. This matter is brilliantly worked out in William Bowsky, "Florence and Henry of Luxemburg, King of the Romans: The Rebirth of Guelfism," *Speculum*, XXXIII (1958), 177–203, which he expanded in his *Henry VII in Italy. The Conflict of Empire and City-State, 1310–1313* (Lincoln, Nebraska: University of Nebraska Press, 1960).

12. Cf. Robert Folz, *L'idée d'Empire en occident du ve au xive siècle* (Paris: Aubier, 1953), 165–6.

13. Cf., for example, Henry IV's letter to Gregory VII in K. M. Setton and H. R. Winkler, eds. *Great Problems in European Civilization* (New York: Prentice Hall Inc., 1954), 141–2. Also the views of one of King John's supporters, *ibid.*, 164–5.

14. A narrative of the Visconti is available in Dorothy Muir, *A History of Milan under the Visconti* (London: Methuen and Co., Ltd., 1924).

15. An account of this constitutional development is to be found in Ferdinand Schevill, *History of Florence from the Founding of the City through the Renaissance* (New York: Frederick Ungar Publishing Co., 1961), 119–284. For a description and analysis of the constitutional machinery as of 1343 see Gene A. Brucker, *Florentine Politics and Society, 1343–1378,* vol. XII of *Princeton Studies in History* (Princeton: Princeton University Press, 1962), 57–71. Cf. also Marvin M. Becker, "Some Aspects of Oligarchical, Dictatorial and Popular *Signorie* in Florence, 1282–1382," *Comparative Studies in Society and History*, II (1960), 421–39, and his article, "The Republican City-State in Florence: An Inquiry into Its Origin and Survival (1280–1434)," *Speculum,* XXXV (1960), 39–50.

16. For a detailed account of this change see Schevill, *op. cit.*, chap. xiv, "Florence Encounters the Problem of the Despot (1313-1343)"; and cf. G. A. Brucker and M. B. Becker, "The *Arti Minori* in Florentine Politics, 1342-1378," *Mediaeval Studies*, XVIII (1956), 93-104.

17. On the collapse and its impact see Brucker, *op. cit.*, 3-56.

18. On the despotism of the Malatesta see P. J. Jones, "The Vicariate of the Malatesta of Rimini," *English Historical Review*, LXVII (July, 1952), 321-51, and his essay, "The End of Malatesta Rule in Rimini," *Italian Renaissance Studies, A Tribute to the Late Cecilia M. Ady,* ed. E. F. Jacob (London: Faber and Faber, 1960), 222-55.

19. The development of this is excellently traced in Daniel Philip Waley, *Mediaeval Orvieto: the Political History of an Italian City-state, 1157-1334* (Cambridge: Cambridge University Press, 1952).

20. On one phase of this oligarchy see William M. Bowsky, "The *Buon Governo* of Siena (1287-1355)," *Speculum*, XXXVII (1962), 368-81.

21. This attempted revival is discussed briefly in *The Cambridge Medieval History*, vol. VIII, *The Close of the Middle Ages* (Cambridge: Cambridge University Press, 1936), 535-8.

22. Short survey in Knut Gjerset, *History of the Norwegian People* (New York: Macmillan Co., 1915), II, 1-15.

23. Short survey in Ragnar Svanström and Carl Fredrik Palmstierna, *A Short History of Sweden*, trans. Joan Bulman (Oxford: Clarendon Press, 1934), 35-42.

24. For an account of this restoration see *The Cambridge History of Poland from the Origins to Sobieski — to 1696* (Cambridge: Cambridge University Press, 1950), 108-47, 167-87.

25. A fine study of this revival appears in *The Cambridge Medieval History, VIII, 587-99.* For a shorter treatment see Oscar Halecki, *Borderlands of Western Civilization. A History of East Central Europe* (New York: The Ronald Press Company, 1952), 79-83, 110-2.

26. Brief introductory survey in Previté-Orton, *op. cit.*, 399-402.

27. An excellent treatment of the subject is to be found in George Ostrogorsky's *History of the Byzantine State*, trans. Joan Hussey (Oxford: Basil Blackwell, 1956), 371-414, 424-75. For a brief survey see Charles Diehl's essay "The History of the Byzantine Empire: An Outline from A.D. 1204 to A.D. 1453," *Byzantium*, eds. Norman H. Baynes and H. St. L. B. Moss (Oxford: Clarendon Press, 1948), 33-50.

28. Kenneth Setton, *Catalan Domination of Athens, 1311-1388* (Cambridge: The Mediaeval Academy of America, 1948), intro. chapter.

29. Cf. Ostrogorsky, *op. cit.*, 428 ff.

30. Cited from Diehl, *op. cit.*, 45–46.

31. For a brief account see Steven Runciman's essay "Byzantium and the Slavs," Baynes and Moss, *op. cit.*, 459–62. Longer treatment in *The Cambridge Medieval History*, vol. IV, *The Eastern Roman Empire, 717–1453* (Cambridge: Cambridge University Press, 1923), chap. xvii, "The Balkan States, 1. The Zenith of Bulgaria and Serbia (1186–1355)."

32. For a full treatment see *ibid.*, and for a brief one see Baynes and Moss, *op. cit.*, 362–5.

33. For a brief introduction see Previté-Orton, *op. cit.*, 405–9, or *The Cambridge Medieval History*, IV, 653–65.

34. For a recent interpretation of this rise of Moscow the reader is strongly urged to consult Michael T. Florinsky, *Russia — A History and an Interpretation* (New York: Macmillan Co., 1953), I, 71–91.

II

International Political Developments on the Eve of the Renaissance

Spain

THE RECONQUISTA In Spain one important development was the continuation of the *reconquista*. The drive against the Moors in the century before the Renaissance may not have been as spectacular as that which ended in the famous battle of Las Navas de Tolosa in 1212 or as that of Ferdinand III (1217–1252) of Castile and Leon, but it continued nevertheless. Alfonso X (1252–1284) of Castile recovered some coastal lands to the west of Cadiz and in the vicinity of Cartagena. In 1292, Tarifa, the key to the Strait of Gibraltar, was captured, and about the same time a treaty was made between Sancho IV (1284–1295) of Castile and James II (1291–1327) of Aragon defining their respective claims to the coast of Africa, Castile reserving the western portion from Muluya to the Atlantic, and Aragon, from Muluya to Tunis. In 1309 another pact was agreed to, and in accordance with its arrangements Algeciras and Almeria were beseiged by Castile and Aragon, respectively, although unsuccessfully; but Gibraltar was conquered in a joint operation. During the minority of Alfonso XI (1312–1350) some of these gains were lost, including Gibraltar (1333); but in the end, as a result of Alfonso's victories at Salado (1340), Palmones (1343), and Algeciras (1344), the *reconquista* was resumed and at the same time a new invasion from Africa (of the Benemerines of Morocco) was thwarted.[1] Thus, though less spectacular than the earlier efforts, the drive against the Moors continued to the end of the medieval period.

THE VENTURES OF ARAGON IN THE MEDITERRANEAN Another significant political development of international character in which an Iberian state was involved during the same period was the Aragonese expansion in the Mediterranean (Plate I).

The Balearic Islands held by the Moors were conquered between 1229 and 1235. For some time they were attached to Aragon as vassal

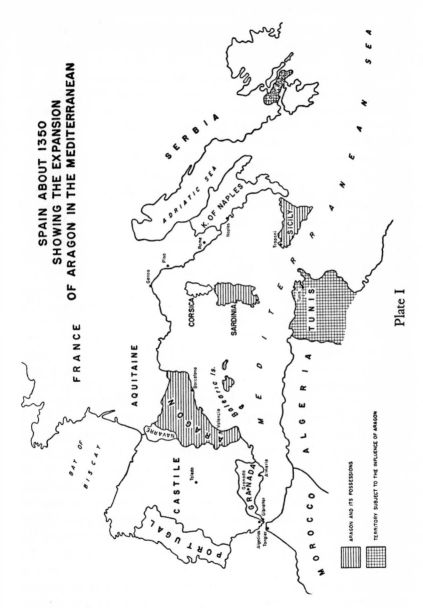

SPAIN ABOUT 1350
SHOWING THE EXPANSION
OF ARAGON IN THE MEDITERRANEAN

ARAGON AND ITS POSSESSIONS

TERRITORY SUBJECT TO THE INFLUENCE OF ARAGON

Plate I

states held by princes of the Aragonese house. But the feudal tie proving to be unreliable, the islands were incorporated into the kingdom in 1343.

Sardinia was invaded even before the Balearics were taken. Although the invader, Alfonso II, did not conquer the entire island, he and his successors clung to the conquest despite numerous rebellions fomented there by Genoa and Pisa. In 1354 Pedro IV invaded the island in person and extended the Aragonese control.

Tunis was made a protectorate in 1280 by Pedro III who had come to aid the legitimate heir against a usurper and secured lucrative concessions. As a mark of his overlordship Pedro was given the right to collect tribute and one-half the wine tax. In addition, he was allowed to maintain consuls in two places and a justice who would administer law among the Christian residents there. Perhaps a more significant advantage was the strategic position in which this intervention placed him with respect to Sicily whither he soon turned his attention.

Sicily, which had been wrested from Frederick II's illegitimate son Manfred by Charles of Anjou, rebelled against the Angevins in 1282 (Sicilian Vespers) and then invited Pedro, Manfred's son-in-law, to assume the crown. Pedro was "accidentally" off the Barbary Coast at the time. He accepted the invitation, landed at Trapani on August 30, 1283, and soon took Sicily. Without tracing the series of wars which this conquest provoked between him and his successors on the one side and the French and the papacy on the other, we may note that by the Treaty of Caltabellotta, Frederick II, then ruler and Pedro III's third son, was recognized as king. Although the terms stipulated that he was to hold the island just for the duration of his life and that on his death it was to revert to the Angevin successors, the Valois, the fact is that the island remained in the hands of Frederick's descendants.

The Treaty of Caltabellotta set the stage for another extension of the Aragonese interests in the Mediterranean. Plagued by the soldiers who were idled when peace came in 1302, Frederick II encouraged the principal company, known as the Catalan Company, to enter the service of Emperor Andronicus II of Byzantium who was seeking mercenaries to oppose the advance of the Ottomans. After serving the emperor well for some time, the Company fell out with the heir apparent, Michael IX, and became rebellious. A great number of its soldiers were massacred, but the remainder, after looting in the empire, sold their services to the Duke of Athens, Walter of Brienne. When Walter failed to pay them, they rose in arms, and on March 15, 1311, destroyed his forces and seized his Duchy. To legalize their acquisition they put themselves under the suzerainty of Frederick II of Sicily. Though the Sicilian rulers did not gain control of the Duchy, through this conquest Aragonese influence extended to the Greek Peninsula.[2]

Thus by 1350 the Aragonese were a major power in the western and central Mediterranean, and their expansion at this time laid the basis for the Italian enterprise later of the great Ferdinand and his successors Charles I and Philip II.

France and England — The First Stage of the Hundred Years' War

A major international development involving France and England on the eve of the Renaissance was the outbreak of the Hundred Years' War. Although the war began in 1337, it was the consequence of more than two centuries of repeated clashes between the two countries. When Duke William of Normandy, a vassal of the French king, conquered England in 1066, he set the stage for an inevitable conflict between France and England. A powerful king of England could hardly be treated like an ordinary vassal, and yet he would always serve as a rallying point for feudal rebellions against the French king. Hence the only solution from the point of view of the French rulers lay in the recovery of the French lands held by the kings of England. But serious as the situation was as a result of William's conquest of England, it became even more critical when Henry, Count of Anjou and lord of Normandy, Maine, and Tourraine, added Aquitaine and Poitou to his domain by marrying Eleanor, heiress to these lands and recently divorced wife of Louis VII of France, and then became King of England in 1154. With half of France and England in his possession (Plate II) Henry overshadowed the French monarchs, and self-preservation dictated to the latter that they should strive to undo this grave situation.

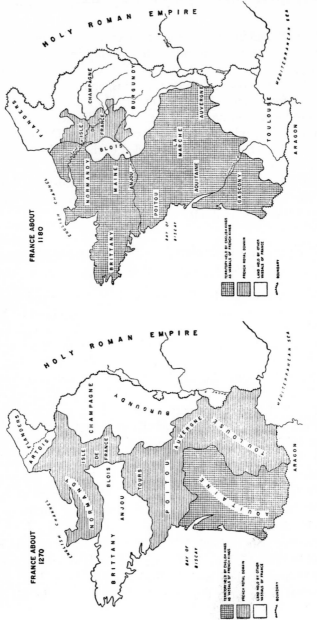

Plate II

FRANCE ABOUT 1180

HOLY ROMAN EMPIRE

FLANDERS

CHAMPAGNE

BURGUNDY

ISLE DE FRANCE

BLOIS

NORMANDY

MAINE

ANJOU

AUVERGNE

LA MARCHE

BRITTANY

POITOU

AQUITAINE

GASCONY

TOULOUSE

ARAGON

ENGLISH CHANNEL

BAY OF BISCAY

MEDITERRANEAN SEA

TERRITORY HELD BY ENGLISH KINGS AS VASSALS OF FRENCH KINGS

FRENCH ROYAL DOMAIN

LAND HELD BY OTHER VASSALS OF FRANCE

BOUNDARY

Plate III

FRANCE ABOUT 1270

HOLY ROMAN EMPIRE

FLANDERS

ARTOIS

CHAMPAGNE

BURGUNDY

ISLE DE FRANCE

NORMANDY

BLOIS

ANJOU

TOURS

POITOU

AUVERGNE

TOULOUSE

AQUITAINE

BRITTANY

ARAGON

ENGLISH CHANNEL

BAY OF BISCAY

MEDITERRANEAN SEA

TERRITORY HELD BY ENGLISH KINGS AS VASSALS OF FRENCH KINGS

FRENCH ROYAL DOMAIN

LAND HELD BY OTHER VASSALS OF FRANCE

BOUNDARY

Without detailing the story of these efforts, it is enough for us to know that repeated wars were fought during the next hundred years, that the French kings recovered the lands extending from the Channel south to Poitou, and that by the Treaty of Paris (May 1258 and December 1259) an agreement was reached between St. Louis of France and Henry III of England — Henry at the time was in trouble with his English vassals because of his reliance on foreign councillors (his wife's and mother's friends and relatives) and because of his son's failure to secure the throne of Sicily which the pope offered him for £90,000 and which was costing England more than the barons were willing to contribute — whereby Henry abandoned all claims to the lost lands and in return was allowed to hold Gascony and some neighboring fiefs (Plate III) as a vassal of the French king.[3] In a sense, therefore, if the duration of this stage of the conflict is taken into account it can be said that the French and the English had already fought the first Hundred Years' War (1154–1259).

With the recovery of half of the English holdings in France, it was natural that the reclamation of the remaining territory should be attempted the moment when a less scrupulous man than Louis IX ascended the French throne. This happened when Philip IV became king in 1285. From that date, he and his successors repeatedly tried to recover Gascony by exploiting their suzerain rights over it, but without much lasting success.[4] On the other hand, as the ideas of sovereignty began to crystallize with the passage of time, the English kings strove to undo the terms of the Treaty of Paris and to convert Gascony to a sovereign territory in which their authority would be final.[5] The issue therefore became thoroughly flammable and only needed added aggravations to lead to an all-out war. By 1337 these had appeared, not as new issues but as old issues reaching the breaking point, and the second Hundred Years' War began.

The old issues becoming more critical were threefold. One was the chronic rivalry between the merchant marines of the two countries. From Bordeaux to Calais there were ample opportunities for raids on each other's shipping, particularly when piracy and overseas trading were not distinguished too finely; and they multiplied in number and magnitude and inflamed the national passions. Another issue was the policy which both lands adopted of supporting each other's natural enemies. France, anxious to acquire prosperous Flanders, was repeatedly thwarted by an alliance between the Flemish merchant and laboring groups, who needed English wool for their looms and shops, and the English king who held the threat of embargo over their heads. On the other hand, the English rulers, trying to annex Scotland, found themselves opposing a stubborn Scotland aided by men and money supplied by France. Dictated at all times by self-interest, this policy was really an application of the theory of "balance of power." For England to have abandoned Flanders or for France to have forsaken Scotland would have been tantamount to knowingly increasing the potential of one's natural enemy, and this obviously could not be allowed. A third issue, related to the first two, was the clash over commercial interests. The bulk of the English wine supplies came from Gascony, which was held as a fief of France, and the English kings were anxious to hold on to this source of their wine imports and the resulting tariff revenues. France, interested in this wine trade and also in the salt industry which was located on the shores of Guienne, preferred to have direct control of these. Similarly, there were overlapping economic interests in Flanders. Next to central Italy, Flanders was the most highly industrialized and commercialized region in Europe at the time. Naturally, the French kings were eager to assert their authority over the county, for they were its rightful feudal overlords. But, as stated above, Flanders imported English wool, and England could not afford to have its principal customer pass under French control. Indeed the English had dynastic ties with the Low Countries, Edward III having as wife Philippa of Hainaut, and his sister Eleanor having as husband Reginald, Count of Gelders.[6]

Always present, these issues became exasperating in the early decades of the fourteenth century, mostly because the French kings, taking advantage of the unsettled conditions in England during Edward II's reign, pressed their claims too audaciously. Hence, when Edward III ascended the English throne, he inherited a situation which seemed intolerable. Although efforts were made to negotiate a *modus vivendi* — indeed, even the pope, Benedict XII, who was engaged in promoting a crusade and needed peace in the west, tried to bring the two countries to terms — nothing came of all the efforts. Accordingly, when, upon Benedict's postponement of the departure of the crusading fleet *sine die*, Philip transferred his naval contingent from Marseille to Normandy and also began to send aid to Scotland to block Edward's attempt to plant his satellite John Balliol on the Scottish throne, Edward deemed war with Philip both inevitable and imminent and prepared for it by introducing an issue which became the ostensible cause of the war.

The issue involved the succession to the French throne. From 987 to 1316 the Capetians had had male heirs. In 1316, however, Louis X died without a son. A posthumous son died shortly after birth, and the crown passed to Louis' brother, Philip V, though Louis had a young daughter. Philip also died without male heirs, and the crown passed to the third brother, Charles IV, who died in 1328 leaving daughters only. The question then was who was to succeed. The nearest heir was Edward III of England the son of Edward II and Isabella, sister of the last three Capetian kings. The French would have no part of Edward, declared that a woman could neither hold the throne of France nor transmit any rights to it, and elected a cousin of the last Capetians, Philip of Valois, who became Philip VI (1328–1350). At the time of Philip's elevation Edward was a minor under the regency of his mother Isabella and of her paramour Mortimer, so that the English government could do no more to challenge the French action than to register a diplomatic protest. In fact, in 1329 Edward was forced to do homage to the French king. But by 1336 he was master at home; and when war seemed inevitable to him, rather than fight it as a vassal condemned for contumacy, he preferred to wage it as a rightful claimant to the French throne and proclaimed himself King of France. The issue was therefore joined.[7]

From 1337 until 1360 several campaigns were launched by the English, and a number of engagements were fought.[8] At Sluys on June 24, 1340, the French Channel fleet was destroyed, giving Edward unhindered access to the mainland. On the other hand, the alliances which Edward had arranged with several princes of the Low Countries, with Flanders, and with Emperor Louis IV failed him, and so he accomplished little in this stage of the war. Failing on the northeastern flank of France, Edward seized an opportunity of a disputed succession to the County of Brittany (1341-1342) to establish himself on France's northwestern flank. Then, on August 26, 1346, came Crecy where much of the flower of French chivalry went down before a numerically inferior army that was actually trying to avoid battle but, having been overtaken, was forced to fight, though on ground of Edward's choosing. The English longbow decimated the charging French knights before they could reach the English lines. The battle won, Edward moved to Calais to acquire a port of debarkation. After a stubborn siege of a year Calais yielded (August 4, 1347) and Edward returned home victorious.

Although Edward had two major victories to his credit, he could not force France to come to terms. Hence desultory fighting continued for the next ten years, punctuated by ill-kept truces. Then Edward planned a two-prong attack, one from Normandy and another from Guienne, under his son the Black Prince. The northern project miscarried, but the Black Prince won a spectacular victory over a French army about seven times greater than his, inflicting some 11,000 casualties and capturing an additional 2,000, among them King John himself and a host of his great barons. This was the famous victory at Poitiers in the year 1356.

This disaster precipitated a serious internal crisis in France, and the combination of national defeat and internal strife enabled the English to extort great concessions. By the Treaties of Brétigny and Calais (1360), they secured an enlarged Aquitaine, Ponthieu, Calais, and the County of Guines in complete sovereignty (Plate IV) and a promise of 3,000,000 gold écus (£500,000) as ransom for the captive king.

The terms, though agreed upon, were impossible for any self-respecting country even if ruled by such a chivalric king as John who voluntarily returned to his captivity when ransom payments could not be met. The war was therefore bound to continue. However, the treaties of 1360 brought the first stage of the war to its close and provide a logical termination to our narrative.

Such was the Hundred Years' War to 1360. It had not come to an end, but it already revealed some definite and significant indications.

It presaged the fact that the English might win battles but that they could not conquer France, wherefore the conflict was likely to be a prolonged struggle. Another indication was that France, subjected to repeated defeats, would suffer in international prestige. It had enjoyed European leadership up to the outbreak of the war; that leadership it would now lose.

The Holy Roman Empire and Italy — The Parting of Ways

THE HOLY ROMAN EMPIRE A significant development of international consequences was the abandonment of Italy by the rulers of the Holy Roman Empire. It was not a voluntary or a complete abandonment, for, as was seen, Henry VII and Louis IV actually invaded Italy to keep it in the Empire. But their ventures failed, while the other emperors could not or did not undertake any serious attempts to preserve the union. The result was that Italy, though claimed as part of the Empire, was able to develop well nigh independently. This parting of the ways was important, of course, for it allowed the Italian cities to continue their evolution as autonomous states.

ITALY In Italy itself the prime political fact was the expansion of several of the larger cities at the expense of their neighbors. To relate the story of these expansions in full would be to get lost in interminable detail, but some of the highlights justifiably may be presented.

Genoa and Pisa, which in the late eleventh century had cooperated in recovering Sardinia and Corsica from the Saracens, became bitter rivals in the thirteenth century for the sole occupation of these islands. In addition, they were contenders for Levantine trade and for maritime supremacy in the Tyrrhenian Sea. Clashes were numerous and recurrent, with victories fluctuating. But the issue was decided in 1284 in the naval battle off Leghorn, near Meloria Reef. The Genoese won decisively, destroying some eighty Pisan ships and capturing between 9,000 and 10,000 prisoners. Thereafter Pisa ceased to be a challenger of consequence.

With Pisan sea power destroyed, the maritime rivalry was confined to Genoa and Venice.[9] Here the issue was competition for the Levantine trade. Ever since the Genoese aided the Palaeologi to recover

Constantinople from Venice (1261) and secured extensive commercial privileges as compensation, the two cities were arch rivals. Repeated wars were fought in which, at first, Venice aided by Pisa generally emerged victorious, but when Pisa was eliminated in the battle of Meloria (1284), victory went to Genoa. At the battle of Curzola (1298), off the Dalmatian coast, the Venetian navy was smashed, and some 5,000 Venetians were carried captive to Genoa, among them Marco Polo who whiled away his imprisonment by dictating an account of his journeys to China. But this victory did not cripple Venice permanently, as Venice had substantial resources to draw upon for recovery. Moreover, the Aragonese sided with Venice because of Genoa's opposition to their claims to Sardinia. The result therefore was the prolongation of the conflict, now and then punctuated by truces, into the Renaissance period.

Having become a maritime power, Venice also turned to the mainland. The reasons were compelling, namely the need of a dependable source of food supply and of secure land routes to the Alpine passes. Accordingly, in the second half of the thirteenth century, Istria was subjected, and in 1308 a disputed succession to Ferrara opened an opportunity there. One of the claimants, facing serious opposition from contestants supported by the pope, sold his rights to Venice, and Venice embarked on its second major land acquisition. The resulting war (1308) ended in the defeat of Venice and in the abandonment of its policy; but only temporarily, for in the thirties of the same century, as a member of an alliance of Lombard and Tuscan states, it acquired Treviso from the Scaligers (1339). Possession of this province naturally drew Venetian ambitions farther up the Po and laid the basis for much of the city's Italian policy throughout the Renaissance period.

The expansion of Milan fluctuated with the family fortunes of its Visconti lords as the power politics of Italy affected them. These fluctuations may be omitted; it is enough to mention that towns which had been lost before 1329 were recovered by Azzo Visconti during his lordship. Pavia, Bergamo, Cremona, Vercelli, Vigevano, San Donnino, Como, Lecco, Lodi, and Piacenza were under Azzo's rule when he died. Then, under Luchino (1339–1349), Asti, Bobbio, Parma, Crema, Tortona, Novara, and Alessandria were added. By 1350, therefore,

Milan had acquired much of the central Po Valley, and so assured its position as a great princely state by the time the Renaissance period opened.

Florence, centrally located, found itself cramped by Siena to the south and Pisa to the west. In addition, its commerce with Rome and with the outside world through the port of Pisa was at the mercy of the intervening towns, hence, its policy was necessarily dictated by its location. Pisa and Siena it was not able to reduce before the Renaissance although several attempts were made, usually as by-products of the rivalry between the Guelfs and Ghibellines. But a number of lesser towns were annexed. By 1350 Poggibonsi, Monte Pulciano, Pistoia, Volterra, and San Gimignano were subjected, so that, as in the case of Milan, the major part of Florentine territory was acquired before the end of the Middle Ages.

In general, then, the political physiognomy of Renaissance Italy had begun to take shape before 1350 as a result of the formation of these several large states. After that date came only the "rounding out" of the respective territories.

Scandinavia — Preparation for a Union and the Penetration of the Hansa

In the Scandinavian Peninsula where the significant internal situation was the decline of monarchic authority, there were two important international developments. One development was the preparation of the groundwork for the subsequent formation of the Union of Calmar (1397). The principal step in that direction was the marriage of Magnus (VI), the Lawmender (1263–1280) of Norway, to Ingeborg, daughter of Eric Klipping, King of Denmark, and then the marriage of their daughter, also Ingeborg, to Duke Eric of Sweden, brother of King Birger Magnusson (1290–1319). Their child, Magnus Eriksson became heir to the Norwegian throne and was also elected King of Sweden. This was, of course, merely a personal union. Still, for a while, during Magnus' minority, his mother Ingeborg was regent for him in Norway and also sat with the Swedish Council which governed Sweden in his name. Magnus' two sons ruled the two kingdoms separately, the older boy Eric receiving Sweden as co-ruler with his father and the younger one, Haakon VI, Norway. However, when Eric died in 1362, Haakon was elected as co-ruler of Sweden in his place. In 1363 Haakon married Margaret, daughter of King Waldemar of Denmark, and it was she who eventually organized the Union of Calmar.

While these dynastic ties did not make union inevitable and, indeed, there were wars among the three countries in the course of these ties, still the occasional union of Norway and Sweden could hardly have passed without conditioning the minds of the nobility of all three lands to the idea of a union. If there was no strong opposition from the Swedish nobility to the election of Margaret's son, who was King of Norway, as there was on the part of the French nobility to the candidacy of Edward III who was aiming at a similar dynastic union of England and France, it would seem more than probable that the prior conditioning had allayed the dislike for it.

The other development of international consequence in the Scandinavian countries was the increasing penetration therein of the Hansa merchants. The lack of a substantial native commercial class enabled the merchants of the German Baltic towns to pre-empt the Scandinavian commerce for themselves. Profits from the iron mines of Sweden, from the herring fisheries of Scania, and from the cod catches off Norway attracted numerous German venturers to settle in Scandinavian towns — Stockholm, Oslo, Trondjem, Bergen — and their settlements became commercial outposts for the large continental Hansa centers. In the thirteenth century the Hansa were able to secure privileges for themselves, and by the end of that century they were powerful enough to protect these privileges from the attacks of Scandinavian rulers. Thus, when Eric II (1280–1299) of Norway tried to reduce their position, they imposed a blockade and forced him to confirm their former rights and in addition to exempt them "from many obligations resting on citizens, such as the *leidang* [service in the militia] and the night watch."[10] True, their position in relation to Denmark about the same time was less strong, for the Wendish League had to recognize Eric VI Menved (1286–1319) as overlord. But this subordination proved to be a temporary one, for the failure of Danish monarchy after Eric's death enabled the German towns to regain their independence and in addition to tighten their grasp on the economy of Denmark. It was this resurgence that led Waldemar IV of Denmark to launch the first Hanseatic War some twenty years after 1350.

Central Europe — The Revival of Hungary and of the Slavs

In central Europe the significant development was the rise to power of the three principal Slavic states — Bohemia, Poland, and Lithuania — and of Hungary. Since this rise was contemporaneous with the decline of the two major western powers, France and the Holy Roman Empire, the focal point of European power politics shifted from western to central Europe, for the time being at least.

To account for this rise is not easy though the course of its history is traceable. One factor undoubtedly was the temporary re-establishment of fairly effective monarchies, which was traced in the preceding chapter. Perhaps another was the introduction of some western socio-political institutions into these lands by way of the royal courts. It will be remembered that the Luxemburgers became kings of Bohemia, that the Angevins ascended the throne of Hungary, that the courts of Poland and Hungary were dynastically bound by the marriage of Vladislav IV's daughter to King Charles Robert of Hungary, and that Poland and Lithuania were tied through the marriage of Casimir III to Gedymin's daughter Aldona. Perhaps a third factor was the improvement of economic conditions in these lands in consequence of the influx of German merchants and artisans, including, of course, the penetration of the Hansa into northern Poland. At any rate, whatever the reasons, there is no doubt that these lands rose to international prominence by the end of the Middle Ages.

Translated into action, this increase in power manifested itself in the expansion of Bohemia into Silesia, of Lithuania into White Russia, and of Poland into Little Russia. Hungary did not make any significant territorial gains before the Renaissance, but it directed its interests toward the Balkans and readied itself to challenge the expansion of Serbia under Stephan Dushan. All of these movements pointed to the future when Lithuania and Poland would face the Tartars, and Hungary, with some help from these two lands and from the west, would oppose the Turks.

The fortunes of Poland and Lithuania were affected by the territorial expansion of the Teutonic Knights along the southern bend of the Baltic Sea. The movement had begun with the Christianizing and colonizing efforts of the Danish King Canute IV and the Livonian Brothers of the Sword, and Estonia and Livonia were occupied in the first three decades of the thirteenth century. In 1237, owing to a serious defeat by the natives in the area, the Livonian Order affiliated with the Order of Teutonic Knights which had been invited in 1229 by the Polish prince of Mazovia to war on the pagan Prussians and had been rewarded with the territory of Chulm. Combined, the two Orders pushed steadily into the Baltic hinterland, and by 1310 they had carved out a state extending from Pomerelia in the west to the Gulf of Finland in the north and encroached on the lands of Poland and Lithuania. It will be recalled that it was this danger which in part led to the re-establishment of monarchy in Poland and to the organization of a Lithuanian state first under Mindaugas and then under Gedymin. From that time on the Order and these two monarchies were bitter opponents, with the gains generally going to the Order and preparing, as it were, for the decisive wars that came in the fifteenth century. This movement is, of course, part of the German *drang nach osten* which has led to repeated conflicts between the Slavs and the Germans, even into the modern period.

Balkan Developments — Turks on the Horizon

In the Balkans there was also an ascendence of a Slavic power, that of Serbia under Stephen Dushan. A brief account of its rise has been given in the preceding chapter and will suffice. All that needs to be noted here is that by 1350 Serbia became the greatest power in the Balkans and thereby contributed to the shift of the center of gravity of political power to central Europe.

On the Asiatic side of the Byzantine Empire there was the phenomenal rise of the Ottoman Turks. Appearing in the thirteenth century in Asia Minor as tribal mercenaries of the Seljuk Turks, the Ottomans acquired some fiefs on the Byzantine frontier. Under their second chieftain, Osman I (1290–1326), they won their independence as the Seljuk Sultanate faltered to its close (1302), and captured a number of Byzantine fortresses, including Doryleum (1290) and Brusa (1326). In the reign of Orkhan (1326–1359) the frontier was moved up to the Straits, Nicaea falling to them in 1329 and Nicomedia in 1337. At the same time a related Turkish tribe, the Karasi, were also absorbed. But it was the marriage alliance between Orkhan and John VI Cantacuzenus that gave the former the opportunity he most wanted. Pressed by the invasion of Stephan Dushan and by the opposition of John V from whom he usurped the throne, Cantacuzenus solicited military aid from Orkhan and to secure it agreed to give Orkhan his daughter in marriage, a humiliating bargain with an infidel and an aggressor. In pursuance of this alliance Orkhan supplied 600 troops in 1346 and 20,000 [!] in 1349. These official missions and many other unofficial raids enabled him to gauge the political and military situation in the Byzantine Empire and to embark on his European venture. In 1354 a raiding party seized the fortress of Tzympe and, in the confusion of an earthquake, also the fortress of Gallipoli. From then on there was no stopping the Ottomans. Though this expansion in Europe took place during the period of the Renaissance, it is of course obvious that it was merely a continuation of the expansion that had started in the Middle Ages and had gained for them much of Asia Minor.

Summary

What is revealed by this brief survey of international developments on the eve of the Renaissance is the establishment of trends which could be expected to continue during the Renaissance. Castile and Aragon were squeezing on the Mohammedans until only the small territory of Granada was left to the latter, and logic would suggest that the conquest of Granada would only be a matter of time. Aragon became a Mediterranean power, and by the conquest of Sicily it was knocking at the door of Italy which conceivably might be forced open at some later date. England and France became engaged in a struggle which could not be resolved until either the English were driven out of France or France was conquered, which meant, of course, that the struggle would prove to be a long one. The Holy Roman Empire, for all intents and purposes, was ejected from Italy preparing thereby for two eventualities, the rise of autonomous Italian states and of rivalry among them, and the possibility of an attempt on the part of the Germans to re-establish their control over Italy. The Slavic states saw the coming-of-age, so to speak, and would be expected to assume the resultant political leadership. Ottoman Turkey had begun its expansion and would be likely to continue this program unless stopped. Finally the Scandinavian states were being maneuvered into dynastic union, which would likely be the principal preoccupation of all the Scandinavian lands for some time thereafter. Thus every single international move of the Middle Ages was preparing the groundwork for the international developments in the age to follow.

1. On the importance of the victories of Alfonso XI see Rafael Altamira, *A History of Spain*, trans. Muna Lee (New York: D. Van Nostrand Co., Inc., 1949), 238.

2. A detailed history of the Catalan Company is available in Setton, *op. cit.*

3. On the implication of this treaty for both countries see Pierre Chaplais, "Le traité de Paris de 1259 et l'inféodation de la Gascogne allodiale," *Le moyen âge*, LXI (1955), 121–37.

4. On this stage of the conflict see Powicke, *The Thirteenth Century 1216–1307*, 270–318, 644–69.

5. Cf. G. P. Cuttino, "Historical Revision: The Causes of the Hundred Years' War," *Speculum*, XXX (1956), 463–77.

6. On the Anglo-French conflict of interests in Flanders and in the Low Countries see Henry Stephen Lucas, *The Low Countries and the Hundred Years' War, 1326–1347*, vol. VIII of *University of Michigan Publications, History and Political Science* (Ann Arbor, Mich., 1929), 52–90.

7. For a detailed treatment of the events that led to the war see Edouard Perroy, *The Hundred Years' War*, trans. W. B. Wells (New York: Oxford University Press, 1951), 60–100. An up-to-date briefer account is to be found in May McKisack, *op. cit.*, chap. iv, "The Origins of the Hundred Years' War." For a summary analysis see Cuttino, *op. cit.*

8. For an interesting narrative of the war, reflecting the spirit of the times, the student is urged to turn to Sir John Froissart's *Chronicles of England, France, Spain and the Adjoining Countries from the Latter*

Part of the Reign of Edward II to the Coronation of Henry IV, trans. Thomas Johnes (revised ed., New York: The Colonial Press, 1901).

9. A clear narrative of the rivalries of Pisa, Genoa, and Venice is available in Mari' Antonio Bragadin, *Histoire des républiques maritimes Italiennes — Venice, Amalfi, Pise, Gênes* (Paris: Payot, 1955), 56–145. For a more scholarly treatment but with Venice as a focus see Freddy Thiriet, *La romanie vénitienne au moyen âge* (Paris: Éditions E. de Boccard, 1952), 105–68.

10. Karen Larsen, *A History of Norway* (Princeton: Princeton University Press, 1948), 182.

III

International Political Developments during the Renaissance

In our analysis of the political conditions in Europe on the eve of the Renaissance, we first examined the internal situation in each land and then the international developments. For the Renaissance period itself we might reverse the order. The international developments were profound and had widespread repercussions on internal affairs; and inasmuch as they were more generic than derivative, they may well be treated first.

The Hundred Years' War after 1360

THE COURSE OF THE WAR In the west a major international event during the first century of the Renaissance was the continuation of the Hundred Years' War. Its causes, its course to the end of the first stage, that is, to the year 1360 when the Treaties of Brétigny and Calais brought it to a temporary halt, and the almost certain likelihood of its renewal because of the severity of the terms imposed on France have been treated above. The narrative may be resumed from that point.

Within a decade after the year 1360 the war was resumed, and it continued intermittently until 1453, passing through three more stages. The second stage lasted until 1415 and favored the French. They regained some of their strength during the period of peace (1360–1369), and then under the cautious policy of Charles V and of his general Du Guesclin to avoid open battles, they gradually recovered most of the losses, so that by 1375, when a truce was agreed upon, only Calais and coastal Gascony remained in the hands of the English. This state of affairs remained unchanged for the next forty years, for in the reigns of Richard II and Henry IV the English encountered a prolonged domestic crisis. But when the Lancastrians, who had usurped the English throne in 1399, finally established themselves securely, they reopened the war, and its third stage began. This lasted from 1415 to

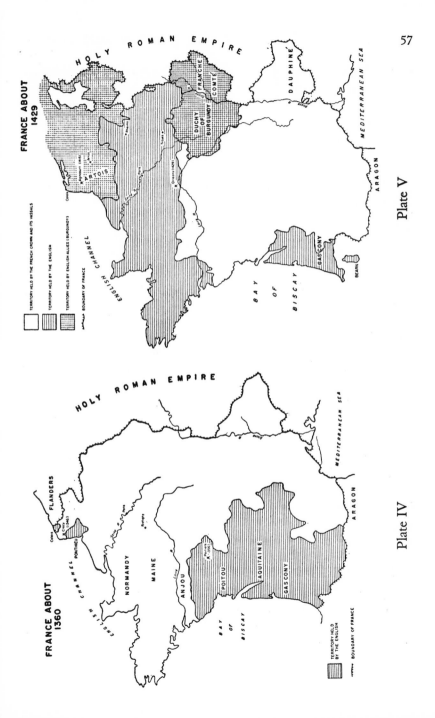

57

Plate V

Plate IV

1429 and brought great success to the English (Plate V). With France torn by a civil war between the factions of the king's uncle (the Burgundians) and the king's brother and nephew (the Armagnacs) for the control of the regency necessitated by the insanity of Charles VI, Henry V was able to win a decisive victory at Agincourt (August 13, 1415), to conquer Normandy, and finally, by the Treaty of Troyes (May 21, 1420), to secure the right of succession to the throne of France on the death of Charles VI and the regency for the duration of the king's life. But Henry himself died barely two years later, before he had time to consolidate his gains, and his spectacular achievement began to crumble, though it was not until 1429, when the war entered upon its last stage, that the hollowness of his victory became apparent. Always overexpanded regarding manpower, and so necessarily dependent on the good will of their Burgundian allies, the English were never really secure. Then, when Joan of Arc, an inspired shepherd maid according to popular tradition but in all probability a princess born to Charles VI's notorious wife and her paramour, the king's gay brother, Louis, Duke of Orleans,[1] revived the hope of the French by leading them successfully to the relief of Orleans (May 1429), the tide of war turned in their favor. This was aided still more when, through the intercession of the pope and the Council of Basel, the Burgundians were detached from the English by some territorial concessions and by the exemption of Philip the Good of Burgundy from vassalage to Charles VII (Treaty of Arras, September 21, 1435).[2] The English, abandoned by their erstwhile allies, yielded ground steadily until by 1453 only Calais remained in their hands; and even Calais would have been lost had it not been surrounded by Burgundian territory which by treaty arrangement was closed to French passage. There was no formal peace concluding the war, but the war ceased when its *raison d'être*, the occupation of French territory by the English, was eliminated.

INTERNATIONAL CONSEQUENCES The war had significant consequences, both for the internal developments in the two countries and for the international situation. Its impact on the internal developments will be treated in the next chapter. But the effects on the international situation need to be considered here.

One of these effects has already been indicated, namely, the expulsion of the English from their continental holdings. This was of utmost importance for both countries. As for England, the expulsion freed it from an impossible continental burden and released its energies, when these were revived, for its insular development; and it was this disentanglement that enabled the country later to embark on overseas ventures and to become the guardian of the Reformation and a challenger to Spain. As for France, the ultimate victory in the war contributed to the consolidation of the royal domain and to the revival of monarchic power.

Another direct result of the war was the rise of Burgundy as an important state.[3] Originating in an appanage which John the Good of France created in 1364 for his youngest son Philip the Bold, the new foundation expanded steadily thereafter. Its first sizable addition came when Charles V, John's son and successor, arranged a marriage between Philip and the heiress of Flanders. Intended as a check upon the English, the marriage was obviously part of the strategy dictated by the war. Subsequently, when large-scale fighting was reopened by Henry V, fortunes continued to favor Burgundy. Boulogne, Tournai, and Maconnais were occupied when the royal power lapsed north of the Loire. Auxerre and Macon were transferred to it from the royal domain by Bedford, regent for Henry VI, to retain its friendship. Lastly, in 1435, by the Treaty of Arras, as the price for returning to the royalist side, the French government confirmed the Duchy in the territories which were given to it by the English conquerors and added by way of guarantee the "Somme Towns," a series of fortress towns guarding Artois from Paris. At the same time the treaty exempted the Burgundian prince from vassalage to the crown. The Hundred Years' War therefore contributed to the rise and expansion of the Burgundian state, which later proved to be a grave obstacle to the consolidation of the French kingdom.

Another effect of the war, this time in Europe as a whole, was the reduction, for the duration of the war, of the influence of the two protagonists on the continental political stage. This reduction naturally redounded to the importance of another power area, and that, as has been indicated above, was the central European block extending from

Poland to Serbia. This is why, for example, the crusades against the
Ottomans were conducted by the central powers, and why the west,
which had borne the burden in the medieval crusades, contributed so
little to them.

Consolidation and Expansion of Spain

Another development of major international significance was the
rise of Spain as a great European power. This was not a new movement, for, as was pointed out above, Aragon had established itself
as a prominent Mediterranean power even before the end of the Middle
Ages. But this second growth, though founded on the first, elevated
Spain to a dominant position in all of Europe.

BIRTH OF MODERN SPAIN The initial step in this rise was the dynastic
union of Aragon and Castile brought about by the marriage of Ferdinand of Aragon and Isabella of Castile. Like many other phenomena
of the Renaissance, this step had its roots in the Middle Ages as the
following genealogy clearly indicates:

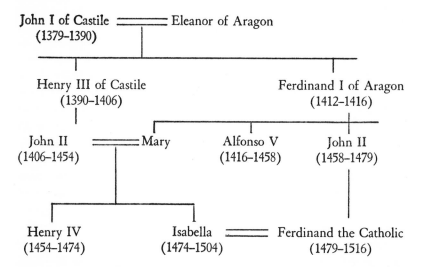

The dynastic unions of Aragon and Catalonia in 1137 and of Leon
and Castile a century later, the cooperation of Aragon and Castile in

the *reconquista,* the increasing acceptance of Castilian as the preferred literary language in the peninsula were all steps in the direction of unification. Much groundwork therefore was laid for this union, and some of it antedates the Renaissance.

The union was not a fusion of states, for, in accordance with the terms of the marriage agreements (1469), the governments, laws, armies, and tax systems remained separate. Still, husband and wife ruled jointly, and it is inconceivable that this partnership should have failed to promote further integration. In Castile, for example, the joint administration of justice and the joint signing of charters when the two sovereigns happened to be together undoubtedly were steps in that direction; while a common foreign policy furthered this still more. But whatever the nature of this union at the time of Ferdinand and Isabella, it gradually became a political reality in the succeeding reigns and served as a basis for Spain's growth as an international power.

The next step in the unification was the annexation of the remaining territories in Spain until the entire peninsula, Portugal excepted, was acquired.

The first of these annexations was that of Granada, the last piece of Spanish territory held by the Moors. Weakened by a prolonged civil war between rival claimants to the headship of the state and having repudiated its tribute obligations to Castile, Granada invited war upon itself. At the same time, Aragon and Castile, troubled with a large Moorish minority and so apprehensive about the ominous surge of Mohammedan Turks in the Mediterranean, were eager to take advantage of these opportunities to eliminate what they deemed to be a potential threat to their security. The war broke out in 1481, and by January of 1492 Granada was conquered. Although the vanquished Moors rebelled shortly thereafter in defense of their right of free worship, which had been conceded to them at the time of surrender, they failed to regain their independence, and Granada became part of Spain.

After Granada came the reannexation of Roussillon and Cerdagne which had been forfeited by Ferdinand's father, James II, to Louis XI of France for a loan of 300,000 crowns. Now, in 1493, by the Treaty of Barcelona, Ferdinand recovered these from Charles VIII as a price for Spanish neutrality in Charles's projected war on Naples. Even though Ferdinand found a way out to interfere with Charles's designs, he held on to the recovered provinces.

The last piece of Spanish territory which Ferdinand added was that of Navarre. Located at the west end of the Pyrenees and controlling the coastal valleys running from Spain to France, the little country was of considerable strategic importance. Throughout history it aligned with France or Spain as circumstances dictated, and during Ferdinand's reign, because its ruling family also held the French counties of Foix and Bearn, it was perforce pro-French. Once France and Spain became enemies, the disposition of Navarre became vital. This, of course, occurred often enough, but it was in consequence of Ferdinand's accession to the Holy Alliance in 1511 against Louis XII that final action was precipitated. Ferdinand's entry into the Alliance alarmed both Louis XII and Navarre and they started negotiations for a mutual defense pact. Louis offered to respect Navarre's rights to Foix and Bearn and to come to the aid of Navarre against Ferdinand who was claiming its crown through his second wife, Germain de Foix, a descendant of a collateral branch of the ruling dynasty. In return, Navarre was to bar Ferdinand's access to France. Ferdinand could not afford to ignore the impending arrangement. He charged that France and Navarre were conspiring to attack him; and getting the support of Pope Julius II and of Henry VIII of England, who had his eyes on Guienne, he invaded and quickly overran the country in 1512. Three years later he incorporated it into the crown of Castile, and with that addition the formal unification of Spain became a reality.

TERRITORIAL AND DIPLOMATIC GAINS LEADING TO SPANISH HEGEMONY

In the meantime Ferdinand had entered upon two other courses which led to Spain's international greatness. One was the acquisition of the Kingdom of Naples. The kingdom had been in the hands of the descendants of Charles of Anjou, its conqueror in 1266, until the death of Queen Joanna II in 1435. Joanna had led a devious personal life, and her politics corresponded to her conduct. At one time she willed the crown to Alfonso of Sicily who was Alfonso V of Aragon and then repudiated her will and transferred the right of succession to a collateral line of Angevins in France. Alfonso insisted on his "rights" and conquered the kingdom in 1443. On his death Alfonso left Naples to his illegitimate son Ferrante who in 1494 was challenged by Charles VIII of France, inheritor of the Angevin claims. The ease with which Charles marched all the way down to Naples and the equally spectacular conquest of Milan by Charles's successor Louis XII necessarily drew Ferdinand into the lists of Italian power politics. Without tracing their course in any detail, it is enough to point out that Ferdinand first entered into a secret treaty with Louis XII (Treaty of Granada, 1500) for the partition of Naples, and then, when Louis ran into difficulties in northern Italy over Milan, conquered the French share of the spoils (1502–1504). Thereafter Naples remained under Spanish control. The other course was the negotiation of dynastic marriages that brought prestige and power to the Spanish crown. Ferdinand arranged the marriage of his daughter Isabella to the Portuguese Infante Alfonso and, when Alfonso died, to his uncle Emmanuel who became King of Portugal (1495–1521). Then, when Isabella died in 1498, he married another daughter, Maria, to the widowed Emmanuel. Ferdinand apparently was determined to have Portugal tied to his family. His marriage arrangements with the Tudors are well known, his daughter Catherine being married first to Crown Prince Arthur and then to his brother Henry VIII. Ferdinand married his son John to Emperor Maximilian's daughter Margaret, and his oldest daughter Joanna, to Philip the Handsome of Burgundy, son of Maximilian. The Portuguese marriage eventually brought Portugal to the Spanish crown; the English connection served as a check on France; while the double marriage into the house of Austria not only detached Maximilian from France but also brought Burgundy within the sphere of Spain and paved the way for the election of Charles, Ferdinand's grandson, as Holy Roman Emperor.

These solid accomplishments of Ferdinand were augmented by his successor. His only son, John, predeceased him (1497) and the crown passed to his daughter Joanna with her husband Philip as consort; but Joanna lost her mind, and in 1516 the crown passed to her son Charles who on the death of Philip also inherited Burgundy. Although Charles was at first opposed in Spain as a foreigner, in the end he quelled all opposition and held on to his mother's rights. Then, in

1519, his money prevailed upon the Electors of the Holy Roman Empire and he was chosen Emperor. With the Empire he also acquired the ancient imperial rights to Italy — he inherited Naples and Sicily from Ferdinand — and strategy dictated that he should secure northern Italy lest it fall to France and become a block to his lines of communication between Germany and Spain via the Mediterranean. Hence throughout most of his reign, Charles strove to get control of Italy for Spain, and in general succeeded in his goal. Western Europe accordingly fell under Spanish ascendancy, with France, alarmed at this state of affairs, trying desperately to counteract it.

Simultaneously with this expansion in Europe Charles secured Spain's position in North Africa; while Spanish explorers and *conquistadores*, Cortez and Pizarro in particular, following the trail blazing of Columbus whom Isabella subsidized, added the precious lands of Mexico and Peru. Spain thus became a veritable giant.

Charles, worn out by the exhaustive wars forced upon him by the demands of the Empire, abdicated in 1556 and left his vast dominion divided between his brother Ferdinand and his son Philip II, Ferdinand getting Germany and Philip getting Spain and the remaining territories. The division did not weaken Spain as much as might be expected, for the two crowns cooperated. Spanish ascendancy therefore continued, at least for a decade or two longer. But the rise was soon reversed, for the Low Countries rebelled against Spain's rule and its religious persecution, while the English seadogs raided its shipping and its colonies, and the two together, coupled with graft and general fiscal mismanagement, drained the country's treasury dry. Even the acquisition of Portugal in 1580 did not stem the decline, for on the other side of the ledger the secessionist movement of the Dutch gained momentum and eight years later, in 1588, came the disastrous defeat of the Spanish Armada. This last event constituted a divide in the history of Spain as a dominant European state and is a fitting place at which to terminate this survey of Spain's rise to power.

Expansion of Turkey

Equally important for the history of Europe was the growth of Turkey and its expansion in the Balkans and in the Middle East (Plate

VII, p. 75). Its emergence in Asia Minor and its occupation of a beach-head on the European continent on the eve of the Renaissance have already been traced. What is needed here, therefore, is a survey of its expansion into the heart of central Europe and around the eastern Mediterranean.

Once on European soil, the Ottomans continued their advance into the Balkans without check until the end of the century. Byzantium was in a hopeless state; Serbia had disintegrated on the death of Stephan Dushan in 1355; Bulgaria was tottering; and the western houses ruling in Greece proper were puny and divided. It was relatively easy therefore for Orkhan's successors, Murad (1359-1389) and Bayazid I (1389-1402), to expand into the interior. Twice the various Balkan powers offered joint opposition, once at Kossovo (1389) and again at Nicopolis (1396) where some western feudal contingents joined them, but to no avail. Both operations failed, with the result that by 1400 Bulgaria was destroyed, a great part of Serbia annexed, and Byzantium reduced practically to the city itself. At the same time some Aegean islands were occupied, Phrygia and Bithynia annexed, and the Greek Empire of Trebizond reduced to vassalage. All that remained in the way was Constantinople, and that was besieged in 1397 and might have fallen had it not been for the timely eruption of Tamerlane's Mongol hordes into Asia Minor. The siege had to be abandoned to meet the new enemy, and in the ensuing clash the Turks were defeated at Angora (1402) and their sultan, Bayazid, was carried away captive. This terminated the first tide of Ottoman expansion. The period from 1402 to 1413 was an interlude in the expansion, the Ottoman world being rent by civil war among Bayazid's sons. But this proved of little advantage to the subjugated Christian lands, for by aligning with what proved to be the losing side they necessarily paid the price of defeat, which meant, of course, continued subjection. With that the interlude of Christian opportunity ended and a second wave of Ottoman expansion got under way.

The second stage, which lasted through the reigns of Mohammed I (1413-1421), Murad II (1421-1451), and Mohammed II (1451-1481), began with the advance of the Ottoman frontier deeper into Serbia and Greece. Next, when the Christians, who had momentarily won a

victory at Varna (1444), were stopped in 1448 at Kossovo, Constantinople was attacked. The capital finally fell in 1453 after a defense that
redeemed the military honor of the decadent empire. After that came
the conquest of the principalities of Athens and Morea and of several
islands in the Aegean. Albania fell next, notwithstanding the heroic
resistance of its national hero Skanderbeg, then Bosnia in the west, and
Azov, Crimea, and Karaman in the east.

Following this stage came a second interlude, that associated with
the reign of Bayazid II (1481–1512). Tradition, originating with
Machiavelli (*Discourses*, I, 19), attributes this lull in Ottoman expansion to Bayazid's alleged pacifism. Perhaps a more compelling reason
was the constant danger that confronted him on all sides and at all
times. For the first fourteen years of his reign the west held a trump
card against him in the person of his brother Jem who, having failed
in his bid for the throne, sought safety with the Knights of St. John in
Rhodes and was later transferred into the custody of Pope Innocent
VIII and Pope Alexander VI and of Charles VIII of France when
the latter invaded Italy in 1494. To prevent Jem's release Bayazid
found it expedient to remain at peace with the west. Nor did he dare
to commit his armies elsewhere, lest the west grasp the opportunity
to launch an attack on his European territory. And this condition
lasted until 1495 when Jem died. Then, from 1503 Bayazid was faced
with a religious rebellion in Anatolia, and with the prospects of war
with a resurgent Persia. Finally, to make matters worse, Constantinople
was hit by an earthquake (1509), while Bayazid's three sons, each
with aspirations to the throne, jockeyed for power and harassed the
country with rebellions. Indeed, in the end, he was actually deposed
by the militant janissaries in favor of his son Selim, the youngest but
the most warlike member of the family. In general, therefore, Bayazid
had little opportunity for aggrandizement. Still, in the interval between
Jem's death and the outbreak of rebellion in Asia Minor, he did manage
to fight a war with Venice and to wrest from it Durazzo and its
Greek bases at Lepanto, Navarino, Modon, and Coron.

Selim I (1512–1520) initiated the third stage of expansion. His own
efforts were directed into Asia and Africa. Upper Mesopotamia was
taken from Persia whose shah had given support to Selim's brother

and nephew; and the whole of the Mameluke empire, comprised of Syria, Arabia, and Egypt, was easily added next (1516–1517), due largely to the preponderance of Turkish fire power. With the latter conquest came the holy cities of Mecca and Medina and the caliphate itself, so that thereafter the Ottoman sultans acted also as religious heads of all Mohammedans. Under Suleiman the Magnificent (1520–1566) the Asiatic expansion was continued in the conquest of Lower Mesopotamia, but it was in Europe that the greatest gains were made. In 1521 Belgrade, gateway to Hungary, was captured. His two attempts on Vienna were turned back; but he did succeed, after a smashing victory at Mohacs (1526) and several other campaigns, in reducing Hungary, part as a vassal state under his appointee Zapolya, and part as a tribute-paying state under Charles V's brother Ferdinand. In addition, he acquired Croatia, Rhodes which had hitherto served as a post for Christian naval operations in the eastern Mediterranean, and the remainder of Venetian Morea and some Venetian islands in the Aegean. Moreover, it was under his aegis that some Mohammedan pirates displaced the Spanish Moslem protégés in North Africa: Kheyr-ed-din, brother of the notorious Barbarossa, occupied the province of Algeria as the sultan's Governor General, and, temporarily, Tunis also; and Dragut mastered Tripoli (1552). Under Suleiman's successor, Selim II (1566–1574), Cyprus was conquered from Venice (1570), but with that the Mediterranean phase of the Ottoman expansion as well as the third stage came to an end. Alarmed by the repeated Turkish naval victories, Spain, Venice, and the papacy combined their naval strength and defeated the Turkish navy at the crucial battle of Lepanto (1571). Even if the allies failed to exploit the victory further, it was decisive in halting the Turkish advance in the Mediterranean. In the opinion of Cervantes who fought in the Spanish ranks, the victory was "the most glorious event that the present and the past ever saw or will ever see."

Since the European and the Mediterranean phases of Turkish expansion occurred during the Renaissance period, Turkey must undoubtedly be recognized as a Renaissance star. Still, it must not be forgotten that the initial growth of Turkey in Asia took place in the later Middle

Ages, and that its successful expansion in Europe was paved by the Fourth Crusade (1202–1204) and the power vacuum which the Crusade created in the Balkans and in Greece.

Territorial Consolidation of the States in Italy

The consolidation and expansion of Spain and Turkey were paralleled by like movements in the larger states of Italy. But in the case of the latter, these movements were more decidedly continuations from the pre-Renaissance period.

Of the five principal states in Italy, the Kingdom of Naples and the Papal States had attained their maximum extent in the late Middle Ages, and so during the Renaissance their rulers were concerned mostly with the preservation of what they already had. Thus, there is no story of Neapolitan expansion to be told. There were recurrent but unsuccessful Neapolitan encroachments on the papal territory, but these were less expansionist in their aims than products of the rivalry between the two branches of the Angevin family or between the Angevins and the Aragonese for the throne and of the intervention of the popes as feudal lords of the disputed kingdom. The papacy had a somewhat more deliberate expansionist program, but this has already been related in Book II of this series. What remains therefore to be considered is the expansion, or rather the attempts at expansion, of the other three major states.

From the territorial core which Florence had established before the Renaissance, its principal expansion could be directed westward only, as Siena, the papal territory, and Milan blocked the remaining three directions. In 1406, after many earlier wars, Florence finally annexed Pisa, thereby eliminating a Ghibelline stronghold and gaining a seaport. It added Leghorn in 1421, but its attempt on Lucca (1429–1433), according to Machiavelli's account (*History of Florence*, Bk. IV, chaps. 4 and 5), failed miserably. The largest addition, that of Siena, was not acquired until shortly after 1550. Bitter foes throughout their history, Siena being generally a Ghibelline outpost, the two cities had engaged in many wars, but Siena was able to preserve its independence until the advent of Charles V in Italy. Then, in the 1550's, in the war between Henry II of France and Charles V, Siena made the

Plate VI

mistake of repudiating Spanish hegemony and accepting French help. Cosimo de'Medici, the first Duke of Tuscany and the Emperor's protégé, promptly entered the war against Siena, and when the struggle was over in 1555, Siena was made part of Cosimo's dominion, though it was conceded the right to have its own government. This terminated the Florentine expansion, so that Florence may be said to have completed its territorial growth by the end of the Renaissance.

Like Florence, Milan had also established the major part of its dominion before the Renaissance. Thereafter its expansion generally involved Venice and Florence and fluctuated with the fortunes of the resulting wars. Without attempting to trace these wars,[5] complicated as they were by the tortuous activities of the *condottieri* who were employed to wage them but who tried to exploit them to personal advantage,[6] we might note that the big issues between these states were whether the boundary between Milan and Venice should be the Adda River or the more easterly Adige River and whether Milan should be allowed to annex Genoa and to control Liguria to the south. Under Gian Galeazzo Visconti (1378–1402) and then again under Filippo Maria (1412–1447), the Milanese had pushed to the Adige and occupied Genoa. This expansion led Venice and Florence to form a defensive alliance, with other states aligning themselves on one side or the other as their interests dictated. In the end the Milanese lost Genoa and were thrown back to the Adda; and the Peace of Lodi (1454), which finally closed these wars and in which the five principal Italian states were signatories, defined the Milanese boundary as it had existed prior to these attempted expansions. And so it remained for the most part during the next four decades of the precarious balance of power and the subsequent half-century when Italy became the battleground between France and Spain. Hence despite all its efforts at expansion from 1350 to 1450, Milan held no more territory at the end than at the beginning of the Renaissance period.

Venice on the other hand saw its possessions grow on land and decline on the sea. On land, by the middle of the fourteenth century, it had acquired Istria and the March of Treviso. In the first decade of the following century the Carraressi of Padua, its protégés who deserted to the side of Genoa during the War of Chioggia, were liquidated, and Verona, Vicenza, and Padua were annexed. In the next decade, as a result of a war against Emperor Sigismund over the control of the Croatian coast and against the Patriarch of Aquileia because of competing claims to jurisdiction over the Venetian clergy, the regions of Feltre, Belluno, and Udine, and the whole of Friuli were added. Then, as a result of involvement in the wars against Visconti, Venice's western boundary was moved to the Adda, where it remained, with only occasional temporary deviations, until the formation of the League of Cambrai in 1508. This alliance of the papacy, France, Spain, and the Empire was aimed at the dismemberment of Venetian land possessions and indeed succeeded in detaching large areas. But in the subsequent shifting of allies and in the resulting fluctuations of war between the French and the imperial sides, Venice was able to recover most of its losses, so that by the end of the Renaissance it still held most of the territory it had acquired prior to 1450. In that sense, then, the Venetian land empire, although entered upon in the late Middle Ages, was mostly a Renaissance accomplishment.

As to the Venetian sea empire, the reverse is true: most of the acquisitions were made before the Renaissance, although it could not have been known until Genoa's challenge in the Levant was eliminated in the War of Chioggia (1379–1380) whether these would be retained or not, and most of them were lost during the last century of the Renaissance.

The Venetian retreat on the sea was the result of its aggressive expansion in Italy and of the rise of the Ottoman Turks. Of the first, a brief account has been given already. The second has also been treated but with a focus on Turkey and not on Venice as the present topic requires.[7]

Until the reign of Murad II (1421–1451) the attitude of Venice to the Turkish expansion was governed by its trade interests in the Levant. Thus it wrested the island of Tenedos from Emperor John Palaeologus by threatening him with a Turkish alliance and deposition; and again, in the time of the Turkish civil war following Bayazid's defeat at Angora, it negotiated a commercial treaty with the victor Mohammed I. Also, the first major naval battle between the two powers (Gallipoli, 1416) was not planned but was forced upon them by the crews, and the victory which Venice won there was not turned against the Turks but was used to secure an advantageous commercial treaty. But with the resumption of Turkish expansion under Murad, its possessions were recurrently attacked and steadily reduced. Thessalonica, which had been acquired as a grant from the Greeks, was lost in 1430, as well as Modon in Morea. Then, after the fall of Constantinople released the Turkish striking power against the west, Negroponte, Lemnos, and Scutari were lost in a general war that lasted from 1463 to 1479, and Lepanto and some additional cities in Morea, in another war twenty years later (1499–1503). The last post in Morea fell in 1540, and Cyprus, which had been acquired in 1489 from the widow of the last Christian prince, was lost in 1570. Although the Venetians and the Spaniards stopped the Turks at Lepanto (1571), it was only after Venice had been deprived of most of its possessions east of the Adriatic Sea. Thus Venice entered the Renaissance period with a maritime empire and saw much of it gone by the end of the Renaissance.

The Rise and Decline of Central European States

In central Europe, the Slavic lands of Bohemia, Poland, and Lithuania and the non-Slavic Hungary had just entered upon a promising stage of their history as the Renaissance period began. During the two centuries of the Renaissance they saw their role as international powers rise somewhat and then either decline or collapse.

BOHEMIA   Raised to prominence by the great Luxemburger prince, Charles IV who was also elected Holy Roman Emperor, Bohemia quickly lost its position under Charles's incompetent son Wenceslas, a drunkard whose reign ended in civil war and in his deposition. Under his successor, his brother Sigismund, Bohemia was weakened still more by the prolonged revolt of the Hussites, a group whose Czech nationalist resentment against the German nobility and against the established church exploded into bitter war, first against the authority of the Emperor and the church, and then, among themselves. Following these disasters, came the loss of several provinces to the aggressive Hungarian king, Matthias Corvinus, and finally, as the Renaissance period drew to a close, Bohemia actually became an annex of the Polish crown.

HUNGARY The fortunes of Hungary duplicated those of Bohemia, except for the difference that its decline was interrupted by a vigorous period under Matthias Corvinus. Under Lewis the Great (1342–1382) Hungary expanded its territories significantly and became a power to be reckoned with: it wrested Dalmatia from Venice, invaded Bosnia, reduced Wallachia and Moldavia to vassal status, and prepared to resist the Turkish expansion. Under his successors it entered upon a decline for some seventy years. Sigismund and his son Albert of Habsburg concentrated their attention on their imperial interests and treated Hungary merely as a buffer state, while the Polish successor Ladislas III and Albert's young son allowed the baronial opposition to get out of hand. Hence the gains made under Lewis the Great were lost and the defense against the Turks crumbled. The crusades of Nicopolis (1396) and of Varna (1444) failed miserably and left Hungary exposed to constant Turkish danger. Fortunately, this critical situation brought forth a man of promise, the warrior John Hunyadi, whose exploits in defense of the country won for his son Matthias Corvinus the crown of Hungary.

Matthias' reign was the interlude referred to above. Exploiting the nation's reaction to foreign rule, Matthias created a standing army and with it turned against the west, ostensibly, as Hungarian sentiment alleges,[8] to unite Germany and Bohemia with Hungary and to turn their combined power against the Turks. But whatever the reason, the western venture proved successful. From Bohemia, still torn by civil war, Matthias acquired the provinces of Moravia, Silesia, and Lusatia (Treaty of Olomoric, 1478), and from the Habsburgs, after three campaigns, he won Styria and Lower Austria, including Vienna (1485), whither he transferred his capital. But the success was only temporary — the forced union naturally violated the historical separateness of German and Magyar lands and was personal at best, and so when Matthias died (1490) without a legitimate heir, his work died with him. Thus politically, Matthias' period of glory was nothing more than a passing interlude.

Following this brief period of strength, Hungary relapsed into decline. The nation split between those who were prepared to accept a foreign king, Ladislas of Bohemia, in the expectation that he would be too weak to continue Matthias' policy of strengthening central authority, and the nationalists who were no more zealous supporters of centralization than the so-called court party but who did prefer a native king and a more nationally oriented program. In the course of this civil war the Turks resumed their advance up the Danube. In 1526 came the disastrous defeat of Mohacs at the hands of Suleiman, and then the partition of Hungary between the Turks and the Habsburgs. The day of an independent Hungary was over. It had been revived at the beginning of the Renaissance; it existed no more at the end of the Renaissance.

POLAND-LITHUANIA In the case of Poland and Lithuania, the revival of their international position, which started at the beginning of the Renaissance, continued throughout most of the Renaissance period. As noted above, the revival began in the two lands separately and reached its maximum by 1350 or shortly thereafter. Poland succeeded in acquiring Galicia, and Lithuania expanded southward to the Black Sea (Plate VII) by the end of Olgierd's reign (1345–1377). Thereafter, however, to hold these additions against resurgent Tartar power and expanding Muscovy and to ward off the Teutonic Knights, the two states were obliged to form a union. Hence the history of these two lands during the Renaissance is the history of the consummation of this union and of the union's attempts to preserve its territories.

The union began as a dynastic affair — the Polish heiress Jadwiga married Grand Duke Jagiello, the ruler of Lithuania (1386 — though the marriage treaty was signed August 14, 1385). In return for the Polish crown the Lithuanian duke agreed to convert his people to Christianity and to make his lands the fiefs of Poland.[9] At the outset the union was personal, for the chief legal tie between the two lands was the recognition of the same person as chief of state. However, the introduction of the Catholic Church into Lithuania, which this treaty provided for, was bound to serve as a unifying factor beyond the purely personal character of the union. Moreover, pressing needs steadily drove the two cooperating lands to closer political ties. Without tracing in detail the progressive consolidation of this union, we might point to two or three of the principal steps. In 1401, the Lithuanian Prince Vitold, Jagiello's cousin and vicar, after having been de-

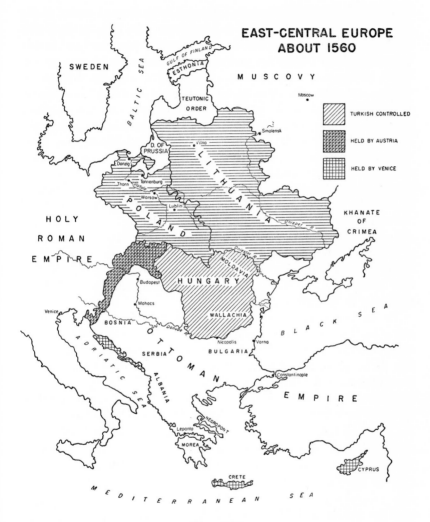

Plate VII

feated in his attempt to separate Lithuania from Poland, agreed to the principle that the union was to be "permanent." In 1413, by the Union of Horodlo, the council of the Grand Duke was recognized as a proper advisory body of the crown, and conferences between Lithuanian and Polish delegates were permitted. At the same time the Lithuanian nobility was given the same privileges that the Polish nobles enjoyed, and the principal noble families were admitted into the nobiliary Polish clans.[10] In 1501, by the Act of Union in Mielnik, when the Grand Duke Alexander, brother of the deceased Polish ruler John Albert, was chosen king of Poland, it was provided that the two offices of King of Poland and Grand Duke of Lithuania were to be one. Finally, in 1569, provision was made for a joint Senate and Chamber of Deputies and a common currency, though the highest state offices, treasuries, armies, courts of appeal, legal codes, and state languages still remained separate. This then is as far as the Union went, union of the crown and parliament. Although otherwise the states still remained separate, the fact that the crown was one meant that the foreign policy was one also; and therein lay the influence of Poland-Lithuania in international politics.

In the course of the consummation of this Union the two lands strove hard to keep their extensive territories and to expand them still more. On the eastern and southern fronts this effort proved unsuccessful. Although in the 1420's Lithuanian and Polish troops marched beyond Moscow and reduced many Russian dukes to vassalage, in the end this suzerainty was repudiated and Muscovy in turn occupied White Russia — including its center, Smolensk. In the south the Turks seized the northern littoral of the Black Sea, cutting off the profitable trade that originated there and moved up the Dnieper and the Bug rivers. The seizure provoked the greatest Polish effort (the "Black Sea Expedition" of 1497) against the Turks to that date, but the expedition turned into a fiasco when the Prince of Moldavia, a Polish vassal, declined to join the march, and Hungary and Muscovy supported his betrayal. But if success was wanting on these two frontiers, it was not wanting in the north. There, the perennial enemy, the Teutonic Order, was finally subdued. In 1410 Jagiello and Witold won a signal victory at Tannenberg, though they gained little from it in the First Treaty of

Thorn (1411) because of their failure to capture the Order's capital, Marienburg, and because the Prussian subjects of the Order, uncertain about the eventual outcome of the war, returned to their loyalty to the Order. The results of the next serious challenge to the Knights were notably different. In a war which began with Casimir IV's acceptance of the lordship of Prussia offered to him by discontented Prussian subjects of the Order, and which lasted thirteen years (1454–1466), the Order was reduced to straits; and when intervention on its behalf by several interested powers was countered successfully by Casimir, it came to terms. By the Second Treaty of Thorn (1461) the Order ceded western Prussia, including the valuable estuary of Vistula, to Poland and agreed to hold the rest of its territory as a Polish fief. Poland thus reacquired access to the sea, which had been lost to it for a century and a half, and became a Baltic power. It is noteworthy that it was Casimir the Great who, without formally renouncing Polish rights to Pomerania, surrendered it to the Order and oriented Polish expansion southward into Ruthenia, and that it was his namesake, Casimir IV, who, failing to hold the gains in the south, turned Polish efforts northward and with success.

Casimir IV's victory did not wholly eliminate the danger from the Order. In general, the Order had moral and diplomatic support of the Holy Roman Empire, and it tried to take advantage of the Muscovite pressure on Lithuania. On several occasions it sought to repudiate the terms of the treaty and actually provoked war, that in the reign of Sigismund I being the gravest. The issue finally came to a close, however, when the Grand Master of the Order, Albert of Hohenzollern, accepted Lutheranism. He declared the Order dissolved and its territory secularized with himself as the first Duke of Prussia, while the majority of the members aligned themselves with him and entered the ranks of the local nobility. The "revolution" alienated and aroused the Holy Roman Empire, wherefore Albert found it necessary to come to terms with Poland-Lithuania. By the Treaty of Cracow (1525), Sigismund accepted Albert's arrangements, and, in turn, Albert rendered homage to him. The dangerous problem of the Teutonic Order thus came to an end.

In addition to this territorial acquisition, Poland-Lithuania during the Renaissance enhanced its role in international politics by successfully placing its princes on the thrones of Bohemia and Hungary. Jagiello's son Ladislas III, who succeeded him as King of Poland, was also elected King of Hungary, largely due to a conjecture of interests of the two countries. Poland felt the need of Catholic Hungary to stem the overflow of Hussitism and to counter the anti-Polish negotiations between the Empire and Moscow, while Hungary needed Polish support against the Ottomans. Since the heir to the throne of Hungary was a minor, it seemed clear that the interests of the two countries might be better served by having the Polish king elected as ruler of Hungary; and this was presently done. The result did not turn out as expected, for the crusade which Ladislas launched ended in defeat and in his own death (Varna, 1444). But though the enterprise did not bring glory to Poland or security to Hungary, it was nevertheless a clear demonstration of Poland's key position in central Europe. Later, while Casimir IV reigned in Poland, his son Ladislas was elected king of both countries (Bohemia in 1472 and Hungary in 1490). Although Ladislas' succession to the throne of the latter country was contested by his own brother John Albert, who had the father's support, in the end opposition was withdrawn and Ladislas ruled both lands. Since Lithuania had a Grand Duke from the same family, practically all of central Europe north of the Danube was ruled by Jagiellonians. If individually some of the rulers were weak, the fact that members of the same family ruled other lands contemporaneously naturally enhanced the influence and prestige of them all. It would not be improper, therefore, to regard north-central Europe during the Renaissance as being under Jagiellonian hegemony.

Scandinavia and the Union of Calmar

In the Scandinavian north the important international developments revolved about the Union of Calmar — its establishment, the unsuccessful attempts of the Danish kings to preserve it, and the chief outcome of its dissolution, namely, the birth of a dynamic Sweden.

The inception of this Union[7] has already been studied, and its roots, it should be remembered, go back into the late Middle Ages.

Its realization fell within the Renaissance period and was the work of Margaret, daughter of Waldemar of Denmark and wife of Haakon of Norway.[11] When her father died in 1375, Margaret prevailed on the Danish nobility to elect her son Olaf as king. Five years later, when her husband died, Olaf became King of Norway also, and in 1385 she had Olaf assert claims to Sweden. All this enterprise was jeopardized when Olaf died, but Margaret was not to be denied. In 1387 she had herself elected regent in Denmark with the title "mistress and ruler with full authority as guardian of the realm"; the following year she acquired the same office in Norway; and in 1389, as a result of a civil war, the victorious baronial party of Sweden which was opposed to a strong central monarchy elected her ruler of Sweden. She then secured the recognition of her grandnephew, Duke Eric of Pomerania, as heir and at Calmar, in 1397, at a meeting of the Scandinavian nobility, Eric was crowned sole king and the terms of the Union were drawn up. The Union was to be perpetual; sons were to succeed in all kingdoms, and in the absence of heirs election was to be in common; and mutual assistance was arranged. Thus the Union was to consist in the unity of the crown and in a common foreign policy, but the laws and the administrations were to remain separate.

Under Eric the Union was tightened by the insinuation of Danes into Norwegian and Swedish fiefs, by the appointment of royal bailiffs, by the establishment of central administrative bureaus at Copenhagen, and by the filling of church vacancies in all three lands with the king's friends. He strengthened the Union further by defeating the Hansa and by collecting tolls from ships passing through the Sound. But that was the height of the Union, for from the 1430's on, recurrent opposition challenged it and reduced it to a precarious state.

In general, the opposition began as peasants' revolts against the increasing impositions of their landlords, some of whom were Danish nobles, but was easily channeled into nationalistic rebellions against the Danish rule. The Danish peasants also revolted. Eric's position became untenable and he fled. The crown passed to his nephew Christopher, nobility's tool. When Christopher died, the succession was contested, and though Count Christian of Oldenburg in the end defeated his principal opponent, Karl Knutsson of Sweden, and became sole ruler of all three lands (1457), his hold remained insecure. Sweden could not be cowed by force, as attempts at repression merely fanned the independence movement. Christian's son Hans, in alliance with Muscovy, was able to defeat the Swedish leader Sten Sture, Knutsson's nephew, and to reassert his kingship (1497), but the work had to be done all over again fifteen years later by Hans's son, Christian II. In 1520 occurred the infamous "Blodbad" at Stockholm, when Christian, after having beaten the opposition, summoned the leaders to a conference and had a great number of them executed in cold blood. The blood of these "martyrs" drowned the Union in Sweden. In 1521 Gustaf Eriksson, known as Gustavus Vasa, with his yeomen and burgher supporters began the "War of Liberation"; on June 7, 1523, he was elected king; and one month later the last Danish garrison capitulated. So far as Sweden was concerned this was the end of the Union.

Norway, much poorer and weaker than Sweden, its nobility riddled with recent Danish immigrants and so divided between nationalists and unionists, did not succeed in liberating itself. On the contrary, when Christian III succeeded in establishing Lutheranism in Denmark and decided to extend it also to Norway, he terminated Norway's separate existence, and declared the country annexed to Denmark (1536). Here, too, then the Union ended, though not in independence as in Sweden, but in annexation.

As suggested above, an important result of the dissolution of the Union was the emergence of a dynamic Sweden. The anti-Union wars, insofar as they were supported by the peasants and the burghers, were themselves evidence of this dynamism. But it was under Vasa that this potential came to life and prepared Sweden to play a prominent part in the Baltic and indeed in Europe at large. Vasa's work, however, was principally internal, and therefore will be treated as part of the next topic.

Decline of the Hanseatic League

Another international factor in the Baltic area, including the North Sea, was the Hanseatic League. Its economic and constitutional phases have been covered in Book I of this series. Here only the political phase receives attention.

The history of the Hansa as a political power of consequence began with the alliance of many of the Baltic and Rhenish towns against Waldemar IV of Denmark whose aggression in the Baltic threatened their commerce and their independence. In the ensuing war the alliance won and dictated the famous Treaty of Stralsund (May 24, 1370). By the terms the League secured complete freedom of trade throughout Denmark, the right to have its own officers in all the German settlements in Scania, exemption from the laws of wreck, and other advantageous arrangements. And, as a guarantee, Denmark was obliged to surrender to the League four of its principal strongholds in Scania for a period of fifteen years and to concede to it the right of participating in the election of Danish kings. This victory and this treaty made the League a major political power in northern Europe, and thereafter, during the Renaissance, it concerned itself with the preservation of this position.

For the first hundred years or so the League was able to maintain its ascendancy. In the Scandinavian Peninsula it participated actively in the various struggles involving the Union of Calmar, always with an eye toward its economic security and always in opposition to any movement which promised to produce a strong power that might threaten that security. On the distant flanks, at Novgorod and Bruges, it successfully employed the commercial blockade to force confirmation of its trading rights. In England it intrigued in the Wars of Roses, helping Edward IV to regain the throne, and secured its trading monopoly there. Thus until 1475, although there were some signs of forthcoming decline — such as the rising Dutch competition and the appearance of disunity among the League members over commercial policy — the League remained a strong force in northern Europe.

From 1475 on, the League's position deteriorated, both economically and politically. The economic impairment was brought about by the mounting competition from the Dutch and English, by the decline of Bruges, and by the closing of the entrepot at Novgorod in 1494. The political deterioration resulted from the nationalistic ventures of the lands in which the League traded. The loss of Novgorod was due to the expansion of Muscovy under Ivan III; the decline of Bruges, while caused in part by certain economic and natural factors, was also due to the promotion of competing centers of trade and commerce by the Burgundian princes; the loss of the Prussian cities was brought about by the enlargement of Poland-Lithuania at the expense of the Teutonic Order which was a constant ally of the League; Vasa's nationalist Sweden, despite the help that Gustavus had received from Lubeck, eliminated the League's privileged position there; and Tudor England, threatening from time to time, actually closed the Steelyard once the Armada was defeated. But in addition to these losses to the rising national states, it was Lubeck's involvement in the Counts' war in Denmark — a dynastic war in which Reformation was an issue — which weakened the League politically beyond repair. It had entered upon this war under the leadership of one Jurgen Wullenweber in the hope of recovering its position in Denmark and then of driving the Dutch out of the Baltic. But the gamble failed. Its forces were defeated, and the cost of war strained its relations with the League members who did not favor the war. This was in the 1530's, and thereafter the League rapidly declined, even though it continued to take part in Baltic politics as late as the Thirty Years' War.

The Habsburg-Valois Conflict[12]

If the Hundred Years' War was the principal international event in the west in the first hundred years of the Renaissance, the Spanish-French rivalry was the major fact in the last sixty years of the period.

CAUSES Protracted as the struggle was, its causes multiplied as new historical circumstances affected it. Appearing at the outset and persisting throughout the entire sixty-year period was the rivalry over the territory of Burgundy. When Duke Charles the Rash of Burgundy, an inveterate enemy of Louis XI of France, died at the battle of Nancy (1477) without leaving a male heir, his lands became the immediate prey of the wily French king. To ward off Louis' aggressive importunities, Charles's daughter and successor Mary married Maximilian, heir to the Holy Roman Empire, who immediately countered Louis. In time, however, the two rivals agreed to divide the spoils. By the Treaty of Arras (December, 1482) Flemish and Walloon Flanders and the Low Countries were assigned to Maximilian; Picardy, Somme towns, Boulonnais, and the Duchy of Burgundy went to France; Franche-Comté and Artois were to go to France upon the marriage of Maximilian's daughter to the Dauphin. But the marriage arrangement was renounced so that Charles might be free to marry the heiress of Brittany, and by the Treaty of Senlis in 1493 the last two counties reverted to Maximilian. In this way the issue of Burgundy entered into the relations between France and the Empire. The issue was passed to Mary's heir, Philip the Handsome, and then to Philip's son by Joanna of Castile, Charles I; it became critical when Charles inherited Spain in 1516 and even more so when he was elected Emperor in 1519. Both sides, for strategic reasons, wanted Burgundy in entirety or as much of it as possible, and so it remained a contentious matter throughout the rest of the struggle.

Another cause was the rivalry over Naples. How the rivalry originated has already been reported in our account of the territorial expansion of Spain. Here we might repeat that the claims of the Angevin line to Naples were inherited by the French dynasty but that Alfonso of Aragon conquered the kingdom, passed it to his illegitimate son Ferrante, and that when the French king Charles VIII sought to seize it, Ferdinand of Spain and Maximilian joined with Milan, Venice, and the papacy to prevent the annexation. Naples thus became a matter of concern both to the Holy Roman Empire and Spain, and when their interests were merged in the accession of Charles to both thrones, it became an even more vital issue.

The third cause was the rivalry over Milan. The French claimed the Duchy on the grounds of the marriage of Valentina Visconti to Louis, Duke of Orleans, whose grandson became Louis XII of France. Spain had no claim to the territory, but it inherited Maximilian's double rights when Charles V became Holy Roman Emperor. One right was the age-old claim that Milan was part of the Holy Roman Empire, and the other was Maximilian's marriage to the daughter of Ludovico Moro of the Sforza family which had acquired Milan in 1450. Moreover, possession of Milan was strategically vital to both powers after Charles became Emperor. Milan was a major link between the Empire and

Spain via the Mediterranean, and Charles could not afford to let it fall into French hands. From the French point of view Milan in the hands of Charles was the link that completed the encirclement of France, and France could not afford to let the Emperor close that link. It is important to recognize that what began as a clash of claims became a bitter struggle over vital strategic territory.

These three causes were united in one major issue, namely, concern of all western powers over the balance of power. At first, the French aggression in Italy constituted the threat. The successes of Charles VIII and Louis XII alarmed Spain and other powers and led to wars against them. Subsequently, when Charles united Burgundy, Naples, Spain, and the Holy Roman Empire under himself, the balance of power passed to Spain and naturally provoked bitter French opposition. The conflict thus became a fight to prevent Europe from falling under Spanish ascendancy.

These were the fundamental causes. A subsidiary cause was the ambition of the French kings Charles VIII, Louis XII, and particularly Francis I. They dreamed of conquests and glory and let their ambition carry them into one war after another.

THE COURSE OF THE CONFLICT The course of the conflict is a complicated one, and only the salient stages can be given here. It falls into two major stages, that against the French kings, Charles VIII and Louis XII; and that between Charles and Francis and its continuation between their respective sons Philip and Henry II.

The clash began with Charles VIII's invasion of Naples in 1494. The field was prepared for him by the disruption of the balance of power in Italy which had functioned quite effectively since the 1450's. After the Visconti line of Milan had expired in 1447 and the Milanese aggression had been stopped by Venice and Florence, a general peace treaty was negotiated (Peace of Lodi, 1454) in which the five major states of Italy — Florence, Milan (then under the Sforza), Venice, the papacy, and Naples — agreed to cooperate against any disturber of peace. Although there were several wars among the signatories themselves during the next fifty years, none resulted in an imbalance in Italy, as the shifting of alliances among them prevented any side from momentarily acquiring real preponderance. But toward the end of the fifteenth century the entente among Milan, Florence, and Naples, which balanced that of Venice and the papacy, began to break up. Ludovico Moro, regent for his nephew Gian Galeazzo Sforza in Milan, revealed what appeared to be intentions to usurp the ducal throne of his ward. But the ward's mother, Isabella, was the daughter of Ferrante of Naples, and Ferrante naturally became suspicious. Since Florence maintained close ties with Naples as a check on the pope who had fallen out with the Medici over some disputed church fiefs which Lorenzo's son-in-law alienated to the detriment of the reigning Pope Alexander VI, Ludovico felt insecure in Milan. To divert danger from himself he encouraged Charles VIII to assert his claims to Naples, and Charles, seeing the rising discord among Italian states and receiving further encouragement from some Neapolitan exiles and from Roman and Florentine intriguers who wished to see their respective governments fall, decided to do so. At the same time, he prepared for the venture by unburdening himself of possible dangers on the three sides of France. By the Treaty of Senlis (May 1492) which released him from his betrothal to Maximilian's daughter so that he would be free to marry Anne of Brittany, Charles returned Franche-Comté and Artois to Maximilian and apparently agreed to Maximilian's "designs" on Venice and thereby removed the danger from the east. In November of the same year he signed the Treaty of Étaples with Henry VII of England which provided for cessation of hostilities between the two countries — over French seizure of Brittany — and for an annual subsidy of 50,000 francs to Henry. In the southwest, by the Treaty of Barcelona (January 1493), he ceded Rousillon and Cerdagne to Ferdinand of Spain and in return got what he believed to be Ferdinand's neutrality.[13] With his European frontiers safe and Italy beckoning, Charles moved into the peninsula and the conflict was started.

Charles's descent into Italy proved easy. Milan, Florence, Siena, and Rome opened their gates to him perforce, and Naples had to be abandoned to him by Ferdinand II (Ferrantino), son of Alfonso II who only recently had been forced to abdicate because of the nation's dislike for him. But Charles's "promenade" south turned into a hasty retreat. Alarmed at his swift success, Milan, Venice, the pope, Ferdinand of Spain, and Maximilian leagued against him, and Charles, fearing to be cut off from his home base, beat a fast retreat. He was intercepted at Fornovo, but due to imperfect coordination of the intercepting armies he was able to repel his interceptors and to continue his withdrawal. In the meantime Ferdinand II, helped by the Spaniards, re-entered Naples. Charles's invasion was over, but at the same time it uncovered all the political "sores" which were to plague Italy and Europe for a long time.

Charles died in 1498 and was succeeded by his cousin Louis of Valois-Orleans as Louis XII. Since Louis was a descendant of Valentina Visconti, he claimed Milan in addition to Naples. To attain his objective he first dissolved the League of Venice: he detached Venice by promising it some Milanese territory west of the Adda; he bribed Pope Alexander VI by promising to help him establish his son Cesare as a prince in Romagna; and he appeased Maximilian, who was preoccupied with a Swiss rebellion, by surrendering some towns in Artois to his son Philip of Burgundy. Feeling secure, he descended into Italy and occupied Milan (1499). Momentarily he appeared to be solidly entrenched, but he risked this position when he agreed with Ferdinand of Spain to partition Naples (Treaty of Granada, 1500). The two powers presently occupied Naples, but within two years they disagreed about the division and engaged in war, Louis losing his share of Naples. Writing off his loss in Naples, Louis reconciled with Ferdinand and joined with him and Maximilian, and with the Pope and Florence in the League of Cambrai (1508) for the recovery and partition of the Italian lands which Venice had wrested from its neighbors in the past century. In the ensuing war with Venice Louis' forces carried all before them, but his very success proved his undoing. Alarmed at his extensive annexations, his former partners in the rape of Venice formed the Holy League against him (October 1511), prevailed on the Swiss to switch to their side, and drove him out of Milan (1512). At the same time Ferdinand seized Navarre, while northeast France was invaded by Maximilian and by Henry VIII who won the Battle of the Spurs (August 16, 1513). The pressure was more than France could bear, and though Louis momentarily regained Milan, he was decisively defeated at Novara (June 1513) and driven out of Italy for good. For the second time France was checked by a concert of powers, of which Spain and the Empire provided the striking force and the papacy the political and diplomatic initiative.

Although Louis XII had restored peace with all his enemies, his successor — his cousin and son-in-law Francis I (1515–1547) — resumed the struggle. But with the accession of Francis and that of Charles as King of Spain and later as Emperor the struggle became more European than Italian as it had been hitherto.

Francis reopened the Italian issue by conquering Milan (Battle of Marignano, 1515). His victory was decisive and crumbled all opposition for the time being. The pope, the Emperor, and the new Spanish king, Charles, each made peace, recognized the occupation of Milan, and settled other differences. Outstanding among these arrangements was the Concordat of Bologna by which Francis renounced French recognition of the principle that a church council is above the pope and, in return, secured papal approval for the crown's nominations to bishoprics, abbeys, and priories, a concession which formalized royal control of the church in France. But everything changed when Charles, who was already ruler of Burgundy, Spain, and Naples, was elected Holy Roman Emperor in 1519. Francis regarded this as encirclement, and a sense of urgency grew upon him as he saw Henry VIII of England accepting Charles's bid for an alliance and saw his Italian opponents preparing to challenge his occupation of Milan. Since Charles was at that time faced with the Lutheran problem in Germany and with a civil war in Spain, Francis decided to anticipate the contest and reopened the war.

He began hostilities on three fronts, in Navarre, Luxemburg, and north Italy. None succeeded. His forces were checked on the first two fronts, and his allies lost in Italy. Francis tried to retrieve his situation in Lombardy, but lost all. He was thoroughly defeated at Pavia (February 1525) and was carried away prisoner. Charles as victor and captor was in a position to dictate his own terms. He was urged to be severe but decided on more honorable terms. By the Treaty of Madrid (January 1526) Francis was released, though he had to leave his two sons as hostages, to surrender all claims to Italy, Burgundy, Flanders and Artois, and to consent to a marriage with Charles's widowed sister Eleanor of Portugal.

Francis was not a man to take his oaths seriously, particularly if he felt that they were wrung from him under duress. Hence, once on French soil, he repudiated his promises and set to work to renew the struggle. Europe was alarmed at Charles's great victory and presently a league was formed (League of Cognac, 1526) including the pope, Milan, and Florence. At the same time Francis invited Suleiman to undertake a simultaneous operation against Charles, and so the sides were drawn up for the resumption of the struggle.

The War of the League of Cognac lasted until 1529. Charles reestablished his control of Milan (1526), and his army moved toward Rome to detach the pope from the League. It was an angry force that marched southward, unpaid at the moment and ready to exact its price from the enemy. Rome was sacked (1527) — Cellini was one of the defenders and he brags in his *Autobiography* how he fired the shot which killed Charles's general, the French Duke of Bourbon who had deserted to Charles when Francis deprived him of the Bourbonnais. Though the French forces were able to recover much of the lost ground, eventually, when the Genoese Admiral Doria who directed the naval operations for Francis deserted to Charles because of inconsiderate treatment, all was lost again. The pope signed the Treaty of Barcelona (June 1529) agreeing to recognize Charles's claims to Naples and to crown him Emperor. Two months later Francis signed the Peace of Cambrai. He was allowed to retain Burgundy and his two sons were to be released upon the payment of an agreed ransom, but once more he had to agree to the surrender of all claims to Italy, Flanders, and Artois. In Italy, Charles reinstated the Sforza in Milan, compelled Venice to restore the papal and Neapolitan towns it had seized, and forced Florence to take the Medici back as its dukes. In a word, Charles remained master of Italy, and this was symbolized by his coronation by the pope as King of Italy and as Holy Roman Emperor.

The very fact that Charles remained master meant that all the French fighting to date had been in vain, and this made renewal of the struggle inevitable. Hence, although the two kings were at peace from 1529 to 1535, Francis was preparing for another attempt, intriguing with Charles's enemies, particularly the Lutherans and the Turks, and waiting for an opportune moment to resume the desperate contest.

The moment appeared when the restored Sforza dynasty came to an end in 1535. Francis claimed Milan for his second son, and since Charles was preoccupied with the Protestants and with the Turks, Francis reopened the war. Engagements were fought in north France, in south France, and in Italy, but no decisive victories were won. In the meantime, the Turks had driven the Venetians out of the Aegean and completed their occupation of Morea. This Turkish surge westward caused alarm in Europe. Accordingly, Pope Paul III was persuaded to join Charles, Charles's brother Ferdinand of Hungary, and Venice in a league against Turkey, and in turn succeeded in negotiating a truce (Truce of Nice, January 1538) which confirmed the terms of the Peace of Cambrai and allowed the belligerents to hold what they had conquered.

Although the two years' war had not been decisive, actually it had brought advantage to Francis, for he had occupied Savoy and about two-thirds of Piedmont and was allowed to hold them. Since this gave him control of the approaches to Italy, he was not unwilling to sign a truce on these terms, as he could use the interval to prepare for another trial. Hence, while entertaining Charles's overtures for peace, he arranged a dynastic alliance with the House of Cleves, one of the few strong Lutheran opponents of Charles, and bided his time. That time came when Charles, discerning Francis' insincerity in the negotiations concerning the final disposition of Milan, withdrew his offers of compromise on the issue and invested his son Philip with the Duchy. Francis regarded that as *casus belli* and reopened the war when news reached him that Charles's expedition against the Mediterranean pirate Barbarossa ended in failure.

The new war began in 1541, though it was not officially declared until July 12, 1542, and lasted until 1544. After some early reverses Charles moved deep into France, and his ally, Henry VIII of England, laid seige to Boulogne, while Francis' ally, Barbarossa, who was operating from the French port of Toulon, was prevented from seizing control of western Mediterranean. At the same time Charles's diplomacy succeeded in isolating France. The German Protestants were won over by the suspension of anti-Lutheran measures (Diet of Speyer, 1544) and by the spectre of the Turkish advance, and Denmark and Sweden dropped their opposition when Charles withdrew support of his niece's claims to their thrones. Francis was ready to talk peace, and Charles, who wanted a free hand to deal with the problem of Lutheranism in Germany, agreed to give honorable terms. Accordingly, in 1544, war was terminated by the Treaty of Crespy. Charles renounced claims to Burgundy, and Francis to Naples, Flanders, and Artois. Milan was to be renounced by Francis if his son were to marry Charles's niece, daughter of his brother Ferdinand of Hungary. Savoy and Piedmont were to be restored to the house of Savoy. In addition, Francis promised to help against the Protestants and the Turks.

The peace between the two powers lasted until 1552 and then war was resumed, provoked largely by Charles's success against the Protestants after 1544. They were defeated in the Schmalkaldic War (1546–1547) and had to accept the *Interim* (1548), a definition of dogma which was strongly pro-Catholic. Discontented, they sought for allies and found Francis' successor, his son Henry II, receptive. By the Treaty of Friedwald (January 1552) Henry was promised Cambrai, Metz, Toul, and Verdun and in return agreed to aid them against Charles. Henry invaded Lorraine to occupy his prize, and the war began.

The war with the Protestants went against Charles and led him to agree first to the Treaty of Passau (August 1552) and subsequently to the Religious Peace of Augsburg (September 1555) which recognized each prince's right to determine the church for his subjects. This left the French to carry on the war alone. Battles were fought on the eastern front and in Italy, but there was no Marignano or Pavia, although the recovery of Siena which had expelled the imperial garrison at the promptings of France was a signal victory. Accordingly, in 1556, The Truce of Vaucelles was concluded but with no alteration in the status quo.

Even before the truce was signed, events were preparing for another and final clash in this series of wars. When Paul IV (1555–1559) was elected Pope, he undertook to free Italy from Spanish domination. He entered into conversations with the Lutherans and the Turks, and made a secret treaty with Henry II, agreeing to invest Henry's son with Naples if the Spanish were driven out. War broke out in the following year, with Philip in charge of the Spanish interests, as Charles had abdicated in 1556. Once more the French and their allies were stopped in Italy, while in northeastern France they were defeated at St. Quentin (1557) and at Gravelines (1558), though they captured Calais in the meantime. Since a decision could not be forced, the belligerents decided on peace.

The lack of a decisive victory was not the only reason why the war ended when it did. There were at least two additional reasons. One was the death (November 17, 1558) of Mary Tudor, Queen of England, Philip's wife and partner in the war. Mary had drawn her people into the war on Philip's side against their wishes, so that the war was unpopular with them. Now Mary's death and Elizabeth's accession injected uncertainty as to the direction of England's foreign policy in the immediate future. As a child of Anne Boleyn and Henry VIII, whose marriage led to the establishment of Protestantism in England, Elizabeth might be expected to adopt an anti-Catholic, and so an anti-Spanish, policy. Indeed, it was not beyond possibility that she might even combine with the continental Protestants. On the other hand, because the great majority of her subjects at the time of her accession were Catholic and she was known to be a realist, Elizabeth might be expected to be circumspect about joining the anti-Spanish side. Moreover, it was clear, if Elizabeth hoped to recover Calais from the French, that she could not afford to alienate Spain. Thus there could be no certainty as to what Elizabeth's policy might be; and until Elizabeth revealed her hand more clearly, Spain and France could not afford to prolong the fighting. Peace under the circumstances was therefore more feasible than war. The other reason, and in the opinion of some authorities perhaps the main one,[14] was that France and Spain had exhausted their financial resources in the 1550's and were in a state of bankruptcy. In the last two or three years of the war both states had defaulted on some of their financial obligations and had to "refinance" their outstanding debts. As the "refinancing" entailed a deliberate scaling down of former debts, the value of the royal bonds naturally dropped, bringing ruin to many bankers and scaring capital away. Although some foolhardy creditors were found who were willing to advance new loans in the hope of protecting the old ones, the amount of capital that could be raised under the circumstances was clearly insufficient to keep the war going. Hence the peace.

The peace was signed at Cateau-Cambrésis in February 1559. By its terms France was allowed to keep Calais and the three bishoprics of Metz, Toul, and Verdun, but had to renounce all claims to Italy and restore Savoy and its holdings in Piedmont to the House of Savoy. Since both nations were presently torn by internal conflicts — France by the Wars of Religion, and Spain by the revolt of the Netherlands — large-scale war between them was out of the question for the time being, and so the era of bitter rivalry came to an end.

The long rivalry, we noted, was over Italy, Burgundy, Flanders, Artois, and in general over balance of power. As to the territorial issues, they ended in a draw, for Spain kept Flanders and Artois and Italy, and France got Burgundy. As to the other issue, Spanish ascendancy was definitely weakened. But the war's by-products were most important. Because of the conflict, Italy lost its independence for another three hundred years, Lutheranism survived, Venice was driven out of the eastern Mediterranean, and the Turks entrenched themselves in the Danube. Truly it was a momentous international struggle.

Overseas Expansion[15]

While undoubtedly the principal factors that shaped European political history during the Renaissance were European, there was one development of signal importance which extended beyond the embattled continent. It was the "expansion" of Europe.

PRE-RENAISSANCE VENTURES This "expansion" started long before the era of Diaz, Da Gama, and Columbus. In fact it started before the Renaissance, in the twelfth century, when in the course of the Crusades Europe expanded into the Levant. It continued into the interior of Asia even when the Crusader states were lost; for, with the appearance of the Mongols under Genghis Khan in western Asia, efforts were made by the papacy and the French king to enlist their aid against the common enemy, and this led to the opening of Asia. Although this penetration was not political, as some of the later ones became, it was important as a prelude to the expansion later in the

Renaissance period. It fired the imagination of the west with visons of a fabulous Orient and it stimulated the missionary zeal with prospects of whole empires to convert.

The commercial phase of this penetration is rightly associated with the two overland trips to distant China which the celebrated Polo adventurers made between 1260 and 1269 and between 1271–1295. They were not discoverers of new trade routes or markets, for the overland routes from Peking to Caffa in the Crimea or to Trebizond were used before them and the East was known as a lucrative market.[16] Indeed, there are reports of a Genoese ship headed by the Vivaldi brothers attempting to reach the Indies by sailing westward from Gibraltar. But their trips "dramatized" this "eastern" orientation and stimulated the intercourse. Before long, there were Italian trading posts in India, central Asia, and China; and the overland traffic came to be regarded as a matter of course. The Florentine merchant Pegolotti, for example, made the casual entry in his book that the route to Peking was "quite" safe." Hence, as far as the western commercial interests were concerned, Asia was not a closed land.

The religious phase of this ingress occurred simultaneously with the commercial penetration. In 1245 the Franciscan John of Plano-Carpini journeyed to the Khan as Innocent IV's envoy, and in 1252 Friar William of Ruysbroeck was sent by Louis IX of France to seek the Khan's permission to bring Christianity to his people and to invite him to join with the Christian West against the Moslems. Although the alliance did not materialize, Christianization found considerable success, as missions were founded in Persia, India, and China, and an archbishopric with seven suffragans was established in China.

This first stage of European penetration of Asia ended shortly after 1350. The fall of the Mongols in China (1355–1368) to the nationalist Ming Dynasty, who naturally turned against things foreign, led to the closing of the Christian missions there; while the acceptance of Islam by the Mongols of Persia terminated the Christian enterprise there. Moreover, the eruption of Tamerlane in western Asia in 1369 dislocated all established relations between the West and the East. Yet, although the European withdrawal from central and far eastern Asia actually took place, Europe retained its interest in that fabulous continent. Knowledge of the vast trade possibilities in Asia remained strong, and it was this knowledge that later induced the Europeans to return there.

PRINCE HENRY THE NAVIGATOR AND THE PORTUGUESE EXPANSION The new movement, anticipated by the discovery (sometime between 1320 and 1339) of the Canaries by some Genoese navigators in the employ of Portugal,[17] began with the steady advance of Portuguese sailors southward along Africa's Atlantic coast. The moving spirit behind this exploration was Prince Henry the Navigator (1394–1460), the youngest son of John I. He gathered around him skilled navigators and cartographers, equipped the necessary ships, and inspired all with an ardent zeal for exploration.

His motives were several. For one thing, he simply wanted to discover the unknown. Secondly, he still had the crusader's desire to subdue the Moslems; and to do so he thought it necessary to know how far south the territories of the Moors extended, which could be determined by sailing down the west coast of Africa and then penetrating into the interior of the continent. He was also anxious to bring the Cross to the heathen; and the tales of a Christian king, Prester John, ruling over a nation of Christians somewhere in central Africa, or perhaps Asia, spurred him on. Then, of course, he was keenly aware of the economic profits to be gained from opening new trading areas. All these strong motives he communicated to his associates and subordinates, both native and Italian,[18] and they responded with the courage and labor necessary for the task.

Although each of these intrepid sailors serving under Henry deserves to be honored individually, we can only report the sum total of their accomplishments. By the time of Henry's death in 1460, the principal island groups off Africa — Azores, Madeira, Canaries, Cape Verde — were rediscovered or discovered for the first time and their colonization undertaken; the African equatorial coast was skirted far beyond Cape Bojador, a legendary danger point, probably even down to the Gulf of Guinea; and trading posts were established and trade in gold dust and slaves was opened.

Following Henry's death this movement continued, though at a slackened pace at first. Notable was the crown's employment of "private enterprise" to promote further exploration. In 1469 Alfonso V leased the trading rights to the Gulf of Guinea to Fernão Gomes of Lisbon for ten years with the stipulation that each year he explore one hundred leagues of the coastline. This brought the exploration to the equator. Then, in 1482, Diogo Cão advanced to the mouth of the Congo and farther south to Cape Cross. Under John II the tempo increased. Bartholomew Diaz rounded the Cape of Good Hope in 1488, and Vasco da Gama duplicated the feat and then sailed north to the east African ports of Mozambique, Mombasa, Malindi, and thence across the Indian Ocean to Calicut, India, and home again (July 1497–September 1499). The Portuguese arrived in the Orient and they got there by outflanking the Mohammedans. Thereafter, exploration yielded to "empire building."

The "empire building" was that of a commercial and not of a territorial nature, and its establishment was the work of several bold men. Pedro Alvares Cabral founded a trading factory at Cochin, India, after having bombarded Calicut where the opposition to European encroachment began to mount under Mohammedan animus. Francisco de Almeida undertook to establish Portuguese monopoly of trade in the Indian Ocean. He instituted a system of licensing which intruded on the carrying trade of the Egyptians, hitherto the principal middlemen between the European merchants and the Indian trade, and reinforced it with a smashing victory over the combined fleets of the Indians and Egyptians (Diu, February 2, 1509). Alfonso de Albuquerque seized Goa, which was converted into a key outpost, and extended the empire farther east by occupying Malacca and by imposing Portuguese overlordship on Sumatra and Java (1511). He planned to divert all trade that went by way of Egypt and Syria by gaining control of the Persian Gulf and the Red Sea. By seizing Ormuz (1515) he secured the first objective, but he failed to take Aden and so the Red Sea trade eluded him.

From the foundations laid out by the foregoing, the empire was extended. Along the Asiatic coast posts were established in Ceylon, Burma, China, and finally Japan, and in the Indies more of the islands were incorporated. By the end of the Renaissance then the Portuguese empire in the East was completed.

In addition to this Eastern empire, Portugal also staked out a claim in the West. In 1500 Cabral's expedition to India touched Brazil, perhaps accidentally but possibly by design, as reports of explorations by Columbus' successors along the north coast of South America must have been known in Portugal by that time. Cabral sent a ship back with the information, and in pursuance of the news the crown dispatched an expedition to explore the coast and to establish trading posts and forts. However, the relative poverty of the discovered land as compared with the wealth of the Orient discouraged extensive occupation, and the colony remained more or less dormant for the next two decades. Only the threat from French intrusion and Spanish penetration led to a determined program of exploration and colonization under John III (1521–1557). The French were checked and the country was organized for purposes of government and development. In 1532 it was divided into fifteen fiefs, each fifty leagues wide along the coast but of indefinite depth into the interior, and granted to interested parties (*donatarios*) on condition that they explore, colonize, and govern their grants. Some grantees made an effort to comply with the terms, with the result that several settlements came into being, the most promising being Martin Affonso de Souza's São Vincente and Santos and Duerto Aoehe's Pernambuco where a thriving sugar industry developed. But the system as a whole failed in its intent, and John decided to put Brazil under royal control. The fiefholders were deprived of their political functions, though not of their fiefs, and all authority was vested in a governor-general subject to the crown. Under this system as a crown colony Brazil had new life breathed into it and was saved for Portugal.

SPAIN IN AMERICA AND IN THE PACIFIC While Portugal was establishing itself in the Orient and in Brazil, Spain, which had the same objectives, established itself in the West. Christopher Columbus had prevailed on the Court of Castile to sponsor an expedition to sail to India by way of the west. In the fall of 1492 he touched the Bahamas, Cuba, and Haiti but thought that he had reached some outlying fringes of Japan and so reported to the authorities when he returned to Spain. On his second voyage he founded a settlement in Hispaniola, and on this and on the two subsequent voyages he explored the West Indies and touched the mainland. Alfonso de Hojeda with Amerigo Vespucci in his company explored the coast of Venezuela and established the colony of San Sebastian on the Gulf of Uraba (1509). Juan de Esquivel started a settlement in Jamaica (1509) and Diego Velasquez began the colonization of Cuba (1511). Vasco Nuñez de Balboa in search of precious minerals traversed the Isthmus of Darien and sighted the Pacific (1513). He also founded the city of Darien. Juan Ponce de Leon discovered Florida, and Juan Diaz de Solis reached the Rio de la Plata. Pedro Arias de Avila, appointed governor of Darien, founded Panama City (1519) and through his subordinates, Gil Gonzalez de Avila and Hernandez Gonzalo de Cordoba, pushed the conquest of Central America. The brilliant Hernando Cortez added the rich Aztec kingdom of Montezuma with its capital at Tenochtitlan (Mexico City) between 1519–1521. From there, explorers and conquerors moved in every direction. Francisco Vasquez de Coronado carried the Spanish claims northward into what today are the states of Arizona, New Mexico, Texas, and Kansas; Hernando de Alarcon explored the Lower Colorado; and Cabrillo and others moved up the coast as far as Oregon. To the south, Guatemala, Honduras, and Yucatan were also occupied. Originating not in Mexico but in Cuba was the expedition of Hernando de Soto which traversed much of southeastern United States. Francisco Pizarro, a man of daring and determination, after repeated failures, finally reached the land of the Incas (1527) and conquered it (1532–1533). From Peru, Chile was invaded and the cities of Valparaiso, Santiago, and Concepción were founded, but full occupation was bitterly resisted by the natives. Sebastian Cabot ascended the Parana and the Paraguay (1528), and within a decade a permanent colony was founded at Asunción. Finally, in the 1540's, the two streams of Spanish penetration, one from Peru and the other from the South Atlantic coast, met, thereby completing the process by which Spain staked out for itself all of South America except Brazil.

While these conquerors were opening new lands and subjecting strange peoples, a newly naturalized compatriot of theirs, Ferdinand Magellan, challenged the uncharted seas and circumnavigated the globe.

Magellan was a Portuguese and had served his country with distinction in its colonial enterprises in India and in the Spice Islands. But when he lost favor with the court, possibly because of allegations that he traded with the Moors, he gave up his Portuguese citizenship and offered his services to Charles V of Spain, promising to lead a Spanish expedition to the East Indies by way of the west. His offer was accepted, and on September 20, 1519, he started on his quest with five small ships.

The venture proved to be very hazardous. It took him fourteen months before he located the passage, now bearing his name, that carried him from the Atlantic to the Pacific. Then followed a long journey across the Pacific, fraught with starvation and disease. In March of 1521 he finally reached Guam where he revictualed, and the following month he arrived at Cebu in the Philippine Archipelago. While there, he joined its chieftain in a war on the neighboring island of Mactan where he and many of his crew met death. The survivors sailed on, touching Borneo and Moluccas where one of the two remaining ships and its crew stayed behind because the ship proved unseaworthy. The one remaining ship pressed on around the Cape of Good Hope and finally reached home late in the summer of 1522.

Magellan had died, but he had found what all western Europe was looking for — a route to the Orient by way of the western seas. In addition, he added the Philippines, the Marianas, and other Pacific islands to the Spanish empire.

It is to be noticed that while the two Iberian nations divided the Orient and the New World between them, the empires which they created were different. Portugal, as was stated above, established a commercial empire with only a minimum of territorial occupation. Spain, on the other hand, conquered and claimed vast territories for itself. Perhaps the difference lay in the fact that, except in Brazil, the Portuguese ran into populous and organized societies who tolerated the establishment of trading posts but would not tolerate occupation, whereas the Spaniards in America, in spite of the vaunted glories of the Aztecs and the Incas, had really little effective opposition to their ventures. Certainly the opponents which fell before the small Spanish contingents led by Cortez and Pizarro could not have been powerful.

At the same time the presence of precious metals, both in finished form and in deposits, made occupation of the land desirable. The *conquistadores* were hungry for gold, and to get it they claimed the land for their king. Spain thus emerged as a territorial empire.

FRENCH VENTURES The stupendous successes of Spain and Portugal naturally tempted other Western powers to enter the race. Francis I of France was sure that Adam did not make a will "bestowing the world on these two neighbors."[19] Accordingly he dispatched navigators into the unknown West. In 1524 Giovanni da Verrazano probed the east coast of North America for a passage to Asia, but other than providing France with a claim to the northern half of North America, he found little of value. More solid was the achievement of the Breton, Jacques Cartier. In three voyages (1534, 1535, and 1541) he explored Newfoundland, Prince Edward Island, and the Gaspé, sailed up the St. Lawrence River as far as present-day Montreal, and planted a post at the present site of Quebec, thereby establishing French claim to what later came to be Canada. But that was an insignificant acquisition in comparison with the empires carved by Spain and Portugal. Besides, the work of colonizing the Canadian wilderness had to be resumed by Samuel de Champlain in the following century. Hence, other than establishing a claim to parts of North America, France had no overseas empire during the Renaissance period. That was to come later.

ENGLISH VENTURES England proved even less successful as an "empire builder" during the Renaissance. In 1497 and 1498 John Cabot had received the blessings of Henry VII and the money of some Bristol merchants to seek a northwest passage to Cathay, but, other than probing the coastline of America from Labrador to Chesapeake Bay and providing England with a claim to Canada, he achieved little. Nor was the voyage of John Rut (1527) of any greater consequence. Like Cabot he was sent out to find the northwest passage, and like Cabot he merely explored the eastern coast of North America. It was not until after 1550 that England sponsored overseas ventures again.

The ventures were threefold. One was the resumption of the search for the illusive northwest passage. Martin Frobisher (1576), John Davis (1585–1587), Henry Hudson (1610–1611), and others later on probed the waters north of Canada and gave their names to some bays and straits, but that was all. The second venture consisted of the attempts to get to Cathay by way of the waters north of Eurasia. This was equally futile. Sir Hugh Willoughby and his seventy men perished in the Arctic cold (1553); Stephen Burrough could not pass through the Straits of Waigatz (1556); and an elaborate expedition prepared by the Muscovy Company and led by Arthur Pet and Charles Jackman (1580) failed there also. A by-product of this search for a northeast passage was more profitable. Willoughby's companion, Richard Chancellor, had been able to reach the White Sea and thence he journeyed to Moscow where he negotiated a trade treaty with Ivan III. This gave rise to the Muscovy Company (1555) whose trade with Russia via the White Sea outflanked the monopolizing Hansa merchants as well as the political disturbances in central Europe. Shortly thereafter this trade led to Anthony Jenkinson's trip across Russia to Bokhara (1557) and to Persia (1561) to open contacts with the Persians, and this in turn helped to prepare the ground for the future trade with India and for the founding of the East India Company. But that, of course, was still in the future. The third venture consisted of trade interloping in the Portuguese and Spanish imperial reserves. Between 1530 and 1544 William Hawkins of Plymouth and other merchants of London and Southampton made several trading voyages to Brazil which, while not furtive, were nevertheless illegal according to the international principles of the day. More daring were the trading expeditions which Thomas Wyndham, John Lok, William Towerson, William Garrard, and their associates conducted between 1551 and 1566 in the Portuguese territories along the Gulf of Guinea, for Portugal took steps to protect its claims to trade monopoly in the region. The climax of this interloping was reached in the 1560's and 1570's when John Hawkins, Francis Drake, Andrew Barker and others openly challenged both Portugal and Spain. Hawkins raided the coast of Guinea for Negro slaves and then sold them, some at the point of guns, to the settlers in the Spanish Main. This trade was combined with piracy; and to this, Drake devoted much of his time, daring, and ingenuity. He tried to seize one shipment of the Peruvian treasure at the Caribbean port of loading, Nombre de Dios, then to waylay another shipment in transit across the Isthmus, but failed in both attempts. In the third attempt he succeeded and hauled away as much gold as could be carried. After his Isthmian raids proved hackneyed, Drake decided, with the approval of the English government, on the bold scheme of striking at the source of the treasure by way of the Straits of Magellan. He did so in 1577, raiding the Spanish settlements along the eastern coast of South America, capturing a treasure ship of great value, and then sailing northward along the coast of California, westward across the Pacific, around the Cape of Good Hope, and back home (1580). The circumnavigation naturally posed a threat to Spanish interests. This was followed by a big raid in 1585 on Santo Domingo, Cartegena, and St. Augustine which, in Drake's own words, opened "a very great gap — little to the liking of the King of Spain." Then came 1588, and the defeat of the Spanish Armada.

If that event is taken as the terminal date for this survey of English "empire building," it is obvious that England had no empire during the Renaissance. At the same time it is equally clear that the exploits reported above, whether licit or not, were preparing for the day when England would have an overseas empire. It was necessary first to challenge Spain's and Portugal's claims to monopoly, and it was principally this that was being accomplished during the Renaissance period.

Developments in Diplomacy and War

The foregoing international political developments were accompanied by changes in two important instruments of international politics, namely, diplomacy and war.

DIPLOMACY[20] In the Middle Ages diplomatic business was generally handled by ad hoc embassies. When an issue arose, envoys were dispatched to negotiate concerning it; and when they discharged their duty, their diplomatic function terminated. The same men might be sent to deal with the same or some other issue, but each assignment called for a new appointment. In short, diplomacy in the Middle Ages was casual.

Although there were no permanent diplomatic agents accredited from one court to another, there were representatives who occasionally approached that status. The consuls of the Italian mercantile communities in the Levant and the branch managers of Italian merchant houses doing business in other European countries may be cited as one type of resident representatives. Neither had diplomatic functions as such; for the first were concerned chiefly with the adjudication of disputes between the members of the settlement and the second managed the business operations of the branches under their care. However, both were sometimes requested to represent their mother cities at the capitals of the countries where they happened to be located, in which case, while not diplomats, they performed the functions of diplomats. Another instance of this is to be found in the diplomatic function of the procurators whom James II of Aragon (1260–1327) maintained at the papal court and the English kings, Edward I and II, kept at Paris. James and Pope Boniface VIII had interests in Sicily, James as a claimant of the throne and Boniface as feudal suzerain, and both found themselves in common opposition to the ruler of the island kingdom. It was natural therefore for James to have a resident representative at the papal court to attend to his interests. The two Edwards were vassals of the French kings, so in respect to their fiefs in France they were subject to the jurisdiction of the highest French court, the *Parlement* of Paris. Since the French kings sought to annex these fiefs, they repeatedly encroached on them and provoked incidents and jurisdictional disputes which they hoped to exploit to their advantage as suzerains. To thwart these designs both Edwards maintained legal experts at Paris who represented them at the bar of the French *Parlement.* To perform this function adequately these representatives tried to secure all the information possible about French actions, present and future, and to relay that information to their home government. Thus these procurators, although essentially advocates at law, were actually doubling as diplomats.

While the above functionaries were resident representatives who acted in the capacity of diplomats, their operations should not be regarded as the inception of permanent diplomacy. In both instances the diplomatic functions were incidental, and the system of resident procurators actually terminated with the kings in question. Thus, at the most, the diplomatic roles of these officials may be taken only as a prefigurement of permanent diplomatic service.

In the Renaissance period ad hoc embassies continued to be used, as indeed they are to this day. But with the growth of international relations due to the consolidation and expansion of the states they were found wanting and were gradually replaced by more or less permanent representatives who could keep constant watch on all things likely to affect the interests of their respective countries. The great demands for information concerning the actions and plans of other states and the constant need to cultivate the good will of these states or to counteract their hostile designs could no longer be met by casual diplomacy, and so resident representatives who could devote full time to these tasks had to be instituted.

This transformation took place first in Italy where the multiplicity of states occasioned numerous disputes and rivalries and shifting alliances, all of which required constant attention. And the first state to employ permanent diplomatic representatives was Mantua. Bordering on aggressive Milan, this little state became fearful for its safety and sought security in an alliance with the Holy Roman Empire. To preserve this alliance it kept a resident agent in the court of Louis IV. Milan was next to adopt permanent agents but for a somewhat different reason. Under Gian Galeazzo Visconti, Milan embarked on a program of territorial aggrandizement, and to expedite this expansion it employed resident agents in several neighboring states. Subsequently, as a result of the second wave of Milanese expansion — that under Filippo Maria Visconti — and of the creation of the League of Lodi (1454) to prevent future aggressions, resident diplomats of the principal states were to be found in each other's courts.

Toward the end of the fifteenth century the practice of having resident agents was introduced north of the Alps. With France casting furtive eyes on the territories of Naples and Milan, the princes of these threatened states established permanent representatives at the court of Burgundy, France's bitterest enemy at the time. Subsequently, when the threatened invasion actually materialized, other Italian states followed suit, mostly in consequence of the feverish jockeying for alliances, and before long most of them had resident representatives in the principal European capitals. In return, these European powers assigned agents to Italian courts; and later in the first half of the sixteenth century, they extended the practice to other European governments. By the end of the Renaissance period therefore permanent diplomatic representation was an established system.

As this practice grew in usage, approved diplomatic procedures and the necessary diplomatic machinery began to evolve. The rights and honors of the ambassadors in the host countries steadily gained in definition and uniformity; an accepted mode of transacting diplomatic business began to be worked out; and the two trends together laid the basis for uniform diplomatic conventions. At the same time the necessary instruments for the maintenance of contact between the ambassadors and the home governments were devised and formalized. Finally, in a number of states separate departments were established for the administration of foreign affairs. The result of all this was the standardization of the diplomatic arm which thereafter was the normal agency through which states conducted their international relations.

Brought forth by the chronic strife of the fifteenth and sixteenth centuries, diplomacy naturally partook of the charged atmosphere of the contentious era. The endless interstate thrusts and parries and the deep suspicions they engendered imparted to diplomacy a character of deviousness. It relied on subtlety and secrecy, and at times stooped to intrigue and duplicity. The spirit animating it seems to have been how to thwart or outsmart a rival without being outsmarted, and this, often without concern for moral rectitude or for legal niceties. Of this lack of scruple there is ample evidence, but perhaps none more revealing than the reply with which Ferdinand of Aragon is said to have parried a courtier's report that Louis XII of France accused Ferdinand of having deceived him twice. "Tell the king he is a liar," he allegedly retorted, "I have deceived him at least ten times!" Ferdinand did not have a monopoly on perfidy; most other courts gave him a run for the dubious honor. Except for greater regard for international law, morality, and public opinion, modern diplomacy has retained most of its Renaissance traits.

WAR The developments in war were no less significant.[21] In the Middle Ages, until the beginning of the thirteenth century, war was conditioned by the feudal organization of society and the martial habits of chivalry. The castle and the feudal levy determined its nature. If armies met in the open, the battle consisted of a collision of two bodies of mounted knights where the momentum of the charge and the skill and courage of the individual rider determined the outcome. What infantry there was served merely as auxiliaries, mostly as bowmen. If the enemy retreated behind castle or town walls, the battle then became a siege with the attacker trying to starve the besieged into submission or to force entry by opening a breach, sapping, going over the top, or by getting a traitor inside to open a gate. Where the battle deteriorated into such a siege commoners were employed in greater numbers to meet the increased demands for labor.

From the thirteenth century on, a significant change began to take shape. While feudal cavalry still retained its prime position, the use of infantry as an integral part of the fighting force began to increase.

In some places geography dictated the adoption of this change. When Edward I of England embarked on the conquest of Wales and Scotland, two mountainous regions, he soon found that the terrain would not permit heavy cavalry charges and that, indeed, knights sometimes had to dismount and fight on foot. Moreover, because the Welsh and the Scots, short on cavalry, avoided battles in the open and retreated into their mountain fastnesses in the hope of outlasting the invasion, Edward realized that he could not hope to win the war unless he maintained an army in the field for a long time and unless he flushed the enemy out of its retreats. Since according to custom the feudal levy had to be compensated if it was kept under arms for longer than forty days and the cost of maintaining a man-at-arms was great, and since cavalry by itself could not catch up with the enemy and defeat it, Edward naturally turned to a less costly and a more useful type of soldiery, namely, footmen armed with bows and arrows. He inaugurated a civilian training program in archery and then mustered the trainees into the army as an indispensable complement to the men-at-arms. With their help he reduced the Welsh and defeated the Scots; and so infantry in England came into its own.[22] Naturally, once the value of the longbowmen was established, the English kings made good use of them on the continent in the Hundred Years' War. The victory at Crecy (1346), largely due to the effectiveness of their firepower, proved their indispensability.[23]

Switzerland was another area where the terrain dictated the change. If the Austrians still relied (blindly, it would appear) on the mounted knight, the rebellious Swiss mountaineers made use of infantry. But instead of emphasizing bowmen they preferred pikemen, probably because at the battles of Morgarten (1315) and Laupen (1339), before there was any firm policy as to the type of infantry to be developed, it was the hand-to-hand fighter that carried the day. Thereafter the Swiss naturally turned to foot soldiery and developed their famous pikemen.

In other places it was the political nature of the belligerents which determined what type of forces would take the field. Princes and kings fighting each other would have feudal levies, but if a town and a king got into war, the town would have to depend on its citizen militia, for, in general, it had few if any vassals. This situation is exemplified well in the battle of Courtrai (1302) which was fought between Philip IV of France and the rebelling Flemish towns. The rebels, aware of the king's superiority of horse and of the lack of training of their own militia, had to call on nature to correct the imbalance. They, therefore, took their stand behind some swamps which, they hoped, would slow down and disorganize the charge of the horsemen, and when the impulsive French chivalry obliged them by galloping into the morass, the Flemish carried the day.[24]

Italy, studded with rising, independent city-states, also turned to the town militia and so to infantry. Indeed, it was as early as 1176 and the battle of Legnano, where an alliance of north Italian towns defeated Emperor Frederick I, that the infantry proved itself capable of facing an army of knights. Here, however, the use of infantry did not grow as much as might be expected. The town governments, most of which were controlled by the upper business classes or by rising despots, were apprehensive of developing regular militias lest these citizen soldiers use their indispensability to wrest political concessions, and so they had recourse to mercenaries. As it happened, there were military contractors, the notorious *condottieri*, who had private armies ready and available for hire;[25] but since their troops were comprised of a high percentage of cavalry — the *condottieri* preferred cavalry, perhaps because a cavalry troop, even if small, looked more impressive than a motley crowd of footmen, or perhaps for reasons of mobility — their employment necessarily arrested the development of town militias.[26] That is why Machiavelli later pressed so much for the creation of citizen armies.

The changes adopted in the later Middle Ages were naturally retained and built upon during Renaissance. However, before we examine the continuation of these changes and the appearance of some new developments, one point needs to be affirmed, namely, that cavalry by adapting itself to the changing circumstances, still remained an important, if not the preponderant, element in the armies of the Renaissance period. Thus in France the old feudal levies were supplemented by the lancers, the core of the *compagnies d'ordonnance* created by Charles VII; and in Spain, by the celebrated 2,500 heavy cavalry, called the *guardas viejas*. Italy, of course, had few feudal knights — although the despots, like the Visconti, had more of these than commonly recognized — and so its mercenary horse increased. Then, light cavalry was added to protect the flanks of the men-at-arms or to harass the enemy's flanks or its baggage and supply trains. Spain, imitating the Moors, added the *genetaires,* and employed them in the Italian campaigns. And France, not to be outdone, countered by adding the *chevaux-legers*, while the Germans expanded their corps of *reiters*. Even the introduction of firearms did not displace the cavalry, for the light-armed branch of it was itself equipped with same. The Germans with their corps of "pistoleers" appear to have originated this change, and other armies followed suit. Thus the cavalry — of course no longer as a feudal levy — continued to play an important part in the armies of the Renaissance.[27]

But while the cavalry still retained its importance, it came to be overshadowed by the infantry, and Switzerland led the way. Following the initial victories over the Austrians, the Swiss introduced formal combat training with the pike and developed their famous phalanx of pikemen. Arranged in squares of approximately 6,000 men — 85 men to a row and 70 rows deep — with their forest of pikes before them, they could stop cavalry charges and carry the day. Indeed, as at Sempach (1386), they could even best knights fighting on foot. Their superiority brought them renown and employment opportunities everywhere. Soon they were found in the service of Milan, the pope, France, and Spain.

To counter the Swiss advantage, Emperor Maximilian began to organize a body of fighters similar to the pikemen. These were the *landsknechte*, armed with the halberd, a deadly weapon capable of being used as a pike or as a long-handled battle axe as circumstances required; and before long they gained the reputation of being second only to the dreaded Swiss. Hence they, too, found their way into various European armies, not infrequently fighting for France against their own countrymen in the imperial armies. Spain, too, followed the Swiss. However, it preferred smaller units, and it armed a larger proportion of each infantry unit with firearms as soon as these came into use. Even France, although belatedly, in the reign of Louis XI, trained some pikemen which gave rise to two celebrated regiments, that of Picardy and that of Piedmont (1509).[28]

With Swiss pikemen and German *landsknechte* available for hire there was no great need for other nations to create large infantry forces of their own. Still, in time of war, with demands for manpower mounting, governments raised some additional infantry from among their own subjects. Usually they contracted with professional captains for a certain number of troops, and these men scoured the countryside and hired whomever they could find. There was little of what might be considered national draft armies or even militia. The French had created their *francs-archers*, and in the reign of Louis XI these numbered close to 16,000, but they failed in their one major test, the battle of Guinegate (1479), and were abandoned thereafter. The English, short on resources, relied more heavily on their militia, who, however, had to be pressed into service abroad and were quite raw in action.

But whether mercenary or not, the important fact is that the infantry, although for the most part still equipped with traditional weapons, the pike and the halberd, had deprived the cavalry of its predominant role.

Another change was the introduction of firearms.[29] Cannons made their appearance as early as the battle of Crecy in 1346, but it was not until a century later that their role became significant. By that time their firing accuracy and mobility were improved, so that in addition to their employment in siege battles to bombard fortified places they came to be used as field artillery also. Although Machiavelli dismissed the big guns as more noisy than destructive, they had already proved themselves in the battles of Ravenna (1512) and of Marignano (1515). In the latter especially, French artillery, probably the best in western Europe at the time, cut great gaps in the vaunted Swiss squares and brought victory to Francis I.

Simultaneously with the increased use of the cannon came the arquebus with which part of the infantry was equipped, usually on the flank of the pikemen to ward off the attacks of light cavalry. Subsequently, with the improvement of the firing device, the replacement of the matchlock by the wheel-lock, the pistol was improvised and was added to the equipment of some of the light horse.

All this progress in firepower sounds impressive, and indeed it was soon to revolutionize war, but in the Renaissance days it was just barely making its influence felt: most of the major battles were still decided by the pike and the halberd of the infantry or the charge of the cavalry.

Still another change, a result of all the foregoing developments, was the change in the manner of combat. The frontal cavalry charge as practiced by medieval knighthood, while still employed at times, progressively gave way to tactical deployment of all troops in accordance with the demands of over-all strategy. Battles thus became more and more a matter of tactics.[30]

Finally, the increase in the number of men marshaled and the introduction of new equipment raised the costs of military establishments, making the problem of financing all-important. Revenue from taxes proved to be as inadequate then as it is now. New methods of raising money had to be discovered, and the success of war became more and more dependent on the success of war financing. The two became interrelated; and if battles became a matter of military tactics, warmaking became a matter of the science of financing. This indeed was a significant change.

Thus in diplomacy and in war, the Renaissance saw important innovations clearly foreshadowing their modern character.

1. On this intriguing suggestion see Jean Bosler, "Was Joan of Arc Charles VIII's Sister?" *The Cambridge Journal*, VII (1954), 756–76.

2. A good, summary treatment of the reconciliation is available in Perroy, *op. cit.*, 290–6. For a detailed scholarly treatment including an account of the mediating role of the papacy, see Joycelyne Gledhill Dickinson, *The Congress of Arras, 1435: A Study in Medieval Diplomacy* (Oxford: Clarendon Press, 1955), chap. iv especially.

3. The story of Burgundy is told brilliantly in Joseph Calmette's *The Golden Age of Burgundy*, trans. Doreen Weightman (New York: Norton & Company, Inc., 1963).

4. A fine survey of this expansion is available in L. S. Stavrianos, *The Balkans since 1453* (New York: Rinehart & Company, Inc., 1958), 33–80.

5. These may be followed in Dorothy Muir, *op. cit.*, 88–172.

6. For a revealing statement of the selfish policy which guided their conduct of the campaigns they were hired to wage see the long harangue which Pius II puts in the mouth of Piccinino, one of the most celebrated of these *condottieri*, in "The Commentaries of Pius II," *Smith College Studies in History*, XLIII (1957), 786–8.

7. For a thorough account of the Venetian-Turkish relations see Thiriet, *op. cit.*, 353–91.

8. Cf., for example, *Cambridge Medieval History*, VIII, 617.

9. On this see Halecki, *op. cit.*, 118–9.

10. Cf., *The Cambridge History of Poland*, I, 217.

11. For a brief history of the Union see Larsen, *op. cit.*, 208–40.

12. Recent treatments of the subject are to be found in *The New Cambridge Modern History*, I, chap. xii and II, chap xi, and in Sir Charles Petrie's *Earlier Diplomatic History, 1492–1713* (New York: The Macmillan Co., 1949), 10–67.

13. Until recently these three treaties have been interpreted as Charles's concessions to the neighboring powers. They are now represented as brilliant diplomatic strokes which secured Brittany for France and disrupted an anti-French alliance. See Yvonne Labande-Mailfert, "Trois traites de paix (1492–1493)," *Le moyen âge*, LX (1954), 379–401.

14. For example, De Lamar Jensen, *Diplomacy and Dogmatism. Bernardino de Mendoza and the French Catholic League* (Cambridge: Harvard University Press, 1964), 2–4, where he cites long excerpts from

Philip's letters to his subordinates describing his financial straits; and Henri Hauser and Augustine Renaudet, *Les débuts de l'age moderne*, vol. VIII of *Peuples et civilizations, histoire générale*, ed. L. Halphen and Ph. Sagnac (3rd.; Paris: Presses universitaires de France, 1946), 575–81.

15. The Renaissance phase of this "expansion" is described brilliantly by Boies Penrose, *Travel and Discovery in the Renaissance, 1420–1620* (Cambridge: Harvard University Press, 1955).

16. On these pre-Polo penetrations see Lopez in *The Cambridge Economic History*, II, 313.

17. For the discovery of the Canaries see Charles Verlinden, "Lanzarotto Malocello et la découverte Portugaise des Canaries," *Revue belge de philologie et d'histoire*, XXXVI (1958), 1173–1209.

18. On the important role of the Italians see Charles Verlinden, "Navigateurs, merchands et colons italiens au service de la découverte et de la colonisation portugaise sous Henri le Navigateur," *Le moyen âge*, LXIV (1958), 467–97.

19. Cited from Vera Brown Holmes, *A History of the Americas* (New York: The Ronald Press Co., 1950), 141.

20. An excellent study of the subject is Garret Mattingly's *Renaissance Diplomacy* (London: Jonathan Cape, 1955). The medieval phase is treated in Donald E. Queller, "Thirteenth-Century Diplomatic Envoys: *Nuncii* and *Procuratores*," *Speculum*, XXXV (1960), 196–213.

21. Valuable studies are Charles Oman, *A History of the Art of War in the Middle Ages* (2d ed.; New York: Burt Franklin, no date), vol. II. A more recent work in French is Ferdinand Lot's *L'art militaire et les armies au moyen âge en Europe et dans le proche orient* (Paris: Payot, 1946). More specialized treatments of wars in the Renaissance are Frederick Lewis Taylor's *The Art of War in Italy, 1494–1529* (London: Macmillan and Co., 1921), and Henri Lapeyre's essay, "L'art de la guerre au temps de Charles-Quint," in *Charles-Quint et son temps*, 37–49.

22. Oman, *op. cit.*, II, 57–108.

23. *Ibid.*, 134–47.

24. *Ibid.*, 112–8; Lot, *op. cit.*, I, 340–8.

25. On these military companies see Oman, *op. cit.*, II, 288–96.

26. *Ibid.*, 302–4.

27. For some statistics on the actual numbers of cavalry employed see Lot, *op. cit.*, II, 79, 114–26, 210–3, 313–8.

28. On the infantry developments see Oman, *op. cit.*, II, 274–7.

29. See the survey in *ibid.*, 205–29.

30. But cf. Lapeyre, *op. cit.*, 44–45: "It could then be said that strategy in the days of Charles V revealed nothing very original and that it hardly differed from that of the Italian wars *or even from that of the Middle Ages*" [italics added].

CHAPTER IV

Internal Political Developments during the Renaissance

W HILE THE INTERNATIONAL activities discussed in the preceding chapter were shaping the destinies of nations and of the world itself, there were certain internal political developments in each European nation, more or less related to these activities, which stimulated this process.

Consolidation of Royal Absolutism in Spain

In Spain the important development was the resumption of the growth of a strong monarchy. The gains in centralization which were made earlier by Alfonso XI of Castile and Peter IV of Aragon were soon dissipated, and for a century thereafter, due mostly to intermittent civil wars, the monarchies remained weak. The work of strengthening royal authority therefore had to be started over again.

The work was begun by Ferdinand and Isabella. With some of their achievements — the dynastic union, the territorial consolidation, and the successful international ventures — we have already met. These placed Spain on the map of Europe. Naturally, they also enhanced the prestige of the monarchy at home. It remains for us to see what actions Ferdinand and Isabella took on the home front to add to this prestige and to convert it into actual authority.

One action which this royal couple pursued throughout the reign was the reduction of the overmighty nobles. Adulterine castles were destroyed, and land and privileges which the nobility had usurped or acquired during the chaos of Isabella's predecessor were recovered by law (Act of Resumption, 1480). Naturally, the reversion profited the crown. Then the crusading orders of Santiago, Alcantara, and Calatrava, which were preserves of the nobility, were incorporated into the crown's forces by the simple expedient of Ferdinand assuming the grandmastership of each as it became vacant. This converted the orders from nobiliary to monarchic instruments. Lastly, the sovereigns created a number of court offices and the famous Corps of Gentlemen of the King's House and Guard, which were open to members of aristocratic families only, and in this way many nobles were attached to the crown and in a sense kept under honorable surveillance.

In addition to clipping the wings of the nobility, Ferdinand and Isabella also subordinated the church. This they achieved by acquiring the right of appointment to church offices. For Spain they had the right to supplicate the pope in behalf of the worthiest candidate, which amounted to indirect appointment. In conquered Granada and in the lands overseas, as reward for opening new lands to Christianity, they were allowed to present their nominees for papal confirmation. All officers of the Inquisition were crown appointees also, especially after 1482 when Ferdinand admonished the pope that it would be run "according to his [Ferdinand's] will." With the principal offices of the church filled with royal nominees, the church naturally became a bulwark of the crown. It is not that the monarchs flagrantly imposed themselves on the church, but that in the atmosphere of the *reconquista* the church found it convenient to accept state leadership, as is clearly evidenced by the cooperation of that staunch churchman, Cardinal Ximenes, Archbishop of Toledo. But once this leadership was admitted, the church perforce remained second to the state.

The third institution, the *cortes*, which formerly served as a check on the monarchy, the monarchs used and subordinated. Like the Tudors they represented their centralizing program as a program for order and good government in the country and got the *cortes* to support it. Thus the action against the nobility and the action to create a national host, for example, were authorized by the *cortes*. Then, Ferdinand and Isabella were careful to associate the *cortes* with themselves whenever they needed to take necessary but unpopular measures in behalf of the state, such as raising revenue by increased taxation. By this expedient they diverted some of the onus from themselves unto the *cortes* and at the same time undermined its popularity with the public. Moreover, they summoned it at will, and they did not will to do so often; occasionally they failed to invite one or the other of the estates, presumably to reduce the weight of the opposition; they remodeled the electoral machinery to influence elections in their favor; and they tried to increase and to husband crown revenue to free themselves from dependence on the purse of the *cortes*.

Finally, the monarchy continued to invade the autonomy of the towns. This invasion dated back to the day of Alfonso XI and was sustained in the fifteenth century, mostly because class discord in the municipalities and interurban clashes grew in the period and demanded intervention from some higher authority, even if the authority was nominal only. The form of the intervention was the appointment of crown inspectors (*veedores*), judges (*pesquesidores*), and investigators (*corregidores*) to bring justice and order where there was turbulence. Ferdinand and Isabella merely continued this policy; but their efforts were more effective than those of their predecessors and hence the loss of urban autonomy was correspondingly greater.

Other measures that this enterprising team implemented were the transformation of the royal councils from advisory organs made up of nobles to administrative bodies of civil servants, the majority of which were professional jurists; the multiplication of these councils as bases for bureaucratic government; the revival of the *Santa Hermandad*, a special policy-making committee with the duty of suppressing disorder in the country; the creation of a national army — one man out of every twelve men between the ages of twenty and forty-five was required to serve on demand — and the reform of the fiscal agencies with the view of assuring that the royal treasury received what the crown was entitled to.

In general, the whole program amounted to an effectuation of strong royal government where weakness had formerly prevailed. As in Tudor England, the public craved order and peace after decades of chaos and was prepared to pay the price to get it, the price being the acceptance of authoritative monarchy.

What Ferdinand and Isabella started, Charles I continued. Charles profited from the fact that he was the sole king of all the Spanish lands, though he did not undertake to impose closer political ties on them. But a greater strengthening of the monarchy accrued from the failure of the two Spanish rebellions at the inception of his reign. Charles had made the mistake of appointing foreigners — his compatriots from

Flanders — to important state and church offices in Castile contrary to the established principle that such offices were to be held by natives. In addition, he requested a substantial grant from the *cortes* for his projected visit to Germany to claim the office of Holy Roman Emperor to which he had been elected, and, incidentally, to meet some of the "expenses" which that election entailed. The Castilians interpreted these actions as those of a foreigner who was intent on exploiting them for the benefit of his German and Italian ventures. They therefore rebelled, at Toledo, Avila, Tordesillas, Valladolid, Burgos, and at other cities in what is known as the War of the *Comunidades*. It soon appeared, however, that the "antiforeign" opposition was also an antimonarchic opposition, the rebels demanding, for example, triennial meetings of the *cortes*, free election of proctors, town confirmation of the *corregidores*, and similar other rights, and at first the movement gained in popularity. In the course of the rebellion, however, the nobility and the commoners began to disagree as to objectives, and the disagreement led to a split in the ranks of the rebels. Charles's ministers exploited the rift. They made a conciliatory gesture by appointing Castilians to the two highest offices in the land and succeeded thereby in detaching some of the nobility from the opposition. The rebellion was soon put down, with the commoners suppressed and the privileged classes tied to the crown. The latter discovered that treason with failure meant death — Charles pardoned the rebels except some three hundred of their leaders many of whom were nobles — and that treason with success held the prospect of subordination to the commoners. Hence their only alternative was loyalty to the crown and the recognition of its authority, and this they accepted. The rebellions which occurred in Valencia, known as the Wars of *Germanias*, were more definitely social wars, the hard-pressed workers undertaking to "equalize" property holdings, and there, too, the nobility was won and attached to the crown. The result of both these unsuccessful uprisings is well expressed in the words of Charles's biographer Gomara:

> The Communes of Castile began their revolt, but after a good start had a bad ending, and exalted, beyond what it had previously been, the power of the King whom they desired to abase.[1]

With the nobility and the church bound to the crown, with the municipalities chastened and the *cortes* reduced to a nominal position, Charles's Spain passed to a man who believed that it was the sovereign's duty to attend to all government functions personally and to use his authority and his dominions in the service of God. The man, of course, was his son Philip II.

Philip continued with the centralizing programs of his forbears. He completed the formation of the central bureaucracy with its Council of State for all the Spanish lands; its separate councils and chancelleries for each of the states over which he ruled, i.e., Castile, Aragon, Italy, Flanders, Portugal, the Indies; its councils of war and of trade; and its several judicial councils, including that of the Inquisition.[2] Next, he advanced the principle that all important matters — and in Philip's eyes almost all matters were important — be referred to the sovereign in person. However, one should promptly add that this assumption of personal responsibility was not all prompted by Philip's craving for autocracy: it also served him as a means of bringing some unity to his segmented empire and some effectiveness to his government. Thirdly, he reduced Aragon to the same subordinate status to which Castile was subject, and at the same time affirmed the primacy of the crown. His private secretary, Antonio Perez, was arrested on charges of actions prejudicial to the state but escaped to Barcelona where the Justiciar of Aragon gave him sanctuary in accordance with the ancient liberties of Aragon that appellants seeking justice at the court of the Justiciar were entitled to protective custody and to justice. Philip demanded the return of the fugitive, but some of the local authorities and the populace contrived Perez' escape to France with whom Philip was then at war. Angered by the rebuff, Philip had his army "pacify" the defiant townsmen, while the guilty officials were executed. He did not withdraw the "rights" of Aragon, but the "pacification" served as a reminder to all Spain that the interests of the crown took precedence over local rights. One more indication of Philip's view on the question of the subjects' loyalty to the crown was his removal of the seat of government from Toledo, the leading city in the War of the *Comunidades* and so a symbol of disloyalty to the monarchy, to Madrid, a small town with no ancient rights to flaunt in the face of the sovereign. Philip did not wish anybody or anything to stand in his way of serving Spain and God.

With Philip authoritarianism in Spain had reached its highest level. Thereafter it was to fossilize, at the same time that the nation, exhausted and indolent, went to sleep.

Failure of Monarchy in Portugal

The political developments in Portugal during the Renaissance did not give rise to a strong monarchy. There were periods when strong rulers advanced the cause of effective central authority, but these periods were invariably followed by others of weakness when the gains were dissipated.

The periods of centralization were three. The first (1279–1367), already examined in an earlier chapter, began before the Renaissance and lasted through the reigns of Dinis, Alfonso IV, and Peter I. Another was that of John I (1385–1433), an illegitimate son of Peter I; he usurped the crown with the help of the commoners of Lisbon, restored Portuguese independence from Castile, aligned Portugal with England (Treaty of Windsor, May 9, 1386), and, basking in the favor of the capital, began to extend royal jurisdiction — this latter, however, mostly against the old nobility who had opposed his usurpation. A third period was that of John II (1481–1495) and Manuel I (1495–1521). The former had to reduce some of the new nobility elevated by his namesake, John I, particularly the Braganca family which was related to the royal line, and sought to have his representatives enter the lands of the immunists. The latter reduced the rights of Lisbon in punishment for its maddened pogrom against the Jews (1506); assumed the mastership of the Order of Christ, in imitation of Ferdinand of Aragon, and prepared the way for the incorporation of the other orders with the forces of the crown (1551); and extended royal justice still further by providing magistrates for all communities of twenty to two hundred inhabitants situated more than a league from the nearest town.

But, as suggested above, these efforts at centralization were repeatedly interrupted by periods of weakness stemming either from civil conflicts over regencies, or from futile foreign wars, or from incompetents occupying the throne. Thus between 1367 and 1383, the country was rent by civil war and harried by Castilian invasion because Ferdinand I married another man's wife and repudiated his Castilian fiancée. Again, between 1438 and 1448, the court and the country fell prey to a contest over regency and succession between the ruling line represented by John's brother Peter (Prince Henry the Navigator was the youngest of these three brothers) and the descendants of the illegitimate line of John I, the Braganca family. This decade of discord was followed by the reign of the weak Alfonso V (1438–1481). This incompetent pandered to the nobility to the extent of provoking the *cortes* of 1460 to demand that he "have a firmer hand in the affairs of the crown with which he should sustain his estate as his predecessors had done, and not give them away with such freedom and so unnecessarily."[3] At the same time he wasted the nation's resources and honor in waging a futile war with Castile to assert his claims to its throne. Finally came the period of complete collapse, from the time of John III's death in 1557 to 1580 when Portugal was annexed by Philip II of Spain. The period opened with a conflict over regency during the minority of Sebastian and ended with Sebastian's crass mismanagement of the expedition against the Moors in Africa. The fate of Portugal was sealed at the battle of Alcazar-Kebir (1578) where out of an army of more than 20,000 scarcely a hundred escaped, Sebastian himself and some 8,000 men being killed and some 15,000 being captured. With the king dead, its army lost, and its court and councils divided, Portugal easily yielded to Philip who claimed it through his mother, princess Isabella.

The collapse of Portugal was furthered by another condition, generally overlooked, namely, imperial overexpansion. In fact, Portugal provides a classic answer to the question of "at what price empire."

As pointed out earlier, Portugal acquired a number of posts on the coasts of Africa and Asia, from Ceuta, opposite Gibraltar, all the way to China. Although it did not strive for a land empire, these far-flung outposts required constant defense, and the demands rose as the natives increased their pressure on the posts. The demands for manpower soon exceeded Portuguese supply, so that mercenaries had to be hired, the cost of which soon became prohibitive. In addition, the long sea voyage exposed its merchantmen to devastating piracy, and to the actual losses on the high seas, which in 1530 reached the staggering total of three hundred ships, had to be added the costs of increasingly greater provisions for defense. The net result was a mounting fiscal deficit which could only be met by costly short-term loans, followed by repudiation of debt, and then by bankruptcy. Moreover, expectation of profit from overseas commerce, however illusory, drew people from the farms, and agriculture languished. With a bankrupt treasury and a failing agriculture, collapse was inevitable.[4]

Revival and Growth of French Monarchy

In France the history of the monarchy during the Renaissance falls into two distinct periods. One period was that of the Hundred Years' War which lasted close to a hundred and twenty years, from 1337 to 1453. The other was the interval between the Hundred Years' War and the outbreak of the so-called Wars of Religion, approximately a century in length and covering the reigns of Louis XI (1461–1483), Charles VIII (1483–1498), Louis XII (1498–1515), Francis I (1515–1547), and Henry II (1547–1559).

MONARCHY AND THE HUNDRED YEARS' WAR   In the first period the cardinal fact was the failure and the recovery of monarchic power. The severe defeats at Crecy and Poitiers had adverse effects on the prestige of the monarchy. Although the institution itself was not challenged by the shocked French subjects, there were those who would have put the monarchy "in commission." Taking advantage of the popular protests against the heavy war taxes which failed to bring victory, of the captivity of King John, and of the enmity between the regent — John's son Charles — and Charles of Navarre, a frustrated aspirant to the French throne, these reformers wrested a number of concessions at the expense of the monarchy. At the Estates General of 1355 the third estate, echoing for the most part the demands of the Paris merchant society and led by the provost of Paris, Étienne Marcel, secured the principles that subsidies and armies voted by the Estates were to be collected and managed by the Estates and that henceforth levying an aid or summoning the *arrière ban* was to have its approval.

At subsequent meetings in 1356 and 1357 the additional demands that the king's administration should be reformed and that the representatives of the Estates be admitted to the royal council were conceded in the name of the king. Thus, because the monarchy had failed to manage the affairs of state successfully, it was to have an active partner in this management, that is, the monarchy was to be limited. Although it was rescued from this condition by the careful administration of Charles V who recovered Paris from Marcel and his associates, eliminated the danger from Charles of Navarre, and regained much of the territory lost to the English, it soon relapsed into a worse condition. With the insanity of Charles VI and the struggle for regency between the party of his uncle — Burgundians — and the party of his brother — Orleanists — and with the loss of France north of the Loire to Henry V of England, the position of the crown deteriorated seemingly beyond repair, and this sorry condition continued until 1429 and the appearance of Joan of Arc.

Joan's appearance roused the nation into action. Inspired by her leadership, it first broke the back of the English at Orleans and then rallied behind its lawful sovereign Charles VII by having him crowned at Rheims, an act symbolic of the restoration of the monarchy.

Once the crisis was turned, the nation, and with it the monarchy, began to recover. The English were driven out, the dual monarchy — French in the south and Anglo-Burgundian in the north — was terminated, and a single administration was installed. To protect the countryside from the ravaging bands of discharged and jobless soldiers a standing army was created — *ordonnances* of 1439, 1445, 1448, and 1455 — and the tax system was broadened, and both the army and taxes passed increasingly under the direct control of the king. At the same time, the sensible policy which Charles VII devised for the mutual restoration of the confiscated property between the followers of the French crown and those who had aligned with the Anglo-Burgundian alliance increased public confidence in the government.[5] Finally the clash between the Council of Basel and Pope Eugenius IV provided the monarch with an opportunity to "liberate" the church in France from the papacy and incidentally to subject it to the control of the state (Pragmatic Sanction of Bourges, 1438).

This revival, although substantial if the postwar position of the crown was compared with its miserable state during the war, still left the monarchy quite limited in power. And much of this limitation was due to the very cause which contributed to the regeneration of the monarchy, namely, the Hundred Years' War. Burgundy, a by-product of the war, was a constant threat to the security of the crown as it incited some French nobles to disloyalty. At the same time the princely houses which had supported Charles VII in the war — Orleanists, Bourbons, Angevins — could not be denied their "just" rewards either. Their demands and their interests could only be satisfied at the expense of the monarchy. Then also the war left the heritage of provincial institutions which hindered national consolidation. When Charles's control was limited to the territory south of the Loire, he had to replace the old Paris *Parlement* by a comparable institution in Languedoc; but then, when he recovered Paris and re-established the traditional *Parlement*, he soon discovered that political interests required the retention of the *Parlement* in the south. Again, when Aquitaine and Normandy were reconquered from the English, to make his regime acceptable, he found it necessary to guarantee to these *pays* their ancient customs. Hence, although the monarchy emerged out of the Hundred Years' War stronger than it was before the war, it was nevertheless as a monarchy of a congeries of appanages and separatist *pays*. This must be kept in mind if we do not wish to exaggerate the position of the French rulers at the end of the first period.

INCEPTION OF ROYAL ABSOLUTISM The second stage in the development of French monarchy during the Renaissance, extending from the accession of Louis XI to the death of Henry II, is generally viewed as one of great growth. And there is certainly much to support this view.

One indication is the steady extension of the royal domain. In the reign of Louis XI the counties of Anjou and Maine reverted by escheat to the crown. Next, as a result of the failure of one of the several baronial rebellions that plagued the wily monarch, the lands of the Dukes of Alençon and of Nemours and of the Constable of St. Pol were annexed. In addition, although Louis' bid for all the lands of Charles the Rash of Burgundy was checkmated by Maximilian's marriage to the heiress, Louis did get, by the Treaty of Arras, Picardy,

Boulonnais, the Duchy of Burgundy, and the Somme towns. To be sure, as pointed out above, this acquisition became a bone of contention between the French crown and Charles V of the Holy Roman Empire, but in the end it remained with the French. Likewise, if Louis failed to reduce Brittany to the status of a subject province by attempting to foist the status of a "subject" on its duke,[6] Charles VIII, Louis XII, and Francis I added it by the forced marriage of the heiress, first, to Charles, and upon his death, to Louis, and then by the marriage of their daughter to Francis. At the same time, when Louis of Orleans ascended the throne as Louis XII, his lands were added to the crown also. In the reign of Francis I the extensive territories of the Constable of Bourbon were confiscated in reprisal for his defection to the side of the Emperor — the Constable was alienated when, on the death of his wife, Francis laid claim to some of her holdings. Although, by the terms of the Treaty of Madrid and the Treaty of Cambrai, Francis was required to restore the confiscated lands to the Constable, in the end, on the death of the latter, in consequence of some interchange of territory which Francis made with the Constable's relatives, most of these lands were recovered. Finally, in the reign of Henry II Calais was reconquered from the English, and the bishoprics of Metz, Verdun, and Toul were cut off from the Holy Roman Empire. Thus, by the end of Henry II's reign, most of France had become royal domain.

Another indication of the strengthening of the monarchy is the progressive subordination of the Estates General.[7] Louis XI called the Estates together when he wanted public support for repudiating his own commitments. Thus, for example, at the meeting at Tours in 1468 he secured the declaration that the monarch should not have alienated Normandy in favor of the king's brother, and yet it was he himself who had granted the Duchy to his brother some time earlier to detach him from the baronial opposition. Two years later, after Louis had been compelled by the Treaty of Peronne to yield once more to his baronial opposition, he got the Estates to release him from the terms of the treaty. But at the same time he dispensed with the practice of securing its consent for raising taxes.[8] In 1483 the regents for Charles VIII called it together to win public support against the machinations of some nobles (League of the Public Weal), but they them-

selves declined to act on its demand for the right to vote on taxes and
to hold regular meetings and dissolved it once the League was out-
maneuvered.[9] Thereafter the Estates was not summoned again until
other regencies occurred and the danger from Protestantism mounted
(1560–1561, 1576, and 1588). But these meetings, while useful for propa-
ganda purposes, merely confirmed the impotence of the body.

Simultaneously with the subordination of the Estates General came
the reduction of the position of the *Parlement* of Paris which was
aspiring to become the highest court of appeal. Louis XI, for example,
removed from its cognizance most of the political suits and transferred
them to a judicial committee of his *Grand Conseil*.[10] Again, when
the *Parlement* protested to Francis I that his Concordat of Bologna with
the papacy infringed upon the rights which the *Parlement* enjoyed over
the church by virtue of the Pragmatic Sanction of Bourges, Francis
rejected the protest with the rejoinder that there was only one king in
France and that the *Parlement* would not be permitted to become
another Venetian senate.[11] Moreover, the personnel of the body came
to be increasingly of royal designation. The king sometimes selected
the members from a list of names provided by the *Parlement* itself;
sometimes he appointed them without consulting such a list; and
sometimes he even sold the posts.[12] Naturally the body tended to
become a royal instrument.

Still another indication of the hardening of royal authority was the
affirmation of its control of the church.[13] The church had been made
subject to the state formally by the Pragmatic Sanction. Now, by the
Concordat of Bologna, the power of appointment was vested in the
crown. Francis I and his successors used the numerous offices at their
disposal to reward faithful servants or to honor their friends and supporters. In that way the hierarchy became creatures of the crown and
inclined the church in favor of the monarchy. In addition, in 1527, all
jurisdiction relative to high ecclesiastical posts was taken out of the
hands of the *Parlement* and transferred to the King's Council. Then,
in 1539, a great part of ecclesiastical jurisdiction was superseded by
royal jurisdiction. Lastly, the clergy became subject to royal taxation.
At first, the tax, in the form of a tithe, was approved by the pope for
the purpose of a crusade and was collected by papal collectors on behalf

of the crown. But Francis went on no crusade, and in 1532 the administration of the tax was transferred to the church in France and the assessment was made by the simple *arrêt* from the King's Council. In the end, therefore, the church was quite dependent on the will of the crown.

Other indications of the consolidation of the monarchy were the steady growth of the administrative machinery both at the king's court and in the provinces, the extension of royal justice into the *seigneuries* at the expense of *seigneurial* justice, and the invasion of royal administrators into the towns.[14]

On the basis of all this evidence one cannot escape the conclusion that the French monarchy had more extensive authority and greater power at the end than at the beginning of the Renaissance. The rule of Francis I, for example, was certainly more personal and dictatorial than that of Philip VI or of John the Good. Yet the conclusion is not to be pushed too far. There were many limitations to the apparent authoritarianism of the crown.

In the first place, there were still some territories which were outside the royal domain and which remained feudal. The *seigneuries* of Condé and Beaujolais, the barony of Enghien, Nevernais, the viscounty of Turenne, and parts of Limousin and Quercy still maintained their feudal status and their rulers still enjoyed the customary medieval feudal rights.[15] Secondly, some of the lands which were annexed to the crown were immediately parceled out among royal relatives and favorites. While the new holders were directly obligated to the king and were less prone to regard themselves as independent feudal lords, nevertheless their land grants increased their resources, prestige, and power and raised their potential as possible opponents of the crown. Moreover, since these same people generally served the king as councillors or as viceroys and belonged to the class which claimed exclusive right to cavalry service and to military office, this potential was even greater. So long as the king was personally powerful, they could be held in check; but once a minor was on the throne and the nobility became divided, the possibility of opposition became very real. One has only to be reminded of the part that the rivalry between the Guise and Bourbon factions played in French politics during the Wars of Religion to be convinced of the truth of this fact. Again, at all times, even in the lands within the royal domain, the people's first contact was not with the royal government but with the administration of the local *seigneurs*. To be sure, the kings had powers of supervision in these areas, but normally these rights were exercised only when maladministration on the part of some *seigneur* required it. Otherwise the crown remained remote, and so the *seigneur*'s influence was paramount. Finally, much of the law in many provinces was not the law of the nation but local customary law. These local customs had been compiled in accordance with the decision of the Estates General of 1454; but while this compilation was ordered with the expectation that it would be followed by a collation of a common body of law, actually the collation failed to materialize so that the codification merely hardened the local law. Hence, strengthened as the French monarchy was during the Renaissance period, it certainly fell short of being absolute.[16]

Tudors to the Rescue in England

The internal political developments in England during the period covered by this survey may be treated in two parts, the pre-Tudor and the Tudor. Generally the two periods are considered as different, one being regarded as medieval and the other as modern. To what extent this is true will soon become apparent.

PARLIAMENT, KING, AND FACTIONALISM IN PRE-TUDOR TIMES[17] In the pre-Tudor period the important political development was the continued nationalization of the monarchy in principle though not in fact. This nationalization took the form of gains that parliament made in relation to the king. Taking advantage of the king's need of money to carry on the Hundred Years' War, parliament wrested from him concession after concession. Without examining the circumstances which occasioned each concession, we may simply note that most of these gains were acquired by the death of the second Lancastrian ruler, Henry V (1413–1422), and that they were fundamental. Parliament secured the principles that no taxes were to be imposed without its assent, that the spending of the tax money was to be for purposes appropriated by it, and that it should have an accounting of the expenditures. It advanced the principle of the responsibility of the executive to the parliament by occasionally compelling the king to dismiss ministers repugnant to it and to accept a standing committee appointed by it to watch that his ministers did not contravene its recommendations to him, and by introducing the practice of impeachment. It increased its role in the field of legislation by submitting petitions for redress of grievances and by declining to vote "money bills" until these petitions were considered. It established the principle of freedom from arrest for its members for the duration of the session, and introduced the idea of freedom of debate. Lastly, in consequence of the revolution of 1399–1400 which deposed Richard II and elevated Henry IV, it claimed the right to determine the succession to the throne.

Impressive as these gains may appear, they were more nominal than real. In the first place, the kings frequently repudiated or evaded these concessions. Edward III, for example, repudiated all the concessions that he had been compelled to make to the parliament of 1341 and then had the parliament of 1343 confirm this repudiation.[18] Thus the measures of the Good Parliament (1376)[19] were nullified by the succeeding parliament largely because the supporter of the first body, the Black Prince, had died in the meantime and his successor in the court, his younger brother John of Gaunt, wanted them nullified. Thus, in 1386, the Lords Appellant, in the parliament called Merciless, forced themselves as chief officers on Richard II and had a number of his ministers impeached and executed; but eleven years later, in another parliament, summoned "to establish the king in his rights," Richard secured the condemnation of these men, obtained a sentence of death against a member of parliament, Thomas Haxey, for criticizing the king's courtly entourage — Haxey being a cleric was spared according to canon law — and, in general, recovered what he considered to be the king's prerogatives — and Richard had very exalted ideas of the monarch's rights.[20] In the second place, the parliament, in spite of the growing importance of the House of Commons, really was a tool of the aristocracy, as this list of reversals clearly shows. When one coalition of magnates gave place to another, parliament responded accordingly by voting the wishes of the new clique in power. Any gains, then, which such a parliament made were more in name than in fact.[21] In the third place, the Wars of Roses which broke out between the Lancastrian and the Yorkist lines for the throne of England reduced the parliament to impotence until it was an echo of the party momentarily victorious in arms. It was called irregularly, every two or three years, instead of annually as before, and sat for short intervals; and about the only function it performed was to serve as a convenient instrument of the party in power for procuring sentences of death and of confiscation of property against the members of the defeated opposition. Fourthly, and because of this parliamentary impotence, the Yorkist kings, Edward IV and Richard III, who finally won out in the Wars of Roses, could and did rule by prerogative. The best evidence of this was the rehabilitation of the Court of Star Chamber in Edward IV's reign. The Court had come into existence in Edward III's time when the Chancery Court branched out of the royal Council to hear the Council's civil cases and left the other cases to be adjudicated by the Council. This latter body held its meetings in the Chamber of the Stars, hence the Court's name, but its distinguishing feature — largely because it was really the king's most trusted councillors acting as a court — was its disregard of the principles of common law. In the reign of Henry VI it fell in abeyance, largely because of the popular opposition to it as an instrument of prerogative, but in Edward IV's reign, when even the baronial opposition was cowed, it was revived.[22]

It seems clear then that the nationalization of the monarchy during the pre-Tudor part of the Renaissance was more theoretical than real. Parliament may have gained important rights limiting the authority of the kings, but these rights were frequently violated while parliament itself became the tool of the kings or of the baronial factions who pretended to speak in the name of the king.

TUDOR "DESPOTISM" The Tudor period began when Henry Tudor, great-great-grandson of John of Gaunt on his mother's side and so a representative of the Lancastrians, defeated the Yorkist Richard III at Bosworth Field in 1485 and won the crown for himself. It continued through the reign of his much-married son Henry VIII (1509–1547) and through the reigns of the latter's three children, the consumptive Edward V (1547–1553), the Catholic Mary (1553–1558), and the wary Elizabeth (1558–1603), first of that name. It came to end in so short a time because Edward died too young, Mary died childless despite her prayerful hopes for a Catholic heir of her body, and Elizabeth remained unmarried for reasons best known to her, be they political or physical or both. But short as it was, it was an eventful era which saw the establishment of a new church order in England, the integration of Wales with England, the rise of England as a sea power, and the beginning of England's richest literary glory. And so, with characters indelible and achievements perduring, the age stands out prominently in the annals of England and is regarded as the inception of its modern era.[23]

Politically the age is judged to be one of absolutism, or as Professor Elton would have it, one in which England became a modern sovereign national state. This trend had started earlier, as was pointed out above. But it was this age that saw the trend develop into an accomplished fact.[24]

The first step in the growth of this absolutism was dictated by the need to safeguard the usurped crown. As the Yorkists before Henry VII had been raised to the throne by one group of rebellious magnates and as Henry himself had acquired the crown with the help of another such group, it was clear that security required the elimination of the striking power of the nobility. Moreover, since the nobility had made shambles of local law and order,[25] the crying need of the countryside was likewise the reduction of the nobility. Hence Henry VII's program. Livery and maintenance, that is, the practice of keeping uniformed men — really private armies or "gangs" — by the nobility was banned, and this time the ban was enforced, largely through the effective operation of the Star Chamber Court which was empowered to handle cases arising from this ban. Nobles with pretensions to the crown were speedily sent to the block, thereby eliminating potential leaders of opposition, and severe treason laws trapped others to their ends. And the new nobles that were created were necessarily creatures of the sovereigns who ennobled them. In the end, therefore, since most Tudors followed this policy, the nobility was reduced in power, and any reduction in baronial power meant a corresponding increase in the strength of the monarchy.

After the reduction of the nobility came the reduction of the church. Hitherto the church in England recognized the pope as its supreme head, was governed by a separate system of law of its own making (canon law), and had large possessions of land. Because of these it seemed like a powerful institution somewhat beyond the reach of the monarchy. Still it was not really as independent and influential as the above might imply, for the monarchs actually controlled the filling of the important church offices in the country and checked on laws passed by the convocations to see that the enactments did not derogate from the dignity and rights of the crown.[26] Moreover, the Wars of Roses revealed the church's powerlessness in the face of force. Nevertheless as an institution which claimed a divine origin and mission and which enjoyed certain rights of long standing, it existed as a challenge to the rising absolutism of the crown. It was this challenge that the Tudors eliminated.[27]

The circumstances which brought about this reduction of the church were twofold. One was Henry VIII's request to the pope to declare his marriage with his brother's widow, Catherine of Aragon, as contrary to the scripture and null so that he might marry Anne Boleyn. The other was the reluctance or the inability of the pope — Rome had recently fallen to the army of Charles V, Catherine's nephew — to comply with Henry's request. To prevail on the pope, Henry began to apply pressure on the church in England. First came measures against excessive charges for the services of burial and for probating wills and against pluralism and nonresidence. Next, the clergy was charged with violating the Statute of Praemunire, but was absolved in consideration of its willingness to pay a fine of £118,840 and to accept Henry as head of the church "as far as the law of Christ allows." Then the churchmen were forced to agree to a revision of the canon law by a royal committee, and Henry secured authority to suspend all payments of annates to Rome as he saw fit. When these pressures failed to bring papal compliance and the marriage became imperative, Henry pushed for a complete break. An Act in Restraint of Appeals (1533), intended to prevent Catherine from appealing to Rome, was inclusive and in principle banned all appeals to Rome. The nation's courts became final. Then, in quick succession, came the Second Annates Act which transformed the permissive character of the first act into a final ban on the annates; the second "Submission" of the clergy whereby Henry was recognized as Supreme Head of the Church, now without reservations; and the Succession Act which made it treason for anyone to act against the succession of Henry's children by Anne and thus tied the hands and the tongues of all those Catholics who looked upon Henry's second marriage as a violation of the sacrament. This was followed by the dissolution of the monasteries, first the smaller ones (1536), and next the larger ones (1539), which amounted to the repudiation of the theories of monasticism and of "good works"; and the formal definition of the doctrine to be allowed in the country (The Ten Articles, 1536; Bishop's Books, 1537; Six Articles, 1539). By 1536 therefore the church in England had been severed from Rome, deprived of one of its branches — the regular clergy — and subjected to the will of the crown. All that remained was to finish the "purging" and to give permanence to the organization of the established church and to the definition of its dogma. The first was accomplished in the reign of Edward VI when the chantries were closed, and the second was completed by Elizabeth in the face of bitter opposition from the Puritans and other Protestant sects. The final act was not a legal one, but one of war, the defeat of the Spanish Armada (1588), for, while the war had imperial and economic causes, it undoubtedly pitted Spain, the self-appointed guardian of Catholicism, against England, an unwitting defender of Protestantism, and when the Armada failed, Protestantism in England and with it the subjection of the church to the crown were assured.

The nobility repressed and the church subjected, remained yet the nation as a whole. It might be driven into opposition, it might be cowed by force, or it might be won for the crown. Brute force was used in the case of the suppression of the Pilgrimage of Grace by Henry VIII, who, after securing the disbandment of the rebels by fair promises, had some two hundred fifty of the trusting folk executed in their villages, presumably to overawe their fellowmen. And it was employed again in the suppression of Kett's rebellion by Warwick, a contender for the office of Protector held by Edward VI's uncle, Thomas Seymour, the Earl of Somerset. In addition, the political murders, the heinous laws of treason, and the burnings at the stake were all of the same stamp. Still, despite these obvious evidences of force, it must be said that in general the Tudors succeeded in winning the nation. They did so in several ways. To the nation as a whole they gave peace and order in place of anarchy and injustice. The law of the land was made king, and the nation which remembered the sad days of Henry VI's reign and of the Wars of Roses, when every nobleman was law, was glad for the Tudors. To the merchant and the industrialist they opened wider opportunities of trade and manufacture. To some members of this class and to the gentry they gave an opportunity to acquire land. In fact most of those who profited materially from the confiscation of the monastic lands had a vested interest in the Tudors: they were bound to them for better or for worse. To the laboring classes they tried to offer protection and bread, however inconsequential the effort turned out to be. They sought to restrict the enclosure movement and so to prevent mass eviction from the farms; they enacted laws to standardize admission to trades on a nationwide basis; they instituted a program of relief (Poor Law); and they tried to protect the housewife and the traveler from harassments by vagabonds. Each of the monarchs contributed to this process, but it was Elizabeth who in the end transmuted the public acceptance of the Tudors into real devotion for them. She did this in part by her personality, and she made sure that the royal rays fell on as many of her subjects as possible by making frequent trips through the country — incidentally, the enchanted hosts along the itinerary fed her court — but her success lay in the fact that in the course of her reign she succeeded in persuading her people that it was she who stood between them and foreign subjection. Patriotism was made to embrace religion, and most Englishmen, even Catholics, were prepared to stand by "good Queen Bess."

To maintain this despotism the Tudors had no standing army other than a small corps of personal guardsmen. Even Mary, the least popular of the Tudor sovereigns, had a ludicrously small force — a bodyguard of four hundred bowmen and eighty gentlemen of the axe, and about 2,200 regulars, 1,200 of them stationed on the Scottish frontier, and 1,000 at Calais and Guines.[28] They depended on a dutiful parliament which voted every measure they requested and so made the absolutism both legal and enforceable. Thus it was by parliamentary enactments that the nobles were stripped of their power and that the church was despoiled and subjected, that the people had their doctrine defined for them, that the prerogative procedures in the Star Chamber Court were sanctioned, and that the vicious laws of treason were raised over their heads. Tudor despotism could therefore be called absolutism by consent of parliament. Secondly, the Tudors depended on the unpaid but doting service of the local officials, principally the Justices of the Peace. The office developed out of an earlier medieval office, that of conservators of peace whose original function was to receive indictments of suspected criminals but whose duties were multiplied to include hearing cases and performing various administrative tasks. In the days of the Tudors their responsibilities were steadily increased until they became the key intermediaries between the crown and its people. The office was unsalaried, but it carried with it social prestige as well as indirect benefits and was eagerly sought by the local gentry. Once the appointees received the honor, they attended to their responsibilities proudly and loyally, with the result that the crown's business was faithfully performed and the absolutism made to function.[29] Of course there was need of a superior body which would stand behind as well as before the doting justices and the willing parliament. That body was the monarch's council, and as needs arose, it gave rise to supplementary councils. The Council of the North, created immediately after the suppression of the Pilgrimage of Grace, saw to it that the north counties bred no more revolts and that the Scottish frontier was safe. The Council of the Welsh Marches, established after Henry VIII integrated Wales into England, enforced peace and order among the restless Welshmen and guarded against the possibility that Wales might be used as a rallying spot for opposition whether foreign or local. The High Commission guarded the established church from attacks by the Catholics and the Protestant dissenters and supervised the operation of the various measures enacted to bring about religious uniformity in the nation. The Court of Star Chamber was another of these councils. Since these councils were at once judicial and administrative bodies and were all creatures of the ruler, the ruler's will was secured.

Such was the famed Tudor absolutism. From the foregoing description it would appear to have been both substantial and thorough. This appearance however should not mislead us into assuming that the system was decidedly new. A comparison of it with the system of government in pre-Tudor days will readily reveal the error of this assumption.

In the first place, the new in the machinery of the Tudor government was not extensive. Some new councils were formed as occasion demanded, as for example the Council of the North following the rebellion in the north against Henry VIII; a new court was established, the Court of Augmentation, to administer the property of the church confiscated by the state; a new office was created, such as that of the Lord Lieutenant whose duty it was to see that the interests of the crown were well served in the counties; and a few other introductions. But obviously these were in large measure merely multiplications or projections of existing agencies. They expanded the machinery but they did not revolutionize it. The royal household, the councils, parliament, courts, and Justices of the Peace remained as of old the principal organs of government.

In the second place, this machinery retained approximately the same relation to the crown as it had in pre-Tudor days. It all existed and operated by sufferance of the king, even the parliaments. In the pre-Tudor days the machinery appeared to be royal, as much of it — though far from all of it — was managed by the king's private household officers under a close supervision of the king himself. In the Tudor days, especially from the time of Thomas Cromwell on, more of the management was entrusted to officers of state and so the machinery began to assume a more national character. Still, the difference, though theoretically significant, was not revolutionary. The king managed as before, except that now he managed more of the state business at one remove, but through intermediaries who were nevertheless of his own making.[30]

In the third place, the philosophy of government remained substantially the same. Edward III and Henry V, for example, regarded themselves as chiefs of state in the same sense that Henry VIII or Elizabeth did. Both the former and the latter considered themselves as the nation incarnate, as the fountains of justice, and as guardians of their people's welfare.[31] The pre-Tudor monarchs paid more respect to their role as suzerains of the feudal estate, but the theory of government in their time did not regard them merely as the apex of the feudal system but also as the true heads of the entire nation. On the other hand, the Tudors, especially Henry VII, actually tried to revive certain feudal rights that were falling into disuse, which would suggest that the feudal concept of monarchy, in practice at least, had not disappeared entirely. And the fact that the objective of this revival may have been fiscal rather than political does not nullify the conclusion, for the legality of these restitutions could only be based on principles of political feudalism.[32] But perhaps the best evidence of the continuity of the old philosophy was the deliberate policy of the Tudors to operate within the constitution. Except in the matter of the church, they proclaimed no revolution, and though they were responsible for more extensive departures than they realized or cared to admit, actually they were very conservative in their notions of government.

There was a substantial difference, but it was in success of execution rather than in principle.[33] Thus while both the pre-Tudors and the Tudors sought to control the magnates in the name of their role as heads of the nation, the pre-Tudors, largely because they were too dependent on the feudatories in the Hundred Years' War, did not succeed, whereas the Tudors, having the nation's support on this matter, did succeed. Thus in the case of the church, the Tudors succeeded in gaining complete control whereas the pre-Tudors had only a partial control through their participation in the appointments to church offices and through their right to permit or deny appeals to Rome. These were substantial gains for the monarchy and they certainly exalted its position in the nation. But they did not revolutionize the monarchy.[34]

Decentralization in the Holy Roman Empire

The political developments in the Holy Roman Empire during the Renaissance differed from those occurring in the other major states in the west. Instead of growing centralization, the Empire witnessed decentralization and a hardening of localism.

FAILURE AT CENTRALIZATION The first process, as observed in an earlier section of this book, was formally admitted in the constitution of the Empire, the Golden Bull (1356), which was prepared by the

Emperor Charles IV. It was enhanced by the incompetence or the preoccupation of his successors and sons. Wenceslaus (1378–1400) was plagued by a steady opposition of the magnates of his native land, Bohemia, who finally forced upon him the principle of government by council with themselves in the council. This preoccupation prevented him from adequately fulfilling his functions as emperor, and his addiction to strong liquor reduced his competence on the few occasions that he might have had for attending to imperial interests. His incapacity finally led to his deposition in 1400, an act, which in itself, reduced the prestige of the emperorship still more. From 1400 until 1411, the Empire was torn by civil war between contestants for the office, first between Rupert, Count of the Rhenish Palatinate, candidate of those who deposed Wenceslaus, and Wenceslaus' son Sigismund, and then, when Rupert died in 1410, between Sigismund and his cousin Jobst, Margrave of Moravia. This decade of civil war and political chaos naturally left its scars on the imperial position. In the reign of Sigismund the situation did not improve substantially. Sigismund gained some international prestige from the active role he took in terminating the Schism, but his authority in the Empire did not increase correspondingly. In fact, considered from the long-range point of view, the imperial position was weakened. As Emperor and so as representative of the German nation, as well as King of Bohemia, he became involved in the ruinous Hussite Wars. Beginning as wars of rebellion against the established church, they soon became wars of nationalism, Czechs versus Germans. Sigismund, although King of Bohemia, could not allow the separatist movement to go unchallenged. Although the rebels were defeated in the end, the martyrdom of Huss and Jerome and the heroic deeds of Ziska fanned Czech nationalism and made Bohemia's membership in the Empire a festering sore. Then, out of consideration for the Hohenzollern support both in war and in his campaign for the emperorship, Sigismund granted an important piece of territory only recently acquired, the Mark of Brandenburg, to Frederick, Burgrave of Nuremberg, and this obviously was a step in the promotion of princely power. The Luxemburg era was no era of strong emperorship.

Under the Habsburgs the process of decentralization continued, although there were some attempts to arrest it and to strengthen central government. Albert II did not rule long enough to affect the situation. However, he was required to agree to a number of measures guaranteeing the quasi-independent position of the princes as the price of his election (*Wahlkapitulation*), and this capitulation served as a precedent at all succeeding elections. In other words, the Emperors were required to bind themselves not to take any measures prejudicial to the princes. Albert's son Frederick III (1440–1493) simply let matters drift as is clearly indicated by the fact that he did not attend imperial diets for twenty-seven years. Perhaps his indolence has been exaggerated, for he did thwart Charles the Bold's attempt to aggress on imperial territory and he did gain, by the treaty with Eugenius (1446) and the Concordat of Vienna, some additional control over the church. Still, the balance, so far as the consolidation of imperial authority was concerned, seems to be against him, as a man who dreamed much and did little. The loss of a great part of his ducal domain, including his capital Vienna, to Matthias Corvinus of Hungary is a good measure of his incapacity. In the reign of Maximilian there were several attempts to reform the imperial government which, if enacted, would have fostered centralization. There were plans for the establishment of an imperial court, an imperial council, an imperial army, and an imperial tax. But except for the establishment of the court (1495), which incidentally could not become an instrument for centralization because the emperor was allowed to name only eight of its twenty-five officers, the plans bore little fruit; the Emperor was unwilling to accept the recommendations of the princes for a council controlled by them, and the princes were opposed to a council subject to the Emperor. Moreover, neither pleas, nor shame, nor threats to the nation from France or Turkey would induce the princes — and the imperial towns for that matter — to provide the Emperor with an army or money. His ventures in foreign policy — marriage, by proxy, of Anne of Brittany, dynastic ties with Spain, promotion of family claims to Hungary, designs on Venice — appeared to them too much like schemes for the aggrandizement of the Habsburgs at the expense of the Empire and to their own jeopardy. They were determined therefore not to give him the instruments of power, and so the Empire floundered.[35] Similar attempts at reform were made in the reign of Charles V, and an imperial council was

actually installed, but its recommendation for a tax and a uniform customs tariff raised violent opposition from the towns and the princes,
and within ten years it died a natural death (1531). And so, with no
reforms to redress the balance in favor of central authority, decentralization under the Habsburgs was as bad as under the Luxemburgers.

Deplorable as the condition was, it became worse in the reign of
Charles. He was repeatedly at war with France and Turkey and
could ill afford to alienate the princes by taking energetic action in
behalf of the central government. And when he did do so in his war
on the Protestant princes, he failed in the end, for by the Treaty of
Augsburg (1555) all princes were conceded the right to decide what
church they would permit in their territory. Thus when Charles laid
down his imperial burden in 1556, he left an Empire whose central
government was practically impotent.

This conclusion may seem to be paradoxical in view of the alarm
of all Europe at the military and political posture of Charles V. But it
will not appear so paradoxical if we remember that the power of
Charles was based on his dynastic possessions — Burgundy, Spain,
Naples and Sicily, and the Habsburg lands — and not on his imperial
office. The Empire brought him prestige and some territorial claims
and resources, but at the same time it burdened him with additional
responsibilities, particularly on the frontier against Turkey, which
consumed so much of his energies and revenues that the Empire was
more a drain on, than an asset to, his actual power.

CONSOLIDATION AND MULTIPLICATION OF MEMBER STATES The second
process, that of hardening of localism, was both cause and consequence
of the weakness of the central government. Because the emperors were
weak they could do little to prevent the growth of princely authorities,
and because the princely states were growing both in autonomy and in
number they steadily undermined the imperial authority, and the
vicious circle went on throughout the entire Renaissance period.

As an illustration of the growth of a principality we may choose
the Mark of Brandenburg. Its origin dates back to Henry the Fowler's
defeat of the Havelli (928–929) and the occupation of their capital
Brennibor, from which the name Brandenburg is derived. The Slavs
recovered their land in Otto III's reign, but in the 1130's the Germans

conquered it once more. The conqueror was Albert the Bear, Count of Bollenstadt, and his descendants ruled the Mark as a unit until 1266. For the next half-century it was held by two collateral lines. On their extinction the Mark was subjected to dismemberment by various neighbors and claimants. In the course of this rivalry the Emperor Louis IV bestowed it on his son, but the family lost it after Louis' death, and his successor, Charles IV, assigned it to his son Wenceslaus, who in turn granted it to his brother Sigismund. Sigismund, as pointed out, gave it to his friend and ally Frederick VI of Hohenzollern, Burgrave of Nuremberg, who became Frederick I of Brandenburg. But by this time the Mark had been reduced from its original size. From Frederick's day on, throughout the rest of the Renaissance period, his descendants labored to establish their authority therein and to enlarge its territory. Frederick II (1437–1470), for example, subjugated the towns which had been enjoying practical autonomy hitherto,[36] established a supreme court, secured the right to appoint bishops in Havelberg, Brandenburg, and Lebus, and purchased the New Mark from the Teutonic Order. His brother Albert Achilles (1470–1486) conquered Krossen, defeated a coalition of northern powers, established a regular budget, and promulgated the principle of primogeniture. His son John extended his authority to all towns and added the county of Zossen (1490); and the latter's son Joachim I (1499–1535) acquired the county of Ruppin. Thus, by the middle of the sixteenth century, the Hohenzollern had established themselves firmly in Brandenburg. Since they had a private army, a private court system, and a private revenue — in a word, since they were autonomous — and since at that time they also had the electoral vote, their position was indeed strong. And insofar as their position was strong and autonomous, they were not likely to support a strong central government which could encroach on their position.

As an illustration of the reverse process, that of multiplication of princely houses, we may consider Saxony. Until 1180 Saxony was a large and growing unit. Then by imperial action it was reduced in size, and in 1260 what remained of it was partitioned into Upper and Lower Saxony, respectively known as Saxe-Wittenberg and Saxe-Lauenburg. From 1285 to 1401 Saxe-Lauenburg was ruled first by three, then by two lines, and finally in 1401 it was reunited again. Saxe-Wittenberg was held by one line until 1422 when the dynasty became extinct. The ruler of Saxe-Lauenburg tried to reunite the two Saxonies but in vain. In 1423 Emperor Sigismund bestowed the vacant Saxe-Wittenberg upon Frederick, Margrave of Meissen, as a reward for his aid in the Hussite Wars. Frederick preferred his new title, and the name Saxony began to be applied to his former holdings. With the grant he also received the electoral vote. Frederick's lands were divided between his two sons, Ernest and Albert, and the division persisted through the next two generations. In 1547, at the battle of Mühlberg the grandson of Ernest, John Frederick the Magnanimous who fought in the Protestant ranks against Charles V, was captured and was compelled to cede some of his lands and the electoral vote to the line of Albert, whose representative at that time was the notorious Maurice, who, though Protestant, had a secret treaty of alliance with Charles. The remainder of John Frederick's holdings, together with a few pieces of territory which were restored to his line later, were divided among his sons, giving rise to several new Saxonies — Saxe-Gotha, Saxe-Weimar, Saxe-Coburg, Saxe-Meiningen, and Saxe-Altenberg. Thus, by the end of the Renaissance, Upper Saxony was divided into five smaller territories. Lower Saxony on the other hand remained intact. Maurice abandoned Charles V in favor of the Protestants and was instrumental in procuring the Treaty of Passau (1552) which enhanced the cause of the Protestants and the interests of Maurice himself. His brother Augustus I, who succeeded him, continued the centralizing policy and also added Neustadt, Vogtland, and parts of Henneberg. Lower Saxony, then, underwent centralization. However, this does not change the fact that where formerly there was one Saxon house, during the Renaissance the number multiplied. Since each enjoyed practical autonomy, the result was an increase in the number of political units which fact was bound to hamper centralization.

The histories of these two houses were duplicated throughout the Empire, and the result was that the Empire became a congeries of principalities, some compact and powerful, and a multitude of small ones, but all more or less independent. It is not surprising therefore that proposals for centralization seldom went beyond unctuous words, and that the Empire, for all practical purposes, was but a name.

If the Empire was in a state of near-dissolution, many of its member units were not much better off. Brandenburg, Austria, Bavaria, and Saxony did move in the direction of governmental consolidation, with a civil service, a territorial judiciary, and a fiscal system to make the princely governments effective. But in the multitude of lesser principalities the local estates of nobles, knights, and towns consistently denied their princes money and arms and jealously guarded and expanded their own rights and jurisdictions. Thus the fragmentation on the imperial scale was duplicated by a fragmentation on the local scale. The Empire therefore was not only a house of various-sized bricks without any mortar to hold them together, but the bricks themselves were in an advanced state of disintegration. Truly a sorry political structure!

Italy

In the various states of Italy the internal political structures during the Renaissance changed least of all. The systems of government which had been evolving during the later Middle Ages had crystallized by the middle of the fourteenth century and continued during the Renaissance without any substantial modifications. Only in Florence were there more than minor changes.

In Milan the Visconti despotism continued until the line died out in 1447. The death of Filippo Maria without heirs prompted the Milanese to re-establish a republican form of government; but the experiment, called the Ambrosian Republic in honor of St. Ambrose, the celebrated fourth-century bishop of Milan, lasted only three years. The party feuds which sprang up among the rival groups seeking to control the republic and the disastrous war with Venice which the republic inherited from Filippo provided Francesco Sforza, the *condottiere* in the city's pay, with an opportunity to seize control of the city. He did so in 1450, and from then until the Habsburg-Valois Italian wars, the Sforza ruled the city and the duchy as despots very much after the fashion of the Visconti.

Venice, having become a plutocracy by the end of the Middle Ages, remained plutocratic during the Renaissance.[37] Big business with the Dieci as its watchdog would not tolerate any departure from the constitution, neither in the direction of despotism nor of democracy. Thus Doge Francesco Foscari, though he had a brilliant reign, was deposed because his toying with the lesser folk made him suspect. On the other hand, even though the plutocracy presided, as it were, at the liquidation of the city's maritime empire and suffered other military and diplomatic defeats in Italy proper, it was able to hold on to the government. If it admitted more families to the list of those eligible for election to the Great Council — 1,671 in 1510 as against 1,107 in 1311 — it was not thereby liberalizing the Council, for those added were wealthy, even if "new," business colleagues and were therefore "safe" politically. Moreover, the old and established families successfully maintained their ascendancy. On the whole, the old government remained substantially the same.

The situation in Florence was not so static. From 1343 to 1378, as pointed out in our first chapter, Florence went through a stage now euphemistically called the "democratic interlude."[38] The priorate was reorganized to give some representation — three out of eight — to the nine lowest gilds; the number of citizens eligible for the magistracies increased steadily, mostly to accommodate the *gente nuova*, the "new" citizens who emerged into prominence as a result of the natural redistribution of wealth following the business crash of 1342 and the Black Death and the accompanying financial repercussions;[39] and the government paid more attention to civic than to partisan interests.[40] If this was a liberalization of a sort, it did not lead to any substantial democratization of the government. Nor did it weaken the hold of the business interests on the government; for they still held a majority position in the priorate and influenced, perhaps even determined, the fiscal and the financial programs of the city;[41] while the *popolo minuto*, the masses, had no representation and were even forbidden to organize.[42] The liberalization was, therefore, quite limited.

So long as this widened ruling segment held together, it was able to keep control of the government. But differences eventually arose over fiscal and foreign policies; and when these were further aggravated by the usual rivalry between the "ins" and the "outs," by the family feuds, and by business competition, they split the caste into hostile factions and reduced its hold on the city. At the same time the lower classes increased their clamor for a "better deal."[43] The result was the Ciompi uprising (1378).

The report of the rebellion need not detain us,[44] as it proved to be a failure. As in other rebellions, the victorious party soon split over policy, conservatives versus radicals, and fell an easy prey to reactionary counterrevolutionaries. In 1382 the old and the new conservatives united and wrested control of the government.

From 1382 to 1434 the government remained strongly reactionary. Without modifying the constitution substantially to assure their control, except for the restoration of the majority of the priorate to the greater gilds, the reactionaries managed to preserve themselves in power. Perhaps the major reason for the acceptance of their domination was the threat from the Visconti, which made internal disunity a luxury that could not be afforded by any class. Moreover, the conquest of Pisa, consummated after many years of struggle, redounded to the prestige of the government also. Certainly this explanation is highly probable, for once the government failed in a foreign policy to which it was strongly committed — namely, the conquest of Lucca — opposition quickly mounted and led to the overthrow of the party and to the rise of the Medici.

Under the Medici, whose regime lasted from 1434 to 1494, the constitution was altered to assure their control of the city. Election by lot was abandoned, and machinery was devised to control elections; the Council of the People and the Council of the Commune, both of which had long since become preserves of the reactionaries and their supporters, were displaced by two new councils, the Council of the Hundred (1458) and the Council of Seventy (1480), both creatures of the Medici; and the office of the *capitano dell popolo* was abolished (1475). But while these changes placed the controls in the hands of the Medici, they themselves preferred to operate from behind the scenes — Cosimo, for example, held the office of *gonfalonier* for six months only. In that way the appearances of a republic were preserved, although the government was operated by an oligarchy of merchants acceptable to, and guided by, the Medici.[45]

Except for two or three crises, like Lorenzo's gamble in personally visiting king Ferrante of Naples in order to get a *rapprochement,* or like the Pazzi plot in which Lorenzo's brother lost his life, the Medici maintained control of the government for sixty years. Then in 1494, as a result of Piero II's surrender to Charles VIII of France when the latter led the first French invasion of Italy, their rule came to an end. The city, by then disenchanted with the Medici, ousted the hapless Piero and returned to a more genuine republic.

The restored republic, combining a permanent executive with a great council patterned after the *Gran Consiglio* of Venice,[46] did not last long. Inspired largely by Savonarola and therefore accepted reluctantly, the constitution lost favor with the public when the fiery preacher was discredited and burned at the stake. But it was war which actually decided the republic's life. Born of a foreign invasion, it was subject to the vagaries of war between the French and the Habsburgs. In the end the Habsburgs won, and the Medici, by then creatures of the victorious Charles V, were reinstated — once in 1512 and then again in 1529 after they had been expelled in 1527 — and the republic suppressed. And so, as in Milan and in many other Italian cities, the republic gave way to a princely state.

Weakness of Monarchy in Scandinavia and Promise of Recovery

The political situation in the Scandinavian lands during the Renaissance may be summarized briefly as the continuation of a weak monarchy. Occasional attempts were made to strengthen it, but in general they were in vain and the repeated failures weakened it still more. Only at the very end of the Renaissance period was there some recovery.

The causes for this sorry state of the monarchy were mainly three. One was the persistence of the elective principle. Election had become the rule in the Middle Ages and continued unchanged until the early sixteenth century. Although in practice sons were sometimes elected to succeed their fathers, their succession was dependent upon election and this led to two or three adverse results. If kings were elected they could also be deposed, particularly if they tried to promote measures prejudicial to the electors. Thus Eric, Queen Margaret's protégé and an open cultivator of monarchic strength, was dropped in 1438 and replaced by his nephew Christopher. Thus, as noted above, Christian II, the ruler who momentarily re-established Danish control in Sweden and who also tried to strengthen the monarchy by taxing the nobility and the church, by surrounding himself with councillors of the bourgeois class, and by issuing codes of law without seeking the approval of the old council of magnates, was driven out (1523), and the crown was given to his uncle Frederick I. Such forced changes naturally provoked civil wars which in turn weakened the monarchy still further by sapping the crown's resources. Another adverse result which derived from the elective principle was the expansion of appanaged feudalism. The reigning sovereigns, uncertain about their sons' successions, tried to prepare for either eventuality by granting them large appanages. This practice multiplied princely houses which were generally a bane to the sovereign whoever he happened to be. Again, because of election, the electors could impose terms of their own making and require the candidate to accept them on oath. These election capitulations went so far as to formally permit the right of revolution against the monarchy, but perhaps equally important was the fact that the acceptance of these capitulations by each monarch kept alive the principle of limited monarchy.

Another cause which contributed to the weakness of the monarchy was the widespread resistance to the Union of Calmar. To preserve the Union the Danish rulers had to keep the inhabitants of Sweden and Norway under control, and the attempts naturally led to friction and to wars. Since the wars generally proved unsuccessful to the Danish kings, they had the effect of weakening the monarchy. Put simply, maintenance of the Union was a greater burden than the Danish monarchy could support, with the consequence that, as the Union went, so went the monarchy.

A third cause was the commercial predominance of the Hansa merchants. They had established their supremacy before 1350, and during the Renaissance they secured it by defeating the Danish ruler

Waldemar IV and by imposing the Treaty of Stralsund which recognized their commercial monopoly. Since they maintained that position throughout most of the fifteenth century, the growth of a native merchant class was both impeded and delayed. This meant that the Scandinavian kings had no substantial middle class to turn to in their clashes with the magnates. In addition, the absence of a rich native commerce which could provide taxes to support an effective monarchy put the kings at the mercy of the Hansa financiers. If the kings needed money, the Hansa could extend loans and secure confirmation of their rights; if the kings threatened the interests of the Hansa, then the latter could subsidize revolts, the classic example of which was the League's support of Gustavus Vasa in Sweden. In either event the monopolistic position of the Hansa actually contributed to the weakness of the Scandinavian monarchy.

This state of affairs continued until about the end of the Renaissance period, when some progress toward stronger central government appeared both in Denmark and in Sweden.

In Denmark the first signs came after Christian III secured the throne in 1536. He had gained it as a result of winning a civil war, known as the Counts' War, in which a faction of nobles aided by some foreign interests tried to restore the throne to the imprisoned Christian II and in which Protestantism was already an issue. Once secure, Christian III took steps which strengthened the monarchy. In 1536 he prevailed on the national assembly to establish the Lutheran Church and to convert the monarchy from an elective to a hereditary institution. To be sure, neither measure advanced the monarchy at once. Indeed, the disestablishment of the Catholic Church profited the nobility more than the monarchy, for it was to the nobles that the bulk of the church estates went, and the monarchy's poverty and impotence were actually so disarming that in 1542 the nobles voted Christian a twentieth part of all their property to relieve him of some of his foreign debts. Still, in the long run, the more thorough subjection of the church to the state and the reduction of succession wars naturally favored the monarchy.

In Sweden, promise of a strong monarchy came with national independence. We have seen the dissolution of the Swedish monarchy on the eve of the Renaissance and its complete eclipse at the inception of the Union of Calmar. We have also seen that it was the Swedish opposition led by such popular leaders as Karl Knutsson, Sten Sture the Elder and the Younger, and finally Gustavus Vasa that brought the Union to its end. With the re-establishment of independence Vasa presently introduced reforms which eventually made Sweden a Baltic power and its monarchy strong.[47]

Since the old council, composed of magnates and prelates, generally supported the Union because it secured to them their rights and their political influence, Gustavus, by destroying the Union, broke the council's power and assumed it for himself. Then, because he needed resources and the church had extensive possessions and was also a spokesman of the old regime, he had it nationalized (Vasteras recess, 1527). Its lands went to the crown as well as the right to determine its personnel and its doctrine. Next, in 1544, by the Act of Hereditary Settlement, the crown was made hereditary. In the meantime, Gustavus crushed open rebellion against his program of nationalization and deprived the Hansa of its crippling commercial monopoly. Finally, although it was with the help of the common folk that he accomplished all this, he eliminated their role in policy making. To the commons of a northern province he reported:

> . . . it behoveth us as a Christian monarch to appoint ordinances and rules for you: therefore must ye be obedient to our royal commands, as well in matters spiritual as temporal.[48]

Thus, when Gustavus died in 1560, he left a nation which was thoroughly subject to the crown.

Poland — A Monarchic "Republic"!

Perhaps the most important political development in Poland during the Renaissance period was the progressive rise of the gentry as the dominant political power. Since this entailed a corresponding decline in the power of the monarchy, the combined process may be regarded as the establishment of limited monarchy. Some historians look upon this development as the transformation of an aristocratic monarchy into a "republic" of the gentry.[49] But whatever the label, the process was the same.

The causative forces were two: the matter of succession from the death of Casimir the Great (1370) to the accession of Jagiello and the needs of an expanded empire. The first originated in the fact that on Casimir's death the crown passed successively to two foreign princes and a girl. Louis of Hungary, Casimir's nephew, was an Angevin and not a Piast, and Jagiello who was invited to become husband of Louis' daughter, Jadwiga, and King of Poland was a Lithuanian and not a Pole. As foreigners they could not be accepted without reservations. They had to bind themselves to respect the rights, customs, and interests of their new subjects, and this was tantamount to the admission that the state came before the crown. Since the state of the time consisted formally of the aristocracy, both lay and ecclesiastical, and the gentry, this meant that the rights and interests of these two classes would not be violated. The accession of a girl added to this process in two ways. One stemmed from the fact that a female sovereign was not in accord with Polish law and custom. To depart from this custom it was necessary to get the approval of the two classes which constituted the state, and they were not likely to grant it without a *quid pro quo*. Thus Louis, in order to get the consent to the accession of his daughter Mary, found it necessary to concede the principle that no taxes were to be imposed without the assent of the state, excepting the nominal imposition of two *groschen* per hide, and to agree that local offices should be held by the local gentry (Charter of Koszyce, 1374). To be sure Mary eventually proved unacceptable because her husband was Sigismund, the future Holy Roman Emperor, and there was enough anti-German feeling in Poland to prevent Poland from falling within the German orbit. But if the opponents repudiated Mary, they clung to the gains secured at Koszyce. They simply had Mary's sister Jadwiga brought to Poland and then married her to Jagiello of Lithuania, but with the stipulation that he underwrite the concessions which they had obtained from Louis. Jagiello confirmed these rights in 1386, and by this act bound his successors to the state. Another way in which the accession of a girl contributed to the advance of the nobility and the gentry was the *interregnum* between the death of Louis and the accession of Jagiello. During the interval, whatever political action was taken in Poland was taken in the name of Jadwiga, but by the nobility. In other words, they ruled while Jadwiga was being prepared to reign.

But greater than the gains made as a result of these issues of succession were the gains which were made in consequence of the country's military needs of men and money. It will be recalled that, beginning with the expansion program of Casimir the Great, the frontiers of Poland had been extended southeastward and eastward, and that in the time of his namesake, Casimir IV, they were extended northward. All this expansion provoked wars with the neighboring peoples, the Tartars, Russians, and the Teutonic Knights, and called for more men and money than the kings could raise. They had to make extraordinary demands, and to obtain them they had to pay extraordinary prices. At the same time, when the gentry assembled as the *levée en masse*, they became aware of their collective strength and so more exacting in their demands. Hence their gains grew steadily.

After the initial gains secured by the Charter of Koszyce came those obtained in 1422 by the Charter of Czerwinsk. The king promised not to imprison any of the gentry without due trial, while the competence of his local officials, the *storostas*, in cases involving the gentry was limited to those of robbery, arson, rape, and armed attack. In 1454 by the Statute of Nieszawa other privileges were obtained. Several articles promised protection to the gentry from abuse in the law courts. Another one bound the king to appoint his local representatives, the *voivodes* and *castellans*, during the sessions of the *seym* (parliament) with its consultation. Since the *seym* was the preserve of the nobility and was soon to include the gentry, this meant that the aristocracy gained a hand in determining the crown's administrative personnel. Still more important was the article which bound the king to consult with the regional assemblies of the gentry (*seymiks*) before summoning the general levy or introducing new legislation. This meant that the aristocracy was given a decisive role in the formulation of policy. Moreover, to facilitate this consultation the *seymiks* were invited to send delegates to the *seym*, and since they came with instructions from their local assemblies which they were bound to uphold, they therefore served to increase the limitation on the monarchy. The result of all these measures was that the Polish monarchy became a parliamentary monarchy. This gain was further confirmed by the Statute *Nihil Novi* (1501) by which the crown agreed that "nothing new may be decided without the joint consent of the members of the Council and the district deputies." By the beginning of the sixteenth century, then, the gentry had become the most powerful political class. Perhaps the reference to Renaissance Poland as "a republic of the gentry" is justified then.

But these gains at the expense of the crown did not stand alone. To them the nobility and gentry also added some gains at the expense of the peasantry and the towns.

As pointed out in the book on economy, it was during this period that the Polish peasantry was reduced to serfdom. In order to assure themselves of the necessary labor to conduct their commercial farming the landlords secured legislation which restricted the mobility of the peasants and deprived them of the right to appeal to the crown courts. At the same time they increased the *corvées* and began to encroach on the possessions of the peasants. Manorialism thus crept in and with it the aggrandizement of the power of the nobility.

The towns were not subjected like the peasantry, but their decline reduced their potential as a counterpoise to the landed aristocracy. The loss of the Black Sea littoral to the Turks deprived the Polish towns of the benefits of the transit trade between the Black and the Baltic. At the same time the gentry secured exemption from custom payments on imports, a privilege which operated to the disadvantage of urban industry. Polish industry, being less advanced than that of Germany and the Low Countries, could not compete with imports from these lands and suffered accordingly. Thus, hit in commerce and industry, the towns lost some of their political vitality and declined in their role as a counterpoise to the aristocracy.

Hence, masters of the crown and of the peasantry, and free from any serious political challenge on the part of the towns, Polish nobility and gentry reigned supreme by the end of the Renaissance period.

Hungary — Limited Monarchy Challenged and Subverted

As in Poland the significant development in Hungary was the preservation of the constitutional monarchy and its ultimate collapse. The difference was that in Hungary this process was temporarily reversed by the hero-king Matthias Hunyadi.

As was noted above, the legal basis for this constitutional monarchy was provided by the Golden Bull in 1222. The privileges of the nobility formalized by the Bull were repeatedly confirmed, and the confirmation which Lewis the Great made in 1351 carried the principle into the Renaissance period. During the reign of Lewis the Great it was advanced further by the establishment of regional assemblies of nobles, known as the *comitatus* and analogous to the Polish *seymiks*. These assemblies acquired extensive administrative functions as well as political rights, and while they could be of service to the central government, they invariably acted as a curb on its efforts at independence. Parallel with these movements there developed a change in the doctrine of the crown. Whereas formerly the crown was conceived as consisting of the king and the great nobles, now it was thought of as consisting of the king and the estates; and since the crown was regarded as the source of all authority, the estates as legal sharers of this authority necessarily functioned as a limitation on the monarchy.

Fostering this idea of constitutional monarchy but at the same time weakening the monarchy itself there were, during the Renaissance period, several factors. One was the recurrence of wars of succession following the death of Lewis the Great (1382). His daughter Mary was opposed by Charles of Durazzo, of the Italian Angevin branch, primarily because her betrothal to the Luxemburger Sigismund excited considerable anti-German feeling always present among central Europeans. When Mary died in 1395 and Sigismund assumed the crown himself, some nobles raised an opponent to him in the person of Charles's son Ladislas, King of Naples. Vladislav I, who was both King of Poland and claimant to the throne of Hungary, was opposed by the supporters of the infant son of the preceding King Albert of

Habsburg. Vladislav II, who was also King of Bohemia, was opposed by the nationalist party led by the House of Zapolya, and Ferdinand of Habsburg ran into the same opposition. These repeated wars of succession weakened the monarchy, and at the same time they kept alive the important constitutional principle that the monarchy was elective, an additional limitation on it. The other factor which contributed to the weakness of the monarchy was the hostility between the magnates and the lesser nobility. Such, for example, was the bitter clash between the Cilli family and the Hunyadi house, which, though itself a member of the magnates, was accepted by the gentry as their leader. These clashes naturally divided the nation and weakened the monarchy still more.

This steady decline of the monarchy was interrupted by Matthias Hunyadi, known popularly as Corvinus and as the promoter of Renaissance culture in Hungary. Elected as a guardian of the national cause, following four successive foreign kings, and as a representative of the gentry as against the high nobility, Matthias pursued a program of strengthening the monarchy. His successful military ventures against Turkey, Austria, and Bohemia enabled him to develop a standing army, to collect extraordinary taxes without the consent of the estates, and to overawe the magnates. As defender of the lesser folk he instituted the right of appeal from the county courts, which normally reflected the influence of the nobles, to the royal curia. Then, as a ruler with autocratic intentions, he promoted centralized administrative machinery. But all this strengthening of the monarchy was contrary to the constitution of the land and too precipitant to last beyond the lifetime of its architect. No sooner was Matthias dead than the nobility brought another foreigner, Vladislav of Bohemia, who was believed to be too weak personally to continue the centralizing program of Matthias. The expectations were more than met, for not only was the new ruler bound by law not to pursue the program of his predecessor and to accept the dictates of the council and the diet, but also he failed to prevent civil war and foreign invasion. The result was victory for the nobility, but death to the country, for it was partitioned by the Turks and the Habsburgs.

Ottoman Turkey — A "Slave" State

Since the Byzantine empire and the former Slavic states in the Balkan area were conquered by the Turks during the period of the Renaissance, they need not be considered here. It is Ottoman Turkey to which we must turn.

The important internal development in this land of the conquerors was the consolidation of the autocracy for which the bases were provided by Orkhan on the eve of the Renaissance. Since the empire was the result of a protracted conquest which lasted for some three centuries, the army naturally became the decisive organ of power in the state. In this connection it should be remembered that the army, made up of *janissaries* and the *spahis*, was not a national force but a force devoted to the sultan in person who actually led it in combat. This, of course, made the sultan a military despot.

Supplementing the fighting force as an instrument of autocracy were two other bodies. One was the corps of administrators and was comparable to the *janissaries*. Captured Christian boys were converted to Islam, trained for various administrative duties, and then assigned to their government posts. Since they were literally "slaves" of the sultan, they naturally reflected his will. The other was made up of native Moslems whose function was to render justice and to preserve the legal, religious, and educational traditions of Islam. Since the principle source of this tradition was the Koran, which was regarded as the Word of God, their decisions were beyond challenge. However, from the time of Selim's conquest of Egypt, the sultan was also Caliph, that is, the successor of Mohammed and so the final guardian of the Koran. Hence, this body too was subject to the sultan's will. In sum, then, Ottoman Turkey developed into a personal, military, and religious autocracy.[50]

This absolutism, however, was not without a weakness. In addition to the limitations inherent in absolutism as such, it had one weakness, which, while not yet fully effective during the Renaissance, had already made its appearance. That was the Law of Succession. There had been fratricidal wars over the sultanate, and in the hope of eliminating them, Mohammed II, the conqueror of Constantinople, issued the rule that "whoever among [his] illustrious children and grandchildren may come to the throne, should, for securing the peace of the world, order his brothers to be executed."[51] This provision naturally provoked much jockeying between the living sons for favorable positions to avoid being caught on the receiving end of the executioner's sword. It also invited rebellion and civil war, but a more serious result was the fact that it provided the *janissaries* with opportunities to interfere in the making of sultans. And once they began to act in that capacity, the power of the sultan was bound to suffer. This, however, was yet to come, although the *janissaries* had already taken part in the elevation of Selim II and in the elimination of his brothers. As yet Renaissance Turkey was beyond question an unmitigated absolutism.

Muscovy — Emergent Czarist Despotism

In the section dealing with political developments on the eve of the Renaissance the initial rise of Muscovy was traced to the reign of Ivan Kalita who already claimed the title of Grand Prince. From his reign on, throughout the period now under consideration, this backward principality continued to expand and to develop as an autocracy.

As the rise of Moscow to pre-eminence was due to the support of the Tartars, so the continuation of this expansion was largely due to the weaknesses of the Tartars once they began to break up into rival khanates. In the first place, the disintegration of the Tartar power invited the princes of Moscow to wage war against the khans in the name of freedom for all the Russians, and the victories which they won, such as that of Prince Dmitry at Kulikovo (1378) or those of Ivan IV (The Terrible) against the Khan of Kazan (1552) and of Astrakhan (1556), naturally raised their prestige and sometimes their power. In the second place, what rights of supremacy they had formerly exercised over other principalities in the name of the Tartars, they now exercised in their own name, and the preponderance they thus acquired they employed to subjugate other principalities. Basil I annexed Nizhy-Novgorod; Basil II, Mozhaisk and Serpukhov; Ivan III (The Great), Perm, Tver, Yaroslav, and the famous Novgorod, both the city and all its northern territories all the way to the Urals and the White Sea; and Basil III, Pskov and Smolensk. Under Ivan IV (1533–1582) this expansion, as intimated above, was directed eastward against the Tartars. Kazan and Astrakhan were conquered outright and the penetration of Siberia was begun. His attempt to move the Muscovy frontiers to the Baltic proved in vain despite extensive fighting; Poland-Lithuania and Sweden prevented him from thus anticipating Peter the Great. Nevertheless, by the end of Ivan's reign, the political arm of the Prince of Moscow extended from Smolensk in the west, past the Urals into Siberia and from the White Sea to the Caspian. Only the Baltic Sea and Black Sea littorals were for the time being beyond his reach.

This territorial expansion was paralleled by the development of absolutism. So long as the Tartars retained their political supremacy over the various principalities, it was natural that they should delegate full authority to a prince whom they could remove at will rather than govern through democratic machinery which would be harder to control and with which, in addition, they had no acquaintance. What authoritarianism the princes were allowed to cultivate under the Tartars, they continued to cultivate when free from the Tartars. The lands they conquered, for example, they considered as their personal possessions, and town governments wherever they were still encountered were reduced.

Thus Ivan III, when he finally broke the back of stubborn Novgorod which had a regular municipal government, insisted that there was "to be no town bell in Novgorod, and no *posadnik*" (mayor), and that "all the sovereignty" was to be his. Similarly Basil III crushed the liberties of Pskov when he annexed it in 1510. Then, the "sovereignty" which they had inherited from their yellow masters they began to claim as theirs by divine right. When the Holy Roman Emperor Maximilian tried to bait Ivan III with an offer of a royal crown in order to get an alliance with him against Sigismund of Poland, Ivan retorted, "We, by God's grace, are sovereigns in our land from the beginning, from our first forefathers, and our appointment we hold from God."[52]

Strongly seconding this authoritarianism was the church in Russia. It realized how necessary was the unity of the Russian people and principalities if they were to liberate themselves from the Tartar yoke, and so it sanctioned Moscow's claim to political primacy and urged the heirarchy and the faithful to be loyal to Moscow's princes. It also urged the replacement of the old practice of dividing the principality among all the living sons of the Grand Duke by something approaching primogeniture. In that way, the church believed, Moscow's strength could be both preserved and augmented for the pursuit of the mission. To be sure the church may have envisioned the need of political unity in order to preserve its own unity. But whatever the motives, the support the church gave to the princes of Moscow contributed substantially to the development of their supremacy and of their autocracy.

A third factor behind this authoritarianism was the Byzantinization of the court following Ivan III's marriage to Princess Zoe (1472), niece of the last emperor of Constantinople. What the introduction of the Byzantine ceremonial apparatus did was to give visible expression to the principle of ceasarship, that is, to the principle that the ruler is exalted above men and is sacrosanct. This exaltation of the rulership was further enhanced by the fact that after Constantinople fell to the Moslems, Moscow represented itself as the inheritor of that city's mantle. As the "third Rome" — an everlasting one, for a "fourth Rome" was never to be — it claimed to be taking the place and the mission of the "second Rome," and its rulers, the august position and the autocratic powers of the Roman emperors.[53]

By the end of the Renaissance, Muscovy was such a thorough despotism that its Czar Ivan IV demanded to "rule however he pleased" and ruled so arbitrarily that he earned for himself the execrated title Ivan "the Terrible." His reign is the clearest testimony of Muscovy's autocracy.

1. Cited from V. H. H. Green, *Renaissance and Reformation* (London: Edward Arnold and Co., 1952), 139.

2. A brief but valuable description of the councils, their personnel and their functions, is to be found in J. M. Batista i Roca's Foreword to Helmut Koenigsberger's *The Government of Sicily under Philip II of Spain* (London and New York: Staples Press, 1951).

3. Cited in Livermore, *op. cit.*, 204.

4. *Ibid.*, 246–7.

5. Overlooked up to the present time, this matter is treated meaningfully in André Bossuat, "Le rétablissement de la paix sociale sous le règne de Charles VII," *Le moyen âge*, LX (1954), 137–62.

6. This attempt is studied in B.-A. Picquet du Haut-Jussé, "Une idée politique de Louis XI: la sujétion éclipse la vassalité," *Revue historique,* CCXXVI (1961), 399–416.

7. On the question of the relations between the crown and the Estates after 1400 see J. Russell Major, *Representative Institutions in Renaissance France, 1421–1559* (Madison, Wisconsin: The University of Wisconsin Press, 1960).

8. Cf. *ibid.*, 54–59.

9. This was the famous Estates General of Tours 1484. For a careful study of it see *ibid.*, 60–116.

10. *The Cambridge Medieval History*, VIII, 296.

11. Henri Hauser and Augustin Renaudet, *op. cit.*, 368.

12. Gaston Zeller, *Les institutions de la France au xvie siècle* (Paris: Presses universitaires de France, 1948), 151–2.

13. For a summary treatment see my *History of the Renaissance*, Book II, *Church and Religion* (Salt Lake City: The University of Utah Press, 1964), 92–97. For a more comprehensive analysis see Zeller, *op. cit.*, 345–64.

14. Cf. Zeller, *op. cit.*, 164–297 *passim*.

15. For a study of one such feudal *seigneury* see Marguerite Boulet, "Survivances et transformation d'une seigneurie médieval au debut du xvie siècle," *Le moyen âge*, LV (1949), 103–26.

16. For a revision of the traditional view that the French Renaissance monarchy was absolutist see Major's work cited in no. 7 above and his articles, "The French Monarchy as seen through the Estates General," in *Studies in the Renaissance*, IX (1962), 113–25; and "The Crown and Aristocracy in Renaissance France," *American Historical Review*, LXIX (1964), 631–45.

17. A fine survey of the period is to be found in E. F. Jacob's *The Fifteenth Century, 1399–1485,* vol. VI of *The Oxford History of England* (Oxford: Clarendon Press, 1961). For a brief treatment of the constitutional developments during this period see Bryce Lyon, *A Constitutional and Legal History of Medieval England* (New York: Harper & Brothers, 1960), 586–612. Indispensable source material for those who can read Latin and medieval French is available in S. B. Chrimes and A. L. Brown (eds.), *Select Documents of English Constitutional History, 1307–1485* (London: A. and C. Black, Ltd., 1961).

18. Chrimes and Brown, *op. cit.*, 66–67.

19. *Ibid.*, 93–110.

20. *Ibid.*, 139–45. There is a valuable narrative treatment of this in May McKisack, *op. cit.*, 442–96.

21. Cf. Lyons, *op. cit.*, 595–8.

22. *Ibid.*, 594–5. Cf. also G. R. Elton (ed.), *The Tudor Constitution, Documents and Commentary* (Cambridge: University Press, 1960), 158–62.

23. An excellent one-volume work on the Tudors, embodying some notable revisions, is G. R. Elton's *England under the Tudors*, vol. IV of *A History of England*, ed. Sir Charles Oman (London: Methuen & Co., Ltd., 1956). Supplementing this is his work cited in the preceding note.

24. This is worked out by Elton in his *The Tudor Revolution in Government* (Cambridge: Cambridge University Press, 1953). It seems that Elton has exaggerated the "revolution" (Penry Williams, "Dr. Elton's Interpretation of the Age"; "The Tudor State"; and G. L. Harris, "Medieval Government and Statecraft," under the general title, "A Revolution in Tudor History?" *Past and Present*, XXV [1963], 3–58).

25. For a first-hand account of this see *The Paston Letters, 1422–1509*, ed. James Gairdner (London, 1901), *passim*.

26. On the relations between the church and the state in pre-Tudor times see the article of Harris cited in no. 24 above, in particular, 13–17.

27. In addition to Elton's *England under the Tudors*, chaps. iv–vi, viii, x, xi, see T. M. Parker, *The English Reformation to 1558* (London: Oxford University Press, 1950) and Philip Hughes, *The Reformation in England* (New York: The Macmillan Co., 1950).

28. Cf. "A Description of English Life and Institutions in the Reign of Mary Tudor," in C. V. Malfatti (trans.), *Two Italian Accounts of Tudor England* (Barcelona: C. V. Malfatti, 1953), 55–56.

29. On the effectivesness of the J.P.'s as royal officials see A. L. Rowse, *The England of Elizabeth* (New York: The Macmillan Company, 1951), 341–51.

30. Cf. Harris, *op. cit.*, 24–34.

31. *Ibid.*, 21–24. Cf. also B. Wilkinson, "The Political Revolution of the Thirteenth and Fourteenth Centuries in England," *Speculum, XXIV* (1949), 502–9.

32. No. 7 above.

33. Cf. Williams, *op. cit.*, 44.

34. This indeed is the theme of the articles of Williams and Harris cited in no. 24 above.

35. For an interpretive study of the movements, of Maximilian's part in them, and of their failure see Hans Baron, "Imperial Reform and the Habsburgs — A New Interpretation," *American Historical Review,* XLIV (1938–39), 293–303. A narrative account, valuable for the many excerpts from the speeches of Maximilian before the Diets, is available in Johannes Janssen, *History of the German People at the Close of the Middle Ages,* trans. M. A. Mitchell and A. M. Christie (St. Louis: B. Herder, 1905), II, 180–264. An up-to-date summary treatment may be found in Hajo Holborn, *A History of Modern Germany. The Reformation* (New York: Alfred A. Knopf, 1959), 37–50.

36. F. L. Carsten, *The Origins of Prussia* (Oxford: Clarendon Press, 1954), 136–40.

37. Cf. James C. Davis, *The Decline of the Venetian Nobility as a Ruling Class,* vol. LXXX of *The Johns Hopkins University Studies in Historical and Political Science* (Baltimore: The Johns Hopkins Press, 1962), 18–33.

38. For a scholarly analysis of this stage see Brucker, *op. cit.* An excellent shorter study is Marvin B. Becker, "The Republican City-State in Florence. An Inquiry into its Origin and Survival (1280–1434)," *Speculum,* XXXV (1960), 39–50.

39. "Shortly after 1343" some 300 individuals were declared bankrupt by the Court Merchant (Becker, *op. cit.,* 47).

40. Exemplified by its actions against the church (Marvin B. Becker, "Church and State in Florence on the Eve of the Renaissance (1343–1382)," *Speculum,* XXXVII [1962], 509–27).

41. Brucker, *op. cit.,* 92 ff.; and Becker and Brucker, "The *Arti Minori* in Florentine Politics, 1342–1378," *Mediaeval Studies,* XVIII (1956), 93–104.

42. Cf. Brucker, *op. cit.,* 48–49, 54–55.

43. For example, *ibid.,* 197–8.

44. The reader will find Machiavelli's treatment interesting; see his *History of Florence,* Bk. II, chaps. ii–v.

45. Cf. L. F. Marks, "The Financial Oligarchy in Florence under Lorenzo" in *Italian Renaissance Studies, A Tribute to the Late Cecilia M. Ady,* ed. E. F. Jacob (London: Faber and Faber, Ltd., 1960), 123–47.

46. On the formation of this new constitution consult Nicolai Rubinstein, "Politics and Constitution in Florence at the End of the Fifteenth Century" in *Italian Renaissance Studies, A Tribute to the Late Cecilia M. Ady,* 148–83.

47. On Vasa's accomplishments see R. Svanström and C. F. Palmstierna, *op. cit.*, 73–89.

48. Cited in *Cambridge Modern History* (New York: The Macmillan Co., 1904), II, 628.

49. Thus J. Siemienski in *Cambridge History of Poland*, I, chap. xx, entitled "Constitutional Conditions in the Fifteenth and Sixteenth Centuries."

50. An excellent account of the Ottoman government in its completed form is to be found in A. H. Lybyer, *The Government of the Ottoman Empire in the Time of Suleiman the Magnificent,* vol. XVIII of *Harvard Historical Studies* (Cambridge: Harvard University Press, 1913). For a fine, brief, more recent account see L. S. Stavrianos, *op. cit.*, chap. vi.

51. Cited in Lybyer, *op. cit.*, p. 94, n. 2.

52. Cited from Bernard Pares, *A History of Russia* (4th ed.; New York: Alfred A. Knopf, 1944), 91.

53. On the Byzantine influences on Russian theory of government see Baron Meyendorff and Norman H. Baynes, "The Byzantine Inheritance in Russia," *Byzantium, An Introduction to East Roman Civilization*, eds. N. H. Baynes and H. St. L. B. Moss (Oxford: Clarendon Press, 1948), 383–6.

CHAPTER V

Political Theory

P OLITICAL THEORY, if it is concerned with real and not with utopian
societies, generally reflects the existing political actualities. Often
it draws on the practices and the thought of the past, and only occasionally does it become so speculative as to be free from historical actualities. This being the case, we should not expect Renaissance political
theory to be revolutionary. To the extent that political realities of the
Renaissance age were new, the political theory may be expected to
reflect some of these innovations. And correspondingly, to the extent
that these realities were still medieval or but minor modifications of
the same, then we should expect the theory to contain much that was
derived from the past. Hence to ascertain the true nature of Renaissance political theory, we need to have some idea of the political
thought of the preceding age.

POLITICAL THEORY IN THE MIDDLE AGES[1]

Factors Shaping the Theory

Medieval political thought was itself an evolving subject drawing
upon tradition and upon the political practices of the day. Its bases
were both age-old and contemporary, and its formal expression at any
given time was generally a synthesis of the several accreting elements.

From the patristic tradition came the idea that the state was the
product of "Man's Fall." Having fallen, man was susceptible to evil
and was in need of some force to restrain him from this inclination.
This restraining force was the state. The state, therefore, had a negative
function to fulfill.

To this negative function Augustine added a positive one. The
state, in his opinion, was also a force for good, for it enabled man to
cultivate right relations with his fellowmen and so with God. Although
he spoke of two societies, the City of God and the Earthly City, to him

they were the same society in two aspects, spiritual and mundane. And although he recognized that they were bound to conflict, he did not view the clash as everlastingly irreconcilable. He saw the possibility of the Earthly City aiding in the attainment of the City of God. The earthly state, therefore, despite its origin, had a good positive end.[2]

From the Germans who displaced the Roman Empire came the notion of an elective monarchy. The idea, of course, was not new, as it was widely explored by Greek and Roman writers; but with the coming of the Germans it became a living fact in western Europe. From them also came the idea that the state is an embodiment of the people's customs, inviolable and so limiting upon the head of the state.

To these ideas were added the notions which grew out of the feudal system. One was the notion that authority was proprietary in character. Another was the principle of the reciprocity of rights between the rulers and the ruled as manifested in the relations between the lords and their vassals. And still another was the idea that the ruler was to counsel with the responsible people of the state. Feudalism therefore brought two contradictory principles: one which promoted unlimited authority, and the other which imposed limitations on the same authority.

With the revival of Roman law in the twelfth century came two more concepts. The state was interpreted as a political community corporately organized for the pursuit of interests common to its members. And the ruler was regarded as the officer in whom this community reposed its governing authority. Hence, in a sense, the state became a conscious work of art.

Then, with the recovery of Aristotle in the early thirteenth century, the idea that the state was natural to man began to gain currency. Man is a political animal, and cooperative existence with his fellowmen is his second nature and enables him to realize himself to the fullest degree. Moreover, being both natural and responsive to man's highest needs, the state was necessarily organic, that is, the state was susceptible to change and evolution. Since Aristotle became central to medieval thought, these ideas tended to displace the earlier notion that the state was the result of man's Fall.

By 1250 all these ideas were in circulation and helped to shape the thinking of the political theorists thereafter. What that thinking was we will soon note when we examine, beginning with Thomas Aquinas, what answers were given to three major political questions: (1) What is the nature of the state? (2) What are the relations between the state and its citizen members? and (3) What are the relations between the state and the church?

Concept of the State in the Later Middle Ages

THE STATE AS A SOCIAL CONSTRUCT Aristotelian that he was, Thomas Aquinas held that it was inherent in man's nature to live socially and to devise his own political system. The state therefore was not a product of man's Fall, but a positive creation by man for his own social, material, and spiritual good. However, since man devises this system in accordance with his God-given reason, the state then is indirectly of God.[3]

More concerned with practical politics than Aquinas, Dante in his writings, notably in the *De monarchia*,[4] combined the views of Thomas with those of Augustine and added a personal view of deep implications. With Aquinas, he agreed that the state was natural; but the kind of state which was natural was the particularistic state, whatever its form. Such a state, while it served man and was necessary as well as natural, actually was inadequate because of man's perverseness. Was not his own misfortune — exile from his beloved Florence as a result of uncontrolled factionalism — proof of this? To overcome this inadequacy a greater state was necessary, a universal state which was more the work of providence than of man. But though of God's origin, this universal state was not Augustine's City of God but a temporal state, indeed, the very Roman Empire which, according to Vergil's prophecy, was destined to bring peace and order to a world torn asunder; and this was Dante's contribution.[5] His unhappy experience with Italian party feuds, due, in his opinion, to the recurrent papal-imperial conflicts over the question of primacy, led him to posit a divinely instituted, universal, temporal state whose function was to aid man in finding his end. Such a teaching was naturally anathema to the papacy, at the time engaged in a bitter conflict with the Holy Roman Emperor Louis IV; and the more so, since it appeared to challenge the church's function here on earth. Accordingly Dante's treatise was burned in 1329 by order of

John XXII, and later, in 1559, because these teachings were revived by the tutor of Charles V, it was entered on the Index.

Less philosophical than Dante but holding to Dante's view of the indispensability of a universal temporal state was the fertile-minded Pierre du Bois, *avocat royal* for Philip IV. It was his duty to protect royal justice from encroachments by the ecclesiastical courts,[6] and out of this assignment, influenced by principles derived from Roman law and from feudal practice and theory, he evolved his theory of the state. He did not work it out formally, but it is implicit in several of his writings, particularly in the *De recuperatione terre sancte* (*On the Recovery of the Holy Land*). It postulates a universal state secular in origin — there were kings before there were priests — with a French king as its natural ruler. And the justification for it was the need of Christian unity to make possible the recovery of the Holy Land. Though the explanation was obviously an apologia for Philip IV's action against Pope Boniface VIII, it nevertheless presented the notion that the state has a positive program which embraces not only temporal affairs but affairs of faith also. Moreover it contains implicitly the Machiavellian thesis that nothing can stand in the way of the state, not even the deeply rooted principle of the independence of the Universal Catholic Church.

A contemporary of Pierre du Bois, known by the names Aegidius of Rome (1246/7-1316) and Aegidius Colonna, wrote for his pupil, the same Philip IV whom Du Bois defended, a treatise on the regimen of the princes, *De regimine principum*. In it he is less blatantly royalist, but his explanations of the origin and the functions of the state, adapted from Aristotle's *Politics*, approximate those of Pierre du Bois. The state is the apex, as it were, of man's natural social institutions, the family and the village, and it serves man's good both materially and morally. One explanation of its origin, although not new, for it was implicit in Roman law and in feudal practices, was the theory of a compact between the people and the ruler. Later, when the clash between Philip IV and the Boniface broke out, Aegidius sided with the papacy (*De ecclesiastica potestate*, 1301) and returned to the Augustinian position which conceived the works of man as corrupted by sin. According to this version the state became a true state only if it were sanctified by divine grace. However, since his *De regimine principum* was widely recognized, his first position continued to exert much influence.

Carrying the concept of the positive nature of the state further was Marsiglio of Padua (1278–1343), an M.D. who became canon, counsellor to Can Grande della Scala and Matteo Visconti, and propagandist for Emperor Louis IV to whose court he fled from the long arm of the church. His principal work, written with the help of the Averroist John of Jandun, was the *Defensor pacis*;[7] and like many other works on political theory, it owed its birth to a bitter clash of the day, that of Louis IV and the Spiritual Franciscans with the papacy. Marsiglio took the side of the papal opponents, and much that he said was undoubtedly called for by the immediate demands of the case. Like his predecessors, he regarded the state as a community cooperating for the sake of sufficient life, spiritual as well as mundane, though with him, the biological and material needs were alone natural and their satisfaction came first, while the social needs were derivative and came second.[8] Moreover, he looked upon it not merely as a passive adapter and coordinator of the prevailing custom, but as the efficient creator and director of new dispensations needed for the better realization of this good life. Then, since custom and law can only derive from the community of men, it follows that the community is sovereign, even though for practical purposes it reposes its own authority in that of a head — *pars principans* — of its own creation. The state thus is a human institution, both in its origin and its operations, and the actions that it takes are based on its own sense of what is needful and good and not on some supernatural values communicated to it from outside. In sum, the state is its own mistress.

STATE — UNIVERSAL OR PARTICULARISTIC? In this survey, we did not take into account whether the temporal state which these writers had in mind was a universal empire, or a particularistic national entity. We need to consider this question as it has a bearing on the distinction that is made between medieval and Renaissance political thinking.

The early medieval theory, influenced by the fact that the late Roman Empire embraced the entire civilized Christian world, held that as there was one Christian church so there should be just one

Christian state, namely, the Empire. Although the fact of the universality disappeared with the dismemberment of the Roman Empire by the Germanic invaders, the theory persisted. Subsequently, the annexation of Italy to France in the time of Charlemagne (774) and Charlemagne's coronation as Emperor of the Romans (800) provided the theory with some basis in fact. It was further strengthened when Italy was claimed and, for a while successfully held, by the German kings. The cooperation between the papacy and the first three Otto's, both within the boundaries of the old Roman Empire and among the Slavs, where the cross and sword traveled together in behalf of Christianity and civilization, naturally reinforced the theory. Additional support for it came from the fact that for centuries much of Christendom faced a common enemy, the Moslems, and on occasion participated, without reference to national boundaries, in common action against them — the crusades. Feudalism, too, with its concept of lordships hierarchically arranged theoretically called for a single suzerain also. Then, on occasion, the Holy Roman Emperors enacted laws in which they insisted on the universality of their authority — for example, Henry VII, in 1312, in preparation for action against Robert of Naples. Thus, throughout most of the Middle Ages the theory of a single Christian empire was kept alive. If it was not an actual reality, it was nevertheless a theoretical ideal which was not beyond all hope. That is why Dante's *De monarchia*, for example, is constructed on the supposition of a single empire, and that is why Marsiglio, who was in need of a universal council to compass reform of the Christian church, admitted, contrary to his expressed preference for the individual state, the universal community — the Legislator — into his theory.[9]

The persistence throughout the Middle Ages of this idea of a single universal empire has been regarded as a mark of medieval political thinking in contrast to the Renaissance political thinking which recognized only autonomous national states. This distinction can be asserted, but only on the mistaken assumption that the theory of a single universal empire was seriously entertained by most of the medieval thinkers. The fact is that the opposite concept, the autonomy of national states, was also recognized. Indeed, it could not be otherwise, since they were everywhere emerging as definite political realities. It is not necessary therefore to wait until the Renaissance to discover the national state as a subject of political thought.

The theory of the autonomous state in contradistinction to the universal empire was not widely propagated in the Middle Ages because, for the most part, there was little occasion for such propagation.[10] The royal kingdoms of Castile, England, France, and Poland, for example, were simply taken for granted, and no defense for their independent existence was deemed necessary. If some canonists argued for imperial supremacy — and some of them were still doing so in the fifteenth century[11] — and if in protocol the kings of such states were known to defer to the Emperor, in practice, as hereditary rulers of their own kingdoms they did not regard themselves in any way subject to the Emperor. This is confirmed by the obvious fact that they governed their realms independently, and by their assertions, whenever they opposed the papal claims to supremacy in matters temporal, that their own authority was derived directly from God.

An early example of the latter claim is to be found in the anonymous *York Tractates* written in support of Henry I of England in his clash with Archbishop Anselm over the matter of lay investiture. The treatise argues for the supremacy of the state over the church, and for the king's right to appoint bishops in his land on the ground that the sovereignty of God is vested in the king as his earthly representative.[12] Obviously such a king could hardly be regarded as subordinate to the Emperor, and his state as a dependency of the Empire.

In the last century of the Middle Ages this theory received repeated affirmation. Thus the compiler of the *Établissements de St. Louis* reported in his work that "the king has no sovereign in temporal things, nor does he hold from anyone but God and himself, nor is there any appeal from his judgment save to God."[13] John of Paris, a student of Aquinas, defending the French King Philip IV against Boniface's invitation to the Emperor to assert his imperial rights to France, argued in his *De potestate regia et papali* (1302) that what the Emperor was to his Empire, the king was to his kingdom. In the Kingdom of Naples, after it was conquered from the imperial line of the Hohenstaufens by Charles of Anjou, there developed a whole school of legists who argued against imperial supremacy and for royal independence.[14] Their position was a natural one, since it was in the interest of their patrons, the recent conquerors, to invalidate the claims of the Holy Roman Emperors to Naples; and it was on the basis of their opinion that Robert of Naples justified his opposition to Henry VII's attempt to restore imperial authority in Italy, Naples included. It was also in connection with this clash that Clement V in order to save Italy from Henry and Naples for the papacy — the popes claimed Naples as their fief — issued the bull *Pastoralis cura* which denied the existence of a universal empire and postulated the existence of autonomous national states.[15] The great scholar of Roman law, Bartolus of Sassoferrato, while paying lip service to imperial authority *de jure*, insisted that the rising city-states of central and northern Italy had *de facto* autonomy and had "as much authority in regard to [their] own people as the Emperor had in regard to the whole."[16] Finally, when the papacy moved to Avignon and revealed itself to be an instrument of the French monarchy, or was assumed to be such, the Germans themselves, first in the Declaration of Rense and the Diet of Frankfurt (1347) and then in the Golden Bull (1356), by repudiating papal claims to imperial suzerainty and to confirmation of Emperors-elect, made out their own Empire to be German and nationalist.

By the time of the Renaissance, then, the modernistic concept of the state was emerging. The idea that the state was a natural institution with a positive, natural objective was widely accepted; the notion that it was secular and autonomous was steadily gaining ground; and the principle that it had the right to preserve itself, even in the face of opposition from the universal church and its claim to represent the ordinances of God, was being voiced here and there. To be sure these notions of the state are not yet that of a Machiavellian state, but that they adumbrate the latter seems to be beyond question.

Relations between the Ruler and the Ruled

LIMITED AUTHORITY OF RULER Throughout the Middle Ages the prevailing theory concerning the authority of the ruler with respect to his people was that it was limited. There were several bases for this assumption.

Most theorists regarded the ruler as the fountain of justice. It followed that he could not take any action against his people which violated justice. Since justice was considered to be comprehensive, including not only virtuous dispensation of law but also nonviolation of the prevailing customs and respect for property rights, the limitations on the ruler's authority were correspondingly broad and firm.

Another source of this limitation were the practices central to the feudal system. According to feudal custom the relations between vassal and lord were reciprocally binding, and the king as lord and suzerain had no right to break these relations without due cause. Since one of these relations consisted of the principle that in breaches of feudal law a vassal must be tried by his peers, the lord's hands were necessarily tied. Again, since in some lands, the feudal practice of the lord consulting with the vassals (*concilium*) came to be regarded as the vassals' right to be consulted, the lord's right to make policy was also limited. The king of course, was a feudal lord, and as such his actions were theoretically bound by these principles.

Still another source was the widely accepted theory that the state existed for man's spiritual welfare. Any state action therefore which endangered the citizen's spiritual well-being was deemed a violation of the state's *raison d'être*. The state's arbitrariness was therefore limited and so also that of the state head.

THEORIES OF ROYAL SUPREMACY But while the principle that the ruler was limited in his actions toward his subjects persisted throughout the Middle Ages, the opposite principle of royal supremacy began to appear also.

One source of royal supremacy was the necessity for the ruler to take action to rectify the ill effects of outdated laws and custom. This idea is recurrently expressed in royal charters. Hugh Capet, for example, reports in one of his charters:

> It is the function of kings, after a sagacious survey of the laws of their kingdom, to take anxious care to cut away the harmful and to give wide effect to all that are profitable.[17]

Thus, instead of merely acting within the limits of existing law and custom, the king assumed the role of a determiner of what constitutes proper custom. In a sense, therefore, kings were above custom. Though they were not arbitrarily above it, for they must be guided by the welfare of the realm, still, in accord with the dictum that "necessity knows no law," they were establishing claims to royal supremacy.

Related closely to the above source was the theory that the general welfare of the state demanded a single head. In part this was based on the philosophical premise that true being is identifiable with unity. In part it was based on practical necessity, it being argued that too many authorities invited chaos.

A third source of this idea that the prince was supreme was the reciprocal interchange, throughout the medieval period, between the church and the state, of titles, insignia, and functions.[18] The ceremonial court practices in the late Roman Empire and the ideas underlying these practices were adopted by the episcopacy, so that the bishops came to be invested with the attributes of princes. On the other hand, the sacerdotal character of the bishops came to be associated with the princes through their coronation and consecration. This invested them with attributes of near-sacrosanctity and elevated them above the mass of the citizens. As a sequel to this early equiparation of prince with bishop and as a result of the investiture struggle, of the growing papal monarchism, and of the crystallization of canon law, the princes borrowed from the chief bishop, the pope, the claim of having the right to judge all and to be judged by none. This claim was further reinforced by the reviving Roman law from whence the civilists got the notion that the judges, and naturally also the princes who were the fountains of justice, were "priests of justice." This reinforcement was important, for it contributed secular foundation to the principle of royal "pontificalism." This "pontificalism" was then gradually transferred to the state, partly through the separation of the office of the prince from the person of the prince and by attributing to the former both ubiquity and immortality. In sum, first the prince and then the state were invested with supremacy.

Although the process of exaltation of the state as the supreme institution was not completed until late in the Renaissance, the fact is, as Kantorowicz clearly demonstrates, that it originated in the early Middle Ages and kept growing throughout the balance of the medieval period. Illustrations of this exaltation may be found in the works of several prominent medieval thinkers. It appears in part in the *De legibus* of the famous legist Bracton.[19] Although the treatise has much to say about limited monarchy and has been properly appraised as one of the strongest expositions of constitutionalism, it also depicts the monarch as an exalted head of the nation. In it Bracton considered government as divided into two spheres called *gubernaculum* and *jurisdictio*. By the first he meant acts of governance identifiable with administrative functions; by the second, ascertainment and enactment of laws. In the first Bracton insisted that the king had no peer, that all administration was his. In the second he admitted that the king was bound by the decisions of his magnates meeting in an assembly. But he also maintained, once these decisions were agreed upon, that the king alone had the right of implementing them. The limitation on the king was therefore only partial. Moreover, since government in the Middle Ages consisted more of administration than of legislation, the limitation was even less extensive than may appear in theory. Hence while positing constitutionalism, Bracton also can be said to have provided considerable support for personal monarchy. A similar position is to be found in Thomas Aquinas. He argued for royal government and defined it as a "regime in which one person excels and the others are by nature constituted to obey."[20] He did not mean by this that the monarch was absolute and irresponsible, for he always insisted that there were rational principles of justice which bound the king, but he did mean that within these principles the royal power was plenary, which is no small support for exalted monarchy. Aegidius Romanus appears to have gone beyond this. He argued that the king "could adjust natural law principles to specific instances" and that he could impart "authority to all positive law."[21] Beaumanior, in the *Coutumes,* which is a study of the feudal law in the County of Clermont and of the relation of the county to the French kings, represented the king "as a legislator *sans pareil*" whose statutes "must be observed because they were the king's and for no other reason,"[22] and the only real limitation on this prerogative was that these statutes be made "for the common good." Pierre du Bois insisted that, once Italy was annexed by the French king, "nothing could authorize [the Italians] to refuse obedience" to him. Here is a notion laden with the implication that might makes right, and which has caused the late Professor Eileen Power to regard its formulator as a man who "delineated the Renaissance Monarch" before such was born.[23]

This brief survey then shows that the theory of royal supremacy was steadily growing. This growth is what one should expect, for theory, if it were not to be dead, had to explain the actualities of practical politics; and in practice the states and their rulers were actually growing stronger from the eleventh century on. However, just as this extension of the power of the rulers was not achieved by any sustained frontal attack on the limitations which custom, morality, and philosophy imposed on it, but within the framework provided by these restraints, so the expression of the theories of royal supremacy generally did not openly repudiate the principles of limitation. Still, it must be recognized that the theory of royal supremacy was steadily gaining ground as the Middle Ages were drawing to their end.

Contributing to this process were the theories brought forth by the recurrent clashes between the temporal authorities and the papacy. This is actually the third question which was proposed at the outset of this survey.

Relations between State and Church

In our survey of political developments during the Middle Ages we met with the issues which drove the two institutions, the church and the state, into collision. One was the question of church taxation and jurisdiction, another was the question of the papal role in the making of Emperors, and still another was the imperial claim to Italy. Although our examination was limited to the period from the late thirteenth century on, the fact is that these issues were quite chronic throughout most of the Middle Ages. There was thus ample opportunity for the development of theories defending both sides.

CLAIMS TO CHURCH SUPREMACY In the early Middle Ages the theory was that which Pope Gelasius proclaimed in the fifth century.[24] According to this theory, the two powers, spiritual and temporal, were coordinate, both deriving their authority from God directly. The spiritual power attended to man's spiritual welfare, and the temporal to his earthly needs. Both functions were necessary and good, and so the two powers were to respect each other's operations. However, because the spiritual needs of a Christian took precedence over his mundane needs, and because the church alone had custody of Christian truth, the temporal power was to defer to the spiritual power in matters affecting man's soul. Indeed, the emperor as a Christian and as a ruler of Christians could not rightly escape sacerdotal guidance.

Practice, however, did not conform to theory. With the disintegration of the Roman Empire, the primacy of the pope lost its efficacy, while the needs of the fledgling churches among the newly converted Germans generally thrust them under the protection of the local powers. At the same time these local powers, whether kings or nobles, needed the educated clergy to help them operate their states. In time, therefore, the two institutions became inextricably interlocked, with the secular powers becoming the more dominant of the two.

Since this interlocking in general tended to despiritualize the church, efforts to revive the true spirit of the church necessitated at least partial disengagement. But any such action was bound to be at the political and material expense of the temporal power and was certain to be opposed, and so the issue was joined. To defend their respective actions the two institutions began to issue explanations and justifications, and these naturally affected the old Gelasian theory.

The natural tendency was for each side to stiffen its claims.[25] Because the temporal authorities were unwilling to surrender what practical control they had over the church, the popes felt compelled to claim supremacy over the state.[26] Their claims were climaxed in the assertion by Innocent the Great that the pope, as head of the institution (church) which alone judged sin and which was answerable to God for this function, was possessed of a plentitude of power (*plentitudo potestas*) which made him the ultimate earthly arbiter. A similar claim, we will recall, was made by Boniface VIII when he clashed with Philip IV of France. To this the kings reacted naturally by insisting on their independence and on their right to manage affairs of state, including the church in it, as they deemed proper.

INDEPENDENT AUTHORITY OF THE STATE In the battle of theories, as in actual fact, the balance, never really decisively on the side of the church, began to tip in favor of the secular authorities from the thirteenth century on and steadily increased as the Renaissance period approached.

With several of the prominent proponents of secular independence we have already met, namely, Pierre du Bois, Dante, John of Paris, and Marsiglio of Padua. On the opposite side there were at least three men who merit recognition. Thomas Aquinas, although recognizing the state's function as the provider of social good, maintained that this was but means to a greater end, union with God. Since this could not be attained without divine help, and divine help came through the ministry of God, it followed that the priesthood had precedence over laity, and that its head had precedence over the highest lay officer — that is, the king was subject to the pope.[27] It must be added, however, that Thomas regarded that supremacy as confined to matters which had a bearing on man's spiritual good only, and not in all affairs. James of Viterbo developed a more subtle argument.[28] He granted, for instance, that the state was also concerned with the spiritual welfare of its people. However, he maintained that its preoccupation with this matter was limited to natural morality. This left matters related to grace to the supervision of the church. As grace stood above natural morality, the church obviously was supreme. In fact he argued that temporal authority was mediated through the papacy. Aegidius Colonna argued that all power derived from God, that it was naturally vested in the church, and that the church delegated it to other agencies. Temporal authority was therefore derivative. Moreover, no one could rightfully exercise that power who was not sacramentally in a state of grace. Since it was through the church that grace was attainable, the church therefore had supremacy.

In connection with the church-state crises that brought forth these opposing theories, a movement appeared prompting a theory which, without explicitly countenancing state supremacy, fostered the notion of the independence of secular from papal authority. This was conciliarism, or a movement for the convocation of a universal council to reform the church, papacy included.[29] Since, from the religious point of view, it was imprudent to concede to a sovereign the right to repudiate papal primacy, those who had reasons to desire such a repudiation argued that an ecumenical council could do so and that the princes could summon it. They contended that the divine spirit was present in the church as a whole and not in a single head, and that a representative body of the church was superior to the pope.

One advocate of this theory was Pierre du Bois. It will be recalled that he advocated French political supremacy in Europe. In that political supremacy he included the authority for a French sovereign to summon a council which in turn could sit in judgment on the pope. Marsiglio of Padua held to a similar point of view. Just as in political affairs the community of citizens possessed sovereignty, so in ecclesiastical affairs the community of Christians had ecclesiastical sovereignty, and the pope was merely its chief officer. Perhaps the most distinguished exponent of this theory was the nominalist philosopher Occam. In his *De imperatorum et pontificum potestate* he recognized the monarchic authority of the pope, and even granted that for the good of the church the pope could act beyond recognized limits; but he insisted that the church as a community, in order to preserve itself, could depose the pope and that it could do so through a council summoned by the Emperor.

While the argument for conciliar supremacy did not propose the supremacy of temporal authority over spiritual authority, it is obvious that any theory that challenged papal claims fostered the former.

Summarizing our survey we can say that, on the eve of the Renaissance, the tendency in political theory was to regard the state as a natural institution capable of positive action, as independent of the Empire and autonomous in its temporal sphere, and as capable of acting in matters of natural morality. The tendency was also to admit that the ruler of such a state was limited by divine law, natural law, and positive law, but at the same time to insist that the ruler did not derive his authority mediately through the church and that within the framework of these limitations he was an absolute administrator answerable to no man.

POLITICAL THEORY DURING
THE RENAISSANCE

Factors Shaping Renaissance Political Theory

The factors which shaped political theory during the Middle Ages, namely, Christian ideals, feudal principles, Aristotelianism, Roman law, naturally did not cease at the inception of the Renaissance; and their influences therefore continued to pervade Renaissance political thought. At the same time, however, there were significant political and cultural developments during the Renaissance, and these were bound to affect the old theories.

One of these developments was the growth of the authority of the states. As the monarchs pressed their encroachment on feudality, they sought to justify their actions by the argument that property rights do not include functions of government. As they expanded and consolidated their administrative machinery and had to find more revenue to finance this expansion, they were obliged to justify an extension of their taxing powers. As certain authorities, especially in Italy, established themselves in power by usurpation and ruled tyrannically, they found it necessary to rationalize their illegal accession and their despotism. In sum, the hardening of state governments, whatever their origin or character, had to find some explanatory justification.

Another of these facts was the diminution of papal participation in the affairs of states and the corresponding increase in royal encroachment on the independence of the church. Both of these movements were bound to find echoes in the theories of the day.

Still another was the influence of humanism. Although interest in classical literature and Roman law antedates the Renaissance, it is a fact that interest in the classics during the Renaissance reached the proportions of a cult; and this increasing intensity was what fostered admiration for Roman history and the lessons in practical politics that it afforded. This was especially true in Italy, and Florence in particular.

Then toward the end of the Renaissance, when the Reformation became a reality, a great number of issues between the newly established Protestant churches and the states had to be resolved, and the resolutions necessarily affected political theory.

How these various factors shaped political thought during the Renaissance can be ascertained by discovering what answers were provided to the same three questions that were examined in connection with our survey of political theory in the Middle Ages.

The Concept of the State

Because by the inception of the Renaissance the state as a natural, autonomous institution was a reality, and because the old papal assertions to temporal supremacy were in practice ignored, there was no compelling reason during the Renaissance to take up the question of the concept of the state. Hence the question was raised only occasionally or treated indirectly as part of the theories of society.

IN ENGLAND — ORGANIZED SOCIETY Illustrations of these occasional and inexplicit treatments are to be found in the views held by some of the foremost theorists during the period. In England, Wycliffe, the fourteenth-century precursor of the Protestant reformers, still held to the early medieval notion that the state was a divine remedy for man's sinful nature.[30] However, because he was opposing the papal church of the time, which he believed to be evil, he contended that the state through its king, holder of God's stewardship (*dominium*) here on earth, could rightfully take action against the church, even to the extent of watching over its morals and of confiscating its property.[31] Wycliffe thus combined the old Augustinian view with the more modern view held by such men as Pierre du Bois or Marsiglio of Padua. Undoubtedly, he was also influenced by the running battle between the Spiritual and Conventual Franciscans, and of both with the papacy on this very question of the right of the church to hold property.[32]

A century later, Sir John Fortescue, chancellor under Henry VII, in examining the institution of kingship, touched indirectly on the nature and origin of the state.[33] It was his view that the state emerged simultaneously with lordship (*dominium*), either through conquest or through an evolutionary process, just as a physical body grows out of its embryo. The nature of this state is a by-product of this origin. It is a society whose rights and property are not subject to the proprietory rights of the ruler. It is a society which exists for its own good and not for the ruler's benefit, and which is protected by its long-time customs and common law. This is a rationalization really of the constitutive principle of a monarchic feudal state as represented by England, and so is quite medieval. If it contained any innovation, it was not in kind but in degree. Based on observation of contemporary political actualities in France and England, the theory admitted the notion that states are subject to social process and that governments must square themselves with this process, that is, the theory was more pragmatic than some medieval theories.[34] However, the difference should not be pressed too far, as the notions that kings can enact laws to remedy outdated custom and that parliaments can enact substantive laws postulate this very theory of accommodation to change; and both of these possibilities were admitted in the Middle Ages.

IN ENGLAND — OF DIVINE ORIGIN A century later, when the issue of a state-church became pressing, the theory of the state as the work of God was widely adopted.[35] Bishop Ponet in his *A Shorte Treatise of Politike Power* (1556) held to the medieval theory that because of man's Fall political authority was ordained by God to secure justice. George Buchanan, the Scottish humanist and defender of the Kirk, contended that God is the author of human society and that the latter shapes itself into a political body in conformity with the Law of Nature which God planted in man. Richard Hooker (1554–1600), the great apologist for the Church of England, in his *The Laws of Ecclesiastical Polity*, which he wrote in defense of the Establishment with the view of satisfying "all tender consciences," argued — since the church was established by the state — that the state originates in the assent of the people to live under authority and that it shapes itself in accordance with divine law, natural law, and reason, reason being not much more than the product of past tradition and the practices of the day.

In general, then, the foremost English thinkers throughout the entire Renaissance period held on to the traditional views on the origin and nature of the state. They were typically medieval in their concept of the state when they regarded it as a society organized for political life or as kingship.

In France — Organized Society France also had theorists who held to the same idea. James Almain of Sens, for example, in his *De auctoritate ecclesiae* saw the state as the result of man's Fall, and its *raison d'être* as the furtherance of common good. Claude de Seyssel, at one time councillor of Charles VIII and Louis XII, and subsequently bishop of Marsielles and Archbishop of Turin, in his *Grand monarchie de France* (1519) — really a eulogy of the French monarchy of the time and a handbook for the instruction of young Francis I — entertained a view which was a combination of Thomism and feudal theory. The state was society — the three estates with their respective rights, pre-eminences, and obligations — organized for the purpose of maintaining peace and order with justice. It was guided by a hereditary monarch whose role was that of "Father of his people" and who was bound to take council with the notables of the land.[36] Guillaume de la Perriere propounded the same theory some three decades later (*Le miroir politique*). Even such scholars of Roman law as Alciatus, his student François Connon, and the great Cujas maintained that the state was a society founded on reason and monarchy which itself originated in the consent of the people.

In France — As Sovereign Power One notable departure was provided by the famous Jean Bodin in his *De la république* (1576).[37] The treatise, like Machiavelli's *Prince*, was a by-product of Bodin's career and of the political troubles — Wars of Religion — that plagued France during his lifetime.[38] Raised and educated as a Carmelite, Bodin, however, withdrew from the order and turned to law and civil service as a way of life. Through his scholarly reputation — he wrote significant works on the science of history (*Methodus*), on jurisprudence (*Juris universi distributio*)[39] and on inflation (*La réponse . . . à M. Malestroit*) — he was able to obtain several government posts, but these were minor and intermittent, as he was suspended on occasion under suspicion of being a heretic or a Protestant "fellow traveler." Until 1574, however, he was able to weather the repeated crises, but in that year as Master of Requests and Councillor of Francis, Duke of Alençon, he was suspected of having participated in an abortive plot to have Francis seize the crown from the rightful heir Henry III, Francis' older brother, and was apparently dismissed from his office. It was to dispell this suspicion and to win the favor of Henry that Bodin wrote the *République* and dedicated it to one of Henry's closest advisers. At the same time as a victim of religious intolerance and strife, he was anxious to see peace and order restored. It was, therefore, natural for him to incorporate both objectives in his treatise; hence his appeal for effective but lawful government, and hence his definition of the state as "a lawful government of many families, and of that which unto them in common belongeth, with a 'puissant sovereignty'" where "puissant sovereignty" signifies the "most high and perpetual power" of commanding in the state.[40] As can be seen, this is not a theory of society but of authority, and in this appears Bodin's principal departure from the traditional view of the state.

His second departure in this connection was his recognition that this body of rightful power was not a fixed thing, but one which adjusted itself to changing conditions — indeed, that was the reason why Bodin invested sovereignty with the right to make law. The state, then, was not a static entity but an evolving one, a product of mundane circumstances even if these operated within the confines of God's eternal order.[41] And to the extent that it was a product of natural processes, it was subject to analysis based on empiricism which is what he himself employed throughout the *République*. This, indeed, is a modern approach to the whole problem of the state.

But significant as these innovations are, his total concept of the state was not as modern as might be expected. Unable to detach himself completely from the past, he retained several notions alien to the modern view. One of these is implicit in the use of the word "lawful." The capacity to act authoritatively must be employed lawfully, and by this he meant in conformity with divine law and natural law.[42] Fundamentally, therefore, the state was not completely sovereign but was subject to the same two limitations which were most universally accepted by medieval political theory. The second notion which conformed to tradition was his view as to the purpose of the state. This, he stated, was the same as the end of man, namely, cultivation of man's virtue and of his well-being.[43] While the second objective may be admitted as implicitly present in the modern concept of the purpose of the state, the first, while desired, is no longer accepted. So again the "modernity" of Bodin's view is limited. Finally, he had the notion that the fortunes of the states were determined by the movements of the planets.[44] While his argument that this influence was not imparted directly but mediately through cosmic forces led him to recognize the role of climate and geography in the shaping of states, which may be acceptable to the modern mind, the general notion, of course, is alien to us as it is grounded on the old Aristotelian-Ptolemaic system of cosmology long rejected.[45]

In sum, therefore, Bodin's concept of the state looks to the past as well as to the future. His innovations are promising and deserve recognition. Yet we should not ignore his traditional notions, for they limit his modernity.

In Germany — Medieval Theories In the Holy Roman Empire, Nicolas of Cusa the conciliarist, Johannes Althusius the civilist, and Erasmus the humanist looked upon the state as a product of a compact between society and its chosen head. Naturally they all adhered to the medieval view that the state served the higher end of good life and justice. Luther's interest in the state was wholly secondary to his interest in religion, and so his concept of it was a by-product of his theology and of the social and political forces that had an impact on it.[46] Thus in the early days of the Reformation when the princes still adhered to Catholicism and threatened to suppress the Lutheran movement, he argued that public authorities had no right to force their beliefs on their citizens. On the other hand, when the princes embraced Lutheranism and became the protectors of the new church against radical sectarianism, then the state — he refers to it as temporal authority — was of divine origin, that it was the Lord's instrument for repressing the godless and for protecting the godly, and that it was to be obeyed. The view resembles that held by Augustine and his medieval followers. Even when he regarded the state from a nonfunctional point of view, that is, from the point of view of its origin, he arrived at the same conclusion. Constitutively the state was a natural evolution of the family, and as the father commands obedience from the members of his family, so the state is to be obeyed by its members. Obedience, however, is God's commandment and so the state has no independent justification.

To Luther, as to the men before him, the state was an aid to man's salvation.

IN ITALY — As SOVEREIGN POWER It was in Renaissance Italy that the concept of the state departed more from the prevailing medieval view. Because a number of the states in central and northern Italy were the creations of enterprising dynasts, these states came to be looked upon as a work of art, as something which man created consciously and deliberately, and not as something which merely appeared as a result of the evolutionary processes of society. This naturally reduced the constitutive role of the people, and so also the limitations which derived from this role. The state, therefore, came to be identified with coercive authority which is both above and independent of society.

This concept began to appear in a mild form in the trecento essays on tyranny.[47] We referred to the treatise written by the famous civilist Bartolus Sassoferrato. We might include as illustrations the *Mirror for Princes* which Petrarch wrote for the Carrara despot of Padua, and Salutati's *On Tyranny*, both of which were written after their authors had earlier shown much sympathy for republicanism. In these essays there is an increasing disregard of the constitutive role of the people and of law and morality as factors in the creation of the state. In Salutati's essay, for example, where he considers the questions whether Caesar was a tyrant and whether his murder was justifiable, the test is not how such a princely state came into being, but whether such a state was accepted by those governed and whether it had effective control over them.[48] The identification of the state with authority rather than with society is quite apparent. It should be added, however, that in the minds of these trecento theorists this modernism in political thinking was still much imbedded in the medieval political notion that the state existed for a higher end, which in this case was assumed to be the preservation of virtue and culture.[49]

What the trecento thinkers began, Machiavelli (1469–1527) completed in his *Il principe* (written in 1513 but not published until 1532).[50] As secretary in Florence's chancery and as ambassador to various states in Italy and across the Alps, he readily discovered that in the game of international politics power was the thing most respected. Without power, he felt, a state could neither preserve itself from extinction nor force others to respect its interests; it would be a "nothing," a *Ser Nihilo*, as his own state was scoffingly labeled by the French who had it in tow since Charles VIII's occupation of it in 1494. In reality, therefore, what gave the state existence was not society, but power, that is, the power-wielding authority which held society together and made it effective.[51]

From this conclusion two other principles naturally followed. First, this power or effective authority was not a means to an end — say, the people's welfare — but an end itself, for once it came into being it could only persist if its principal aim was self-preservation and self-perpetuation. To be sure, in serving itself it could serve society by securing internal peace and order, but these would be ways it would employ to secure itself, and not ends. Second, since it was neither society nor an instrument of society, it was not subject to the system of mores which governed society. It was not bound to follow morality, justice, equity, humaneness if these jeopardized it. On the other hand, of course, if adherence to these ideals were advantageous to it, then they were to be followed. Thus, if continued adherence to a treaty would not serve the best interests of the state, but disengagement would, then repudiation of such a treaty was quite proper, even if fraud had to be employed. Thus, if executions of several persons were necessary to safeguard the state, then it was quite proper to bring about these executions whether they were arbitrarily decided or not. In a word, the determining principle was not morality but "reason of state."[52] As a theory this is obviously quite unmedieval, though of course, in practice one would be hard put to find examples of medieval rulers who were prepared to risk losing their power to command their subjects (the state) to live up to demands of "morality."

Relations between the State and its Subjects

It is customary to take for granted that the strengthening of state authority during the Renaissance reflected itself in Renaissance political thought. That there was greater admission of the principle of authoritarianism is of course unquestioned, but the admission was not nearly as great as might be expected. In fact, the principle of limited authority was very much alive.

In England — Limited Authority In England Fortescue may be chosen as a Renaissance proponent of limited authority. Like Bracton he separated government into the two spheres of administration and legislation — he referred to these as *dominium regale et politicum*, that is, authority royal and constitutional — and like Bracton he ascribed the management of the first to the king and of the second to the king in parliament. On the surface it might appear that their appraisal of kingship as an authoritative office was quite similar. But a fuller examination will show that Fortescue's king is subject to greater limitations than Bracton's. It appears in the sphere of *gubernaculum*. Administration may be the proper province of the king, but in Fortescue's view it was carried out with the help of councillors, and these were protected from royal arbitrariness by two principles: (1) they could be removed from office only for cause, and, (2) the removal of any one required the assent of the entire council. The king therefore was not complete master in his own province. It appears even more in the sphere of *jurisdictio*. In this field, it will be recalled, Bracton argued that the king had to secure assent of his magnates. Fortescue required the assent of the parliament. But although parliament was only a transformation of the assembly of magnates, actually its constitutional position in Fortescue's day was far stronger than that of the magnates in Bracton's day. It had won the right to supervise the king's fiscal program, to defend its members against arrest while in session, to impeach the king's councillors, and even to depose the king and pass the crown to one of its own choice. Fortescue was fully aware of these parliamentary gains. Hence, when he said that in the field of *jurisdictio* the king was bound to the parliament, he meant bound in all these respects. This certainly argues for a greater limitation than that implicit in Bracton's formula, and Fortescue may be regarded as a strong exponent of limited, or, as some might call it, parliamentary or constitutional, monarchy.[53]

Passing over such treatises as Dudley's *Tree of Commonwealth* and Bishop Ponet's *A Shorte Treatise of Politike Power* as essentially medieval in thought, we might next turn to Sir Thomas Smith's *De republica anglorum* and Richard Hooker's *The Laws of Ecclesiastical Polity*. Smith was a humanist scholar of civil law, but he was also a keen observer of the English political system.[54] Being Elizabeth's Secretary of State he naturally recognized the greatness of princely authority. "The prince," he said, "is the life, the head and the authority of all things that be done in the realm of England." He further recognized that to fulfill this role the prince required and actually possessed extensive prerogatives: the right to decide on peace and war, the right to name his own administrators, the right to administer law and justice including the right to dispense from them, the right to coin money, and some other rights. Still, despite this exaltation of the prince, he insisted that the king was not sovereign. Sovereignty, he argued, "consisteth in the parliament." His position then was quite similar to that of Fortescue, authoritative monarchy and sovereignty of parliament, a combination which is sometimes described as "mixed sovereignty." What is new in his thought is his lack of emphasis on divine law and natural law as limiting forces.[55] Hooker was a staunch defender of Elizabethan church settlement, but he was no proponent of arbitrary royal authority. In his view monarchy originated in an agreement between society and its chosen head and so the monarch's authority was derivative and limited. Lawmaking was, therefore, a prerogative of the king in parliament, and royal violation of law so made entailed forfeiture of the office. The king may be supreme over individuals who must accept his dictates in passive obedience, but he was not above the nation as a whole.

In Renaissance England, then, the theory of a limited monarchy was a living principle. This was in keeping with medieval theory. What appears as new in this concept of limitation is the extension of the limiting power of the parliament. But it should be pointed out that even this was not wholly new. For what is parliamentary limitation if not an expanded institutionalized version of the old feudal limitation that in matters of state the king should consult with his vassals?

In France — Limited Authority In France, in practice, as pointed out earlier, monarchy was steadily becoming more authoritarian. But in theory authoritarianism was not the prevailing tenet. There were many spokesmen for limited monarchy.

Gerson, the influential proponent of conciliar government in the church, advocated a monarchy which was bound by the community and even accepted tyrannicide as a means of eliminating an intolerable ruler.[56] Phillipe Pot is reported to have argued in the Estates General of Tours (1484) that the state is an inviolable trust which the people entrust to the king, and that it is duly represented by the Estates General. Claude de Seyssel held that the king as the father of the people and guardian of the public weal was restrained by religion, justice, custom, and the rights of property, truly the recognized medieval forces of limitation.[57] James Almain of Sens, teacher at the College of Navarre, held much the same view; in fact he insisted that since authority originates with the people, asbolute monarchy was a legal impossibility. The civilists Alciatus and François Connon adhered to a similar position. Cujas, too, maintained that the foundation of the state was law, that the prince was not above law, and that he was obliged to keep his oath of coronation.

One of the most renowned French advocates of limited monarchy was the unidentified writer of the *Vindiciae contra tyrannos* (1579). Perturbed by the persecution of his co-religionists by the Catholic kings, he worked out an argument against absolutism on the basis of two compacts. The first compact was a religious one between the king and the people as partners on one side and God on the other. If the king violated his part of the compact, the people, to preserve theirs, had the duty and the right to force him to observe his. The second was a political compact between the king and the people when the commonwealth was being created. If the king violated this, the people had the right to insist that he observe it. To this principle of compacts he added also the principle of trusteeship. The role of the king, he insisted, was that of a trustee of the nation. But his was not the only trusteeship, for the Estates General and the great officers of state were also the people's trustees. Hence if the king attempted to violate his trusteeship, the other trustees, to meet their responsibility to the people, had the duty and the right to correct him, by force if necessary. Even though the author insisted that this right of resistance was not available to the people as individuals or as a mass but only to their legally constituted representatives, the end result of his argument was that the king could be resisted both on religious and political grounds.[58]

It is clear that France had a strong continuing tradition of a limited monarchy.

In France — Absolutism of Ruler From the opposite view, that of an absolutist monarchy, the spokesmen were fewer. Insofar as they were more in number during the Renaissance than in the Middle Ages, it might be said that the trend in favor of absolutism was growing.

Alciatus, whom we included among those who spoke for a monarchy limited by law, included in his political treatises ideas which supported a strong executive. In his *Paradoxa*, for example, where he treated of the location of the *merum imperium* (pure legal or juridical authority), he argued that it was located in the prince and that his subordinates in government had it merely as a delegated function.[59] This represented a challenge to the medieval view that authority went with the fief, and conformed to the growing tendency of the French monarchy to deprive the feudality of its rights of independent jurisdiction.

Stronger advocates of royal authoritarianism were Jean Ferrault, Charles du Moulin, and Peter Gregory of Toulouse.

Ferrault, a licentiate in both laws and Louis XII's attorney in the province of Maine, was thoroughly grounded in canon law and in the political history of his country. Believing that this past history revealed a gradual exaltation of French royal power, and drawing mostly upon medieval precedents, he prepared a treatise — *Insignia pecularia* — on the exceptional privileges and prerogatives of the French kings. Among the twenty which he enumerated were such important religious ones as appointment of churchmen, right to tax the clergy and to award benefices; and such civil prerogatives as the right to levy taxes, to call to arms, to grant safe conduct, to authorize appointments of local authorities and to approve the candidates-elect. Adding, moreover, the claim that the French kings were the only ones entitled "the most Christian," he exalted the monarchy above the French church and people and rated the French monarchs as the highest in dignity in all Christendom.[60]

Du Moulin, in his celebrated commentaries on feudal customs, especially in his *Commentarii in consuetudines Parisienses* (1539), while respecting the feudal theories of property, advanced royal authority in two important ways.[61] Like Alciatus he maintained that feudal jurisdiction did not go with the fief but was a delegation from the king, so that ultimately all feudal law derived from the king. In a sense, therefore, the vassals were no different from subjects. From this followed another boon to monarchic authority: as a father of the state who governed for the good of his subjects, all subjects were to cooperate with him in the fulfillment of that mission even if the demands were extraordinary. Indeed, the subjects should obey him. Here we have an echo of the famous notion, *raison d'état*, and this, as we well know, is an invitation to authoritarianism.

Even stronger was the position taken by Peter Gregory of Toulouse in his *De republica* (1596). While denying that a prince can break a contract and while insisting that government existed for the good of the people, he maintained, nevertheless, that a king can make, interpret, and abrogate law; that he is not required to depend on the counsel of the Estates; and, if his office is hereditary, that he cannot be deposed because his rights derive from God alone.[62]

But the most distinguished French spokesman of strong royal authority was Bodin, the proponent of the modern concept of sovereignty. Like most of the writers, contemporary as well as medieval, who dealt with this question, he admitted the limiting roles of divine and natural laws. He further maintained that the prince could not alter the rules of succession, alienate public domain, tax without consent, seize property without just cause, break his own promise or contract, or ignore the interests of such institutions as the church and gilds. But in spite of these limitations with which he bound the king, Bodin could hardly be regarded as a constitutionalist, for he exalted the king's authority in other respects. He insisted that man lost his liberty with the founding of the state and that, with the exceptions enumerated above, the prince was supreme. The prince was above all; his commands had the force of law; he was not bound by the advice of the Estates except in respect to taxation; the people, including the feudal nobility, were all his subjects bound to him by their respective responsibilities; revolutions against legitimate princes were not valid; and the very notion that the people should control their princes was intolerable.[63] Such a view obviously was not in accord with the medieval concept of a monarch. Rather it epitomized what the French monarchy aspired to become and what the propertied bourgeois wanted it to be.

HOLY ROMAN EMPIRE — LIMITED AUTHORITY   In the Holy Roman Empire opinion for limited monarchy and for authoritarianism was as divided as in France.

One of the spokesmen for limited monarchy was the distinguished conciliarist and reformer Cardinal Nicolas Cusa. Although anxious for an effective imperial government that could bring order to the floundering Empire, he could not conceive of the Empire as anything else but as a product of the people's assent and the elective character of the monarchic office. Such a prince was therefore limited not only by the laws of God and Nature but by the law of the people as well.

Cusa's contemporary, Wessel of Groningen, expressed the view that the ruler-subject relation was in the nature of a contract, and that princely authority was terminable.

The civilists Zasius and Althusius echoed the ideas of Alciatus in France. Althusius, however, appears to have been more Aristotelian than Alciatus, arguing that the fullness of authority lay "in the consent and agreement" of the body politic and that monarchs were accountable and dismissible.

Erasmus, although a universal writer, may be included among the theorists of the Holy Roman Empire. And although a Renaissance humanist in many phases of thought, in political theory he was a traditionalist. According to Professor Born, what prevails in Erasmus' writings which touches on government is "the idea of a limited monarchy, under a good, intelligent, God-fearing prince himself subject to the laws."[64] He even would have deprived the prince of the right to declare war without popular consent.

HOLY ROMAN EMPIRE — SUPREMACY OF RULER   The writers on the opposing side were men of lesser renown with two exceptions, that of Aeneas Sylvius Piccolomini, the future Pope Pius II, and Martin Luther. According to the former the prince was the highest legislator and judge in the land, for what he did, he did by the will of God. Luther, needing the support of the princes to promote the Reformation and to suppress religious deviationism, and alarmed at the irresponsibility of the populace, advocated obedience to the prince on the grounds that man's sinful nature necessitated strong restraining power and that this power was ordained of God. "It is God," he said, "not man, who hangs and breaks on the wheel, decapitates and flogs: it is God who wages war." Man is therefore reduced to the position of a passive subject and a patient sufferer.

ITALY — AUTHORITARIANISM Italy, where dynastic despotisms were current and where feudal principles had not rooted themselves as strongly as in northern Europe, tended to reflect these conditions in theory. Petrarch and Salutati, we will recall, turned from what they believed to be inept republicanism to authoritarianism. Giovanni Conversino da Ravenna, a spokesman for the Carrara despots of Padua, saw in tyranny a force for orderly government and so for security, progress, and patronage. Besides, he preferred one-man government because it conformed with the government of the universe by God. The famous humanist teacher Vergerio expressed a similar view, and his *Vitae principum carrarensium*, where he eulogized the realistic conduct of Carrara despots, is regarded as a prototype of Machiavelli's *The Prince*. There were other notable proponents of authoritarianism, but their arguments were not substantially different from the position of the foregoing, or anticipated those of Machiavelli,[65] and so they may be bypassed. We may, therefore, move on to Machiavelli.

Machiavelli in *The Prince*, it will be recalled, looked upon the state as authority and considered its end to be self-preservation. From these premises it follows as a matter of course that the state comes before the subject. "For reasons of state" the subject must be the servant of the state. This subordination was further justified, in Machiavelli's view, on the ground that human nature is fundamentally base. Man is by nature so selfish and perverse that he could not govern himself even if he were to try his best. Hence there can be only one authority, the state, to order him about. Although theoretically this authority could be republican or princely, Machiavelli's experience with Italian politics in his day convinced him that under the circumstances princely authority was preferable and perhaps the only one possible. Accordingly the prince was practically identified with the state and invested with the same authority relative to the people as the state itself possessed. "For reasons of state" the prince could act without concern for any limitations. He was bound neither by moral law nor by natural law; he had no need for parliaments; and the church and the law were to be used to serve the state rather than the reverse. In sum, the state was absolute and the people were reduced to lowly subjects.[66]

Although written for Italians and dedicated to Lorenzo di Piero de'Medici for personal reasons, *The Prince* soon attracted widespread attention and helped to popularize the theory of despotic rule. Thus, even in distant England, Reginald Pole, in his letter to John Leigh, warned this henchman of Cromwell "against reading the story of Nicolò Matchevello, which had already poisoned England and would poison all Christendom"; while Francis Bacon, with his usual preference for the real, actually acclaimed Machiavelli: "We are much beholden to Machiavel and others that write what men do and not what they ought to do."[67]

ITALY — REPUBLICANISM ADVOCATED But while political theory in Renaissance Italy tended to favor authoritarianism, it was not without spokesmen of limited government, of republicanism.

The foremost proponents of republicanism were a number of Florentine officials, humanist and otherwise, who guided Florence through its wars against the Milanese despots Gian Galeazzo and Filippo Maria Visconti. These Florentines were patriots who looked to the history of Rome for inspiration and found there — for example, in Cicero's resistance to Caesar — a message of republicanism which they deemed useful in fanning the will of their fellow citizens to resist the threatening expansion of Milan. Among these might be mentioned Gregorio Dati whose account of Florence's wars against Galeazzo develops the theme of how an awakened republic, moved by love of liberty, opposed tyranny and saved freedom for itself and for others in Italy. And Dati really regarded Florence as a people's republic. A more influential representative of this school was the humanist historian Bruni. In his *Laudatio*, which he based on a late Greek eulogy of Athens, *Panathenaicus* by Aelius Aristides, he compared the role of Florence in peninsular politics with that of Athens in its opposition to Persia. Both cities, in his view, stood for freedom of the mind and of political life; both cities derived from their love of culture and political freedom the will to resist the advance of authoritarianism; and both succeeded.[68] The lesson is obvious: government by the citizens is preferable, despotism is a blight on man's mind and spirit.

Less doctrinaire about republicanism but apparently a convert to it after his dismissal as secretary of Florence was Machiavelli himself. When he still had hopes of possible reinstatement by the Medici when they should be restored to power, he advocated strong princely rule, but when his hopes were dashed and he gave himself up to the study of Livy and absorbed the liberal influences of Florentine humanism, he was apparently won to republicanism.[69] This change of mind is reflected in his *Discourses*,[70] an analysis of the history of the Roman Republic which he utilized to examine the genesis of a state and the evolution of its government.

In the *Discourses*, Machiavelli maintains that the best form of government is a republic in which autocracy, aristocracy, and democracy have indispensable places. Autocracy provides the resolution necessary for the effective functioning of government, and it could be hereditary or, preferably, an elective monarchy; aristocracy, consisting of enlightened civic-minded patriots, furnishes the dynamic of the state; and democracy, namely, the citizens, provides the good will, that is, the anchor of the state. Although all three elements are deemed necessary, the preference for an elective executive and the recognition of the indispensability of the people's good will envisage a determining role for the citizenry. Moreover, Machiavelli's admission of the usefulness of the public platform as an instrument for political education and his plea for the creation of a citizen army in place of the professionals led by irresponsible *condottieri* suggest that Machiavelli had some faith in the people. Indeed, once a state became well grounded, it was less likely to be disturbed by its citizens than by its prince, for the former collectively have greater constancy and prudence than a prince who is always driven by his ego.[71] Machiavelli, thus, was not for irresponsible despotism as one might gather from his *The Prince*, but for government in which the populace has a substantial role to play. Indeed, even in *The Prince* itself, in the famous exhortation for the liberation of Italy from foreign domination, his call to action seems to be directed as much at the people of the peninsula as it is at the hoped-for princely liberator.[72]

Relations between State and Church

In our survey of the political theory on the eve of the Renaissance we observed that the principles of church independence from the state or of its supremacy over the state were beginning to yield to the theory of the paramountcy of the state. During the Renaissance there were several developments which furthered this trend. One was the continued growth of the state. Another was the deterioration of the papacy in consequence of the several crises recounted in Book II of this series. And the third was the emergence of the Protestant churches. But while these factors furthered the trend in general, there were occasions when they also prompted some writers to revive the earlier medieval theory that the church was supreme.

SUPREMACY OF PAPACY ADVOCATED One of these occasions which resuscitated the theory of church supremacy was conciliarism and its aftereffects. In opposition to the conciliarists who propounded a parliamentary system of church government, the anticonciliarists perforce had to argue for papal monarchy and so for the supremacy of the papal church, if not complete, at least in part. Turrecremata (a fifteenth-century canonist who participated at the Councils of Constance and Basel) for example, while conceding that the pope did not have "full jurisdiction throughout the world in temporals," insisted on the principle that the pope had at least such temporal authority as was "necessary for the conservation of spiritual things, for the direction of the faithful to eternal salvation, for the coercion of sinners, and for the maintenance of peace among the Christian people."[73] It is obvious that these exceptions cover much ground, and that in time of a dispute with the state the initial disclaimer would carry little weight. In essence, therefore, the concession is less significant than it might appear to be, and the medieval position is reasserted. Other clerical supporters of papal primacy might be cited, for example, John of Segovia and Torquemada, but their arguments were essentially the same and need not be spelled out.[74] Even some civil jurists took this position. Étienne Aufreri, for example, in his lectures at Toulouse maintained that "both spiritual and temporal powers reside[d] in the person of the pope" and that the powers which the French kings exercised over the church in France were "only a delegation of the pontifical supreme power."[75] The important consequence of these statements was the revivification of the claims of papal supremacy.

IMPACT OF PROTESTANTISM   A far more important circumstance precipitating the question of church-state relations was the rise of the Protestant churches. If the struggling church depended on the support of a prince for its preservation, then its leaders were likely to claim that the prince could dictate in matters religious and to formulate theories in support of this dictation. If, on the other hand, the sect found itself opposed by the prince, then it sought a theory which justified subversion of the established order, or, if subversion seemed impossible, a theory of noninterference. A survey of the theories of some of the Protestant writers will readily confirm this generalization.

Luther, it has been said before, was not a political theorist, but as the father of the Protestant church in Germany, he had to provide answers to the question of the relation between the church and state.[76] In theory he maintained that the church and the state were independent of each other. Indeed, he even went so far as to suggest that in a true Christian community the state would be unnecessary. But as the community was not truly Christian, some still adhering to the error of Catholicism, others moving in the direction of libertarianism, and still others subverting social order and attacking property (Peasants' Revolts), the state perforce had to be called upon to aid the true church. In the end, therefore, to meet the practical necessity of the time, he admitted the state more and more as the guardian of the church and represented the prince as a divine instrument. The logical climax was the famous principle agreed upon at the Peace of Augsburg, namely, that each prince had the right to determine what church he would admit in his state — *cujus regio ejus religio.*

John Calvin's position derived from his profound theism. Whatever is, he firmly believed, is of God. Everything is for the greater glory of God, including the association of man into society. And naturally society organized as a church is the first and the paramount kind of association. If all members of this organization were free from sin, it would be the only organization necessary; but because some are wicked, there must be a supplementary organization, the temporal state, to restrain them. This secondary organization, however, cannot be distinct from the church, for it is constituted of the same members as the church. The temporal state, therefore, is the church organized for the purpose of employing temporal means and ways to help it fulfill its divine mission. Thus the state is the instrument of the church, the leaders of the church are the directors of the state, and the church is supreme.

That is, of course, how Calvin thought things should be, and he saw to it that they became a reality in Geneva. But what about other lands where the "true church," namely the Calvinist church, was unable to assume this commanding place and was actually persecuted, as in France for example? Calvin did not modify his theory, but provided a rationale for this state of affairs. Because all things are of God, the persecuting Catholic state is also of God. It is God's way of punishing his wayward children. Having earned punishment, they cannot escape it; they cannot rebel against God's provision; they can only bear their burden humbly until God in his mercy sees fit to unburden them. When that happened, the ideal situation would be realized and another Geneva established. Hence where the state seems to be dominant, the domination will be temporary. Eventually the true relation will be restored, the church will assume its rightful supremacy.[77]

From Geneva this political theory took root in Scotland through the writings of John Knox, and for the same basic reason — because the Kirk became the state. But in England the theories depended on the prospects afforded by Tudor policy and Tudor successions and on the sect in question.

When there was hope that Protestantism might be accepted by the living sovereign or by the sovereign next in line, the logic of the situation called for the theory of princely supremacy. The prince was represented as ruler by divine right, capable of dictating in matters religious. If for the time being he was acting despotically, his oppressive actions were to be born passively, for the suffering was God's punishment for man's perverseness. Such was the theory propounded by William Tyndale in *The Obedience of Christian Men* (1528) when there was hope that Henry VIII might see the light. Such was in general the position of the Protestants who fled to Geneva and Strasbourg from

Catholic Mary's persecution. Expecting re-establishment of Protestantism by Elizabeth and knowing that they could not hope to establish
their churches in England without the sovereign's support, they necessarily argued that the prince had the right to dictate in matters of con-
science as well as in temporal affairs. Then, when Elizabeth as queen
adopted a middle-of-the-road policy in respect to the church, those of
her mind, namely the supporters of the Anglican church, continued to
uphold the primacy of the state. Thus Thomas Bilson, Bishop of Win-
chester, went even so far as to suggest that the prince could determine
for his people what the Bible said.[78] Thus also Dr. John Bridges, Bishop
of Oxford, maintained that the magistrate is the Lord's anointed and is
responsible to God alone even in matters of religion.

Somewhat more reserved, but for that reason more influential, was
the position of Richard Hooker in his *The Laws of Ecclesiastical Polity*.
The heart of his argument is that the Church of England is a true
Christian church and that it is established by the people acting naturally
as a state. Logically therefore Englishmen ought to accept it not only
because it is true to Christianity but also because as citizens they must
respect the law of the land. In this argument the role of the state in
determining the church may appear to be less arbitrary than that envisioned by Bilson and Bridges, but it is clearly postulated.

On the other hand, those opposed to *via media*, when they realized
that Elizabeth would make no further reforms, abandoned their earlier principle of "tarrying for the magistrate" and began to agitate for
the separation of church and state and for the right of the people to set
up churches of their choice. This is epitomized in Robert Browne's
Treatise of Reformation without Tarrying for Anie (1582),[79] written
when he was not yet "tamed by time."

In France the issue in the end led to similar modifications.[80] At
first, the Huguenots, entertaining the hope that the Catholic dynasty
might be overthrown — Calvinism was gaining in southern France
and a number of great nobles had joined the movement — advanced
the theory that it was the duty of the people in office to oppose tyranny
and to promote truth. It was a duty because they owed their magistracies to the people. Later, when they perceived that the religious wars
were not likely to bring them a decisive victory but instead were lead-

ing to the decimation of France and to the weakening of the state in general, they began to advocate the separation of church and state and the principle that the state ought to respect a variety of churches — in a word, they argued for toleration. In this, incidentally, they were joined by some Catholic spokesmen of a moderate point of view who also saw what dangers these bitter religious rivalries brought to the state. The message was best worked out by Bodin, who represented the state as an empirical institution whose *raison d'être* was to maintain order rather than to commit suicide by indulging in religious persecutions and wars.

Summary Appraisal

By way of summary we might ask what does this survey indicate about the originality of Renaissance political thought? It shows, without a doubt, that some modern concepts of the state were being enunciated. Machiavelli's principle of the self-centeredness of the state and Bodin's view of the state as authority which demands obedience are new. The disregard of the religious *raison d'être* of the state was steadily mounting. But while these bespeak departure from medieval political theory, the survey also reveals strong currents which carried on the medieval tradition. The theory of a state limited by divine, natural, and customary laws was kept very much alive. The principle that the state is not an end in itself but a means to an end was still widely accepted. The need and the duty of the state to protect the church and to be guided by it was repeatedly aired. In fact, with the coming of the Reformation, the last two medieval principles were vigorously revitalized. The two streams were therefore running abreast. And if there was a revolution in political thought, it was a revolution more in the making than a revolution already consummated.

1. A classic study of this subject is Alexander James and Robert Warrand Carlyle, *Medieval Political Theory in the West* (6 vols.; Edinburgh: William Blackwood & Sons, Ltd., 1903–1936). A good shorter study is Ewart Lewis, *Medieval Political Ideas* (New York: Alfred A. Knopf, 1954). A standard college text that treats the subject acceptably is Charles Howard McIlwain, *The Growth of Political Thought in the West* (New York: The Macmillan Co., 1932).

2. For a fresh interpretation of Augustine on this subject see William Ebenstein, *Introduction to Political Philosophy* (New York: Rinehart & Co., 1953), 56 ff.

3. See his *On Kingship: To the King of Cyprus*, trans. Gerald B. Phelan and rev. Th. Eschmann (Toronto: The Pontifical Institute of Mediaeval Studies, 1949), Bk. I, chap. 1, 2–8; Bk. II, chap. 3, 103–7. For additional argument consult Dino Bigongiari (ed.), *The Political Ideas of St. Thomas Aquinas*, no. XV of "The Hafner Library of Classics" (New York: Hafner Publishing Co., 1953), introduction, vii–xi.

4. There is a recent translation of this work — Donald Nicholl, *Dante: Monarchy and Three Political Letters*, "Library of Ideas" (New York: The Noonday Press, 1954).

5. Ebenstein, *op. cit.*, 86. For a fuller development of this theory see A. Passerin d'Entrèves, *Dante as a Political Thinker* (Oxford: Clarendon Press, 1953), especially chap. ii, "Imperium."

6. A discerning analysis of Pierre du Bois's political views was made by Eileen Power in *The Social and Political Ideas of Some Great Mediaeval Thinkers*, ed. F. J. C. Hearnshaw (New York: Barnes and Noble, Inc., 1949), 139–66.

7. For a challenging philosophical analysis of this work consult Alan Gewirth, *Marsilius of Padua, The Defender of Peace*, no. 46 of *Records of Civilization: Sources and Studies* (New York: Columbia University Press, 1951).

8. *Ibid.*, 85–91.

9. Analysis of his position on this matter in *ibid.*, 125–31.

10. On this subject of the relations between the states and the Empire consult Walter Ullman, "The Development of the Medieval Idea of Sovereignty," *The English Historical Review*, LXIV (1949), 1–33.

11. Cf. Jacques Poujol, "Jean Ferrault on the King's Privileges: A Study of the Medieval Sources of Renaissance Political Theory in France," *Studies in the Renaissance*, V (1958), 21.

12. For the argument consult W. Ullman, *The Growth of Papal Government in the Middle Ages* (New York: Barnes and Noble, Inc., 1953).

13. Cited from Lewis, *op. cit.*, II, 451.

14. For their arguments see Ullman, "The Development of the Medieval Idea of Sovereignty," *op. cit.*, 20–27.

15. *Ibid.*, 25–33.

16. Lewis, *op. cit.*, II, 456. An excellent presentation of Bartolus' treatment is to be found in Cecil Nathan Sidney Woolf, *Bartolus of Sassoferrato* (Cambridge: University Press, 1913), 112–207.

17. Cited from Frederick Maurice Powicke, "Reflections on the Medieval State," *Transactions of the Royal Historical Society*, series 4, XIX (1936), 12–13.

18. The literature dealing with this interchange and a summary survey of the process are provided in Ernest H. Kantorowicz, "Mysteries of State: An Absolutist Concept and Its Late Mediaeval Origins," *The Harvard Theological Review*, XLVIII (1955), 65–91.

19. Bracton's position is brilliantly elucidated by C. H. McIlwain in his *Constitutionalism, Ancient and Modern* (Ithaca, New York: Cornell University Press, 1947), 67–87. McIlwain tends to emphasize Bracton's constitutionalism. For a treatment which tends to emphasize the opposite see S. J. T. Miller, "The Position of the King in Bracton and Beaumanoir," *Speculum*, XXXI (1956), 263–96.

20. Cf. Bigongiari (ed.), *op. cit.*, introduction, xi–xxiii.

21. Cited from Lewis, *op. cit.*, I, 254.

22. Miller, *op. cit.*, 276, 278, 279.

23. In *The Social and Political Ideas of Some Great Mediaeval Thinkers*, 165.

24. On this see Ullman, *The Growth of Papal Government in the Middle Ages*, 17–18.

25. Good account of this whole movement is to be found in *ibid.*, 229–446.

26. How this claim was elaborated may be studied in W. Ullman's scholarly essay *Medieval Papalism, The Political Theories of the Medieval Canonists* (London: Methuen & Co., Ltd., 1949), 76–113.

27. *On Kingship*, Bk. II, chap. iii (Phelan's translation, 58–63).

28. Cf. Lewis, *op. cit.*, II, 523–33.

29. On conciliarism see Emil Lucki, *History of the Renaissance*, Book II, *Church and Religion* (Salt Lake City: University of Utah Press, 1964), 129 ff.

30. Cf. L. J. Daly, S. J., *The Political Theory of John Wyclif* (Chicago: Loyola University Press, 1962), 74–80.

31. *Ibid.*, 63–64, 82, 85–89, 116–20, 142–5.

32. *Ibid.*, 89–93. For a brief treatment of this controversy see my *History of the Renaissance*, Book II, *Church and Religion*, 108–10.

33. See his *De Laudibus Legum Anglie*, ed. and trans. Stanley Bertram Chrimes (Cambridge: University Press, 1949). For an analysis of his theory consult S. B. Chrimes, "Sir John Fortescue and His Theory of Dominion," *Transactions of the Royal Historical Society*, 4th series, XVII (1934), 117–47.

34. This is argued in Arthur B. Ferguson, "Fortescue and the Renaissance: A Study in Transition," *Studies in the Renaissance*, VI (1959), 175–94.

35. For a summary examination of several of these theories see Christopher Morris, *Political Thought in England, Tyndale to Hooker* (London: Oxford University Press, 1953).

36. Cf. John William Allen, *A History of Political Thought in the Sixteenth Century* (London: Methuen and Co., Ltd., 1928), 275 ff.

37. There is an abridged translation of the work — M. J. Tooley, *Six Books of the Commonwealth by Jean Bodin* (Oxford: Basil Blackwell, 1955) and a corrected facsimile reprint of the English translation of 1606 — Kenneth Douglas McRae (ed.), *Jean Bodin, the Six Bookes of a Commonweale* (Cambridge: Harvard University Press, 1962).

38. This relationship is worked out by McRae, *op. cit.*, introduction, A3–A13.

39. These are treated in Julian H. Franklin, *Jean Bodin and the Sixteenth-Century Revolution in the Methodology of Law and History* (New York: Columbia University Press, 1963).

40. For his own words on these points see McRae, *op. cit.*, 1, 84, 88. Cf. also Tooley, *op. cit.*, introduction, xvi.

41. Cf. *ibid.*, xvii, xix, xxiii–xxiv.

42. McRae, *op. cit.*, introduction, A15–A16.

43. Cf. Tooley, *op. cit.*, introduction, xxxvii.

44. For his own words see McRae, *op. cit.*, 561.

45. This subject is studied most thoroughly in M. J. Tooley, "Bodin and the Mediaeval Theory of Climate," *Speculum*, XXVIII (1953), 64–83. Note the concluding paragraph especially.

46. For a recent examination of Luther's theory of the state see William A. Mueller, *Church and State in Luther and Calvin* (Nashville, Tennessee: Broadman Press, 1954), 36–76. This should be compared with Albert Hyma's treatment in his *New Light on Martin Luther* (Grand Rapids, Mich.: Wm. B. Eerdmans Publishing Co., 1958), chap. xi, "Political Ideas." He seeks to minimize the alleged change in Luther's position on this matter.

47. On these consult Hans Baron, *The Crisis of the Early Italian Renaissance* (Princeton: Princeton University Press, 1955), *passim*.

48. See Ephraim Emerton's translation of this essay and his commentary on it in his *Humanism and Tyranny, Studies in the Italian Trecento* (Cambridge: Harvard University Press, 1925), particularly 93–116. Cf. Maude Violet Clarke, *The Medieval City State: An Essay on Tyranny and Federation in the Later Middle Ages* (London: Methuen and Co., Ltd., 1926), 139–42.

49. For other medieval aspects of Salutati's thought in *De Tyranno*, see Baron, *The Crisis of the Early Italian Renaissance*, I, 123.

50. Recently translated by Allan H. Gilbert in his *Machiavelli, The Prince and Other Works* (New York: Hendricks House — Farrar, Straus, 1941). See his introduction for analysis of the treatise.

51. Cf. J. H. Hexter, "Il Principe and lo stato," *Studies in the Renaissance,* IV (1957), 125–6, 130. This is an interesting study on how Machiavelli used the term "state."

52. Cf. *ibid.*, 131–35.

53. A cogent argument in support of the idea that Fortescue's "limited" monarchy was practically identical with what is understood by the terms "parliamentary" or "constitutional" monarchy is presented by R. W. K. Hinton in his "English Constitutional Theories from Sir John Fortescue to Sir John Eliot," *English Historical Review*, LXXV (1960), 410–25.

54. Smith's views are summarized in *ibid.*, 418–20 and in Morris, *op. cit.*, 81–83. Cf. also George L. Mosse, *The Struggle for Sovereignty in England from the Reign of Queen Elizabeth to the Petition of Right* (East Lansing: Michigan State College Press, 1950), 21–25.

55. For a comparison of Smith and Fortescue see G. L. Moose, "Change and Continuity in the Tudor Constitution," *Speculum*, XXII (1947), 18–28.

56. He took this stand at the Council of Constance where the celebrated argument of John Petit in justification of the assassination of the regent Duke of Orleans came under scrutiny.

57. This is worked out in William Farr Church, *Constitutional Thought in Sixteenth Century France*, vol. XLVII of *Harvard Historical Studies* (Cambridge: Harvard University Press, 1941), 22–42. For a succinct statement cf. A. J. and R. W. Carlyle, *op. cit.*, VI, 225.

58. For a fuller development of the argument see Ernest Baker's essay, "A Huguenot Theory of Politics," in his *Church, State, and Study* (London: Methuen & Co., Ltd., 1930), 72–108.

59. On Alciatus see M. Gilmore, *Argument from Roman Law in Political Thought, 1200–1600*, vol. XV of *Harvard Historical Monographs* (Cambridge: Harvard University Press, 1941), 47 ff.

60. Poujol, *op. cit.*, 17–25.

61. Cf. Church, *op. cit.*, 180–94.

62. Cf. A. J. and R. W. Carlyle, *op. cit.*, VI, 441–5.

63. Bodin works these out in Bks. I, chap. viii; II, chap. v (McRae, *op. cit.*, 84–113, 218–30).

64. Lester K. Born (ed.), *The Education of a Christian Prince* (New York: Columbia University Press, 1936), introduction, 6.

65. Cf. Allan H. Gilbert, *Machiavelli's Prince and Its Forerunners* (Durham, N.C.: Duke University Press, 1938), especially the introduction and the concluding chapter.

66. After reading *The Prince*, the student will profit from Friedrich Meinecke's *Machiavellism: The Doctrine of* Raison d'État *and Its Place in Modern History*, trans. Douglas Scott (New Haven: Yale University Press, 1957), 26–40.

67. Citations from William Gordon Zeeveld, *The Foundations of Tudor Policy* (Cambridge: Harvard University Press, 1948), 14, and from Morris, *op. cit.*, 9.

68. For a fuller analysis see Baron, *The Crisis of the Early Italian Renaissance*, I, 163–89.

69. The question whether Machiavelli was converted to republicanism is examined on the basis of the relationship of *The Prince* to the *Discourses*, both as to time of composition and as to central ideas, in Hans Baron's "Machiavelli: The Republican Citizen and the Author of "The Prince,' " *The English Historical Review*, LXXVI (1961), 217–53. This is an important study, but it should be checked against J. H. Whitfield's "Discourses on Machiavelli, VII: Gilbert, Hexter and Baron," *Italian Studies*, XIII (1958), 21–46, even if the latter antedates it, and both should be followed by Eric W. Cochrane's "Machiavelli: 1940–1960," *Journal of Modern History*, XXXIII (1961), 113–36, a brilliant survey of key studies on Machiavelli.

70. For a scrutinizing analysis of this work see Leslie J. Walker, S. J., (trans. and commentator), *The Discourses of Niccolò Machiavelli* (New Haven: Yale University Press, 1950).

71. Cf. *ibid.*, I, 8.

72. On this point see Felix Gilbert, "The Concept of Nationalism in *The Prince*," *Studies in the Renaissance*, I (1954), 38–48.

73. Cited from Lewis, *op. cit.*, II, 552.

74. Cf. Hubert Jedin, *A History of the Council of Trent*, trans. Dom Ernest Graf, O.S.B. (St. Louis, Missouri: B. Herder Book Co., 1957), I, 26–30.

75. Poujol, *op. cit.*, 19.

76. For a concise statement of Luther's thinking on this matter see Thomas Maynard Parker, *Christianity and the State in the Light of History* (London: Adam and Charles Black, 1955), 150–6, and the works cited in no. 46 above.

77. Calvin's position is best expressed in chap. 20, Bk. iv, entitled "On Civil Government," in his *Institutes of the Christian Religion*. For a concise summary see Parker, *op. cit.*, 156–60. For a treatment that draws on all of his works see Mueller, *op. cit.*, 127–63.

78. Cf. Morris, *op. cit.*, 117–9.

79. Cf. *ibid.*, 166–7, and M. M. Knappen, *Tudor Puritanism. A Chapter in the History of Idealism* (Chicago: University of Chicago Press, 1939), 305–10.

80. This is worked out in Parker, *op. cit.*, 160–5.

CHAPTER VI

Summary Survey of Political Developments

O UR STUDY of the political situation in Europe was opened with a glance at the political map of Europe just on the eve of the Renaissance. If we now examine a map depicting the situation some two centuries later and compare the two, we shall discover some substantial changes.

The greatest changes appear at the two ends of the continent, in the extreme west and in the regions east of the Adriatic Sea and of the Oder River. In the west there is Spain, a united Spain embracing the entire Iberian Peninsula except Portugal. Moreover, this newly risen Spain possesses the Low Countries and Naples, dominates the rest of Italy, and has a vast overseas empire in the Americas and in the Pacific Ocean. In the east, specifically in the Balkans, where once were independent Serbia, Bulgaria, Byzantium, and an assortment of Greek principalities, there is a sprawling Turkey. Indeed, it has sprawled over most of Hungary, over extensive territories along the north shore of the Black Sea, and all around the eastern Mediterranean, from Asia Minor to the Persian Gulf and through Syria to Arabia, Egypt, and Libya. Poland-Lithuania, united since 1386, show some change. They lost their Black Sea territory to the Ottomans but pushed their northern border to the waters of the Baltic. Still further east we see a greatly expanded Muscovy where formerly were several independent if related principalities.

The countries between these three newly risen powers reveal less spectacular changes, or hardly any that are readily noticeable. Italy, having fallen under the watchful eye of Spain, still has much the same political physiognomy. Naples, the Papal States, Florence, Genoa, Milan, and Venice reveal rather insignificant territorial alterations as compared with their holdings at the inception of the Renaissance. True, Venice lost most of its maritime empire, but this was in Greece and in the Aegean and the Mediterranean seas and the loss did not affect its territorial position in Italy. Germany remains what it was before, a bizarre land, still fragmented into numerous quasi-independent political units that are only loosely held together as an Empire. Here the only notable changes are the appearance of Switzerland as a distinct political entity and the territorial consolidation of some of the princely states — Brandenburg, for example. France, having expelled the English, shows more fundamental changes. It has advanced its frontier to its natural limit in the west and it has taken the first step to the same effect in the east. On the west the annexation of Gascony, Aquitaine, and Brittany brought it to the Atlantic, and the acquisition of Burgundy and of the Bishoprics of Metz, Verdun, and Toul pushed it closer to the Rhine. England itself shows a less significant change, namely, the annexation of Wales; but a truly important development was the loss of its holdings in France.

Taken as a whole these are noticeably great changes, and so it may rightly be said that the political map of Europe was reshaped during the Renaissance. But while recognizing the import of this reshaping, we must not lose sight of the fact that the bases for many of these changes had been prepared in the later Middle Ages.

While a comparison of the maps can show us the territorial changes, it can tell us little about the internal developments in the various lands. At the most it can only suggest the possibility that where there was territorial consolidation there probably was a corresponding increase in the effectiveness of governments and vice versa.

This supposition, as our study has revealed, is certainly correct. Most of the expanding countries developed governments that were stronger and more effective than their counterparts at the beginning of the Renaissance. Turkey and Muscovy were outright despotisms thriving on the successes of their spectacular expansions. Spain and France acquired more authoritative monarchies but they had not yet succeeded in freeing themselves from the restraints of their medieval institutions. England accepted its dominant, perhaps, even despotic, Tudors and seemed to be content with them, but their authority and despotism were dependent on the approval of the parliament, which, though very much under their influence, was nevertheless a decided medieval curb on any autocratic inclinations that they may have had.

A similar trend toward more authoritative governments was also present in some smaller lands. In Italy, the Republic of Florence became a duchy with Medici despots at its helm, Milan and Venice remained princely and class despotisms, respectively, as they were by the end of the Middle Ages, and Naples and the Papal States were still in pursuit of that fleeting objective just as they were when the Renaissance began. In Germany, many of the principalities, such as that of Brandenburg, were in the process of establishing strong princely governments. But Germany as a whole failed to make its Empire an effective reality. In Sweden this trend came to life under the strong arm of its liberator and founder Gustavus Vasa, who, to save his liberated country from chaos, felt called upon to rule with an iron hand. In much of Europe, therefore, the trend toward effective central governments was very strong.

On the other hand, in central Europe the trend did not materialize or became reversed. The Holy Roman Empire was no more an effective Empire than it was Roman or holy. Poland-Lithuania, which began the Renaissance with prospects of developing a strong monarchy, became, by the end of the period, thoroughly feudalistic. Hungary began as an effective feudal monarchy, saw the despotic rule of Matthias Corvinus pass away like a flashing comet, and then reverted to baronial localism and lost its independence to the Turks and the Habsburgs.

Unique was the emergent federation of the Swiss, though it was soon to have the company of the Low Countries which were just beginning to challenge the Spanish rule as the Renaissance was drawing to a close.

Having summarized both of these developments, the territorial expansion and the growth of strong central governments, we might also bring together the causes behind them.

One general cause was the interacting influence of these two movements, one upon the other, in a kind of cause-effect cycle. On the one hand, territorial expansion redounded to the prestige of the monarchies directing them and justified three measures or policies which made the successes possible and at the same time served to undergird the central governments. One measure was the establishment of national armies, parts of which often remained as standing armies, and the adoption of heavy armaments which only the larger states were able to acquire in significant quantity. Another was the establishment of a permanent national tax to finance these armies and to sustain expanding governments. The third, growing out of the needs of wartime diplomacy and of war treasuries, was the steady increase in the control of the nation's economy by the central government until the maximum was reached in the form of mercantilism. On the other hand, successful implementation of these measures enabled the rulers to muster their nations' strength behind their territorial aggrandizements.

Another general cause, at least as far as the Catholic west was concerned, was the troubled state of the church, brought about by the decline of the papacy at the beginning of the Renaissance and by the disruptive influence of the Protestant movement toward the close of the period. The decline of the papacy, both spiritually and temporally, simply invited increased encroachment by the states on the prerogatives of the church within their borders; and all the states took advantage of this opportunity to do just that. The emergence of the Protestant movement led to even greater encroachment. Whether the states acted as protectors or opponents of the movement, in the end they managed either to extend their control over the church or to subject it completely.

In addition to these general causes, there were specific causes which were applicable to particular countries only. In England the chaos of the last Lancastrian reign and of the Wars of Roses made the public receptive to strong central government. In France it was the successful expulsion of the English in the last stage of the Hundred Years' War that redounded to the prestige and power of the monarchy. In Spain it was the fortunate marriage of two energetic rulers, Ferdinand and Isabella. In Muscovy it was the fortuitous designation, by the Tartars, of its princes as their official collectors of tribute from the other Russian dynasts. In Sweden it was the people's destestation of the Union of Calmar and their indignation at the horrible "Blood Bath." And so on.

All the explanations offered so far were generally of the Renaissance period, and if we looked no further we would have to accept the proposition that both the developments and their causes were products of the Renaissance movement. But we cannot stop with these explanations alone, as there is the additional factor of demonstrable continuities from the Middle Ages, without which some of the Renaissance developments would not have been possible.

The principal influence deriving from pre-Renaissance days was the incipience of the state itself. The state had made its appearance in England and France, in the several Italian bodies politic, in the member units of the Holy Roman Empire, in Spain, and belatedly in Hungary, Poland, and Lithuania. In all of these rising states, as was shown in an earlier chapter, the governments were beginning to become effective even before the Middle Ages came to end. Some were encouraging commutation of the feudal military services for money payments which enabled their rulers to engage some professional troops. Some were in the process of developing a nationwide tax system suggested by the practice of collecting imposts to pay for the crusades. In most of them the theory of kingship as a fountain of justice promoted the encroachment of the kings on the private jurisdictions of the feudal lordships and the introduction of a system of nationwide royal courts. Then, underlying all these developments, was the remarkable transformation of economy and society as manifested in the truly spectacular urbanization which had attained its peak by the first quarter of the fourteenth century, that is, just on the eve of the Renaissance. These causes and others obviously prepared the groundwork for the Renaissance developments we have been summarizing and accounting for. Our conclusion must then be that these developments and the forces behind them started in the Middle Ages and became fullblown during the Renaissance. We must not forget that behind every flower there is a bud. In this case, as in most other phases of the Renaissance civilization, the flower was of the Renaissance; the bud, of the Middle Ages.

Bibliography

The footnotes to each chapter include considerable bibliographical information. Here, therefore, only a select bibliography will be compiled, mostly of works printed in English.

Some Current Bibliographical Aids

Renaissance News, 1948–, a quarterly published by the Renaissance Society of America.

Studies of Philology, the annual April issue.

Studies in the Renaissance, 1954–, published annually by the Renaissance Society of America.

There are extensive bibliographies at the end of Cheyney, Edward Potts, *The Dawn of a New Era, 1250–1453*. New York: Harper and Brothers Publishers, 1936; and of Gilmore, Myron P., *The World of Humanism, 1453–1517*. New York: Harper and Brothers Publishers, 1952.

Works Dealing with Renaissance Politics in Europe in General

Popular as the subject of the Renaissance is, surprisingly there is no comprehensive political history of the period in the English language other than Volume I, *The Renaissance*, of the first edition of *The Cambridge Modern History*, Cambridge: University Press, 1902, which, while still useful, is obviously outdated. For more recent general treatments the reader will, therefore, have to turn to histories which deal with the Renaissance in all its aspects or with the Renaissance and the Reformation. Among these some of the better ones are:

Cheyney, Edward Potts. As cited above.

Ergang, Robert. *Europe from the Renaissance to Waterloo*. New York: D. C. Heath and Company, 1939.

Ferguson, Wallace K. *Europe in Transition, 1300–1520*. Boston: Houghton Mifflin Company, 1962.

Gilmore, Myron P. As cited above.

Green, V. H. H. *Renaissance and Reformation: A Survey of European History between 1450 and 1600*. London: Edward Arnold & Co., 1952.

Lucas, Henry S. *The Renaissance and the Reformation*. 2d ed. revised. New York: Harper & Brothers, 1960.

Potter, G. R. (ed.). *The Renaissance*. Vol. I, *The New Cambridge Modern History*. Cambridge: Cambridge University Press, 1957.

Previté-Orton, C. W. *A History of Europe from 1198 to 1378*. Vol III of *Methuen's History of Medieval and Modern Europe*. New York: G. P. Putnam's Sons, 1937.

Sellery, George Clarke. *The Renaissance, Its Nature and Origins*. Madison: University of Wisconsin Press, 1957.

Thomson, S. Harrison. *Europe in Renaissance and Reformation*. New York: Harcourt, Brace and World, Inc., 1963.

Waugh, W. T. *A History of Europe from 1378 to 1494*. Vol. IV of *Methuen's History of Medieval and Modern Europe*. 3d ed. London: Methuen & Co., Ltd., Publishers, 1949.

Works Dealing with Internal Developments in the Various Nations

Baynes, Norman H. and Moss, H. St. L. B. (eds.). *Byzantium, An Introduction to East Roman Civilization*. Oxford: Clarendon Press, 1948.

Becker, Marvin B. "The Republican City State in Florence. An Inquiry into its Origin and Survival (1280–1434)," *Speculum*, XXXV (1960), 39–50.

Bragadin, Mari' Antonia. *Histoire des républiques maritimes Italiennes — Venice, Amalfi, Pise, Gênes*. Paris: Payot, 1955.

Brucker, Gene A. *Florentine Politics and Society, 1343–1378*. Vol. XII of *Princeton Studies in History*. Princeton: Princeton University Press, 1962.

Calmette, Joseph. *The Golden Age of Burgundy*. Translated by Doreen Weightman. New York: Norton & Company, Inc., 1963.

Carsten, F. L. *The Origins of Prussia*. Oxford: Clarendon Press, 1954.

Chrimes, S. B. and Brown, A. L. (eds.). *Select Documents of English Constitutional History, 1307–1485*. London: A. and C. Black, Ltd., 1961.

Davis, James Cushman. *The Decline of the Venetian Nobility as a Ruling Class*. Series LXXX, No. 2 of *The Johns Hopkins University Studies in Historical and Political Science*. Baltimore: The Johns Hopkins Press, 1962.

Elton, G. R. *England under the Tudors*. Vol. IV of *A History of England*. Edited by Sir Charles Oman. London: Methuen & Co., Ltd., 1956.

Elton, G. R. (ed.). *The Tudor Constitution, Documents and Commentary*. Cambridge: University Press, 1960.

Elton, G. R. *The Tudor Revolution in Government*. Cambridge: University Press, 1953.

Fawtier, Robert. *The Capetian Kings of France*. Translated by Lionel Butler and R. J. Adams. London: Macmillan and Co., Ltd., 1960.

Florinsky, Michael T. *Russia — A History and an Interpretation*, Vol. I. New York: Macmillan Co., 1953.

Holborn, Hajo. *A History of Modern Germany. The Reformation*. New York: Alfred A. Knopf, 1959.

Jacob, E. F. (ed.). *Italian Studies, A Tribute to the Late Cecilia M. Ady*. London: Faber and Faber, 1960.

Jacob, E. F. *The Fifteenth Century, 1399–1485*. Vol. VI of *The Oxford History of England*. Oxford: Clarendon Press, 1961.

Larsen, Karen. *A History of Norway*. Princeton: Princeton University Press, 1948.

Livermore, H. V. *A History of Spain*. London: George Allen and Unwin, Ltd., 1958.

Lot, Ferdinand and Fawtier, Robert. *Histoire des institutions françaises au moyen âge*. 3 vols. to date. Paris: Presses universitaires de France, 1957 ff.

Lybyer, A. H. *The Government of the Ottoman Empire in the Time of Suleiman the Magnificent*. Vol. XVIII of *Harvard Historical Studies*. Cambridge: Harvard University Press, 1913.

Mackie, J. D. *The Earlier Tudors, 1485–1558*. Vol. VII of *The Oxford History of England*. Oxford: Clarendon Press, 1952.

Major, J. Russel. *Representative Institutions in the Renaissance, 1421–1559*. Madison: The University of Wisconsin Press, 1960.

Major, J. Russell. "The Crown and the Aristocracy in Renaissance France," *American Historical Review*, LXIX (1964), 631–45.

Major, J. Russell. "The French Monarchy as Seen through the Estates General," *Studies in the Renaissance*, IX (1962), 113–25.

McKisack, May. *The Fourteenth Century*. Vol. V of *The Oxford History of England*. Oxford: Clarendon Press, 1959.

Merriman, R. Bigelow. *The Rise of the Spanish Empire in the Old World and the New*. Vol. I, *The Middle Ages*. New York: Cooper Square Publishers, Inc., 1962.

Mosse, G. L. "Change and Continuity in the Tudor Constitution," *Speculum*, XXII (1947), 18–28.

Mosse, George L. *The Struggle for Sovereignty in England from the Reign of Queen Elizabeth to the Petition of Right.* East Lansing: Michigan State College Press, 1950.

Ostrogorsky, George. *History of the Byzantine State.* Translated by Joan Hussey. Oxford: Basil Blackwell, 1956.

Rowse, A. L. *The England of Elizabeth.* New York: The Macmillan Co., 1951.

Schevill, Ferdinand. *History of Florence from the Founding of the City through the Renaissance.* New York: Frederick Ungar Publishing Co., 1961.

Stavrianos, L. S. *The Balkans since 1453.* New York: Rinehard & Company, Inc., 1958.

Wilkinson, B. "The Political Revolution of the Thirteenth and Fourteenth Centuries in England," *Speculum*, XXIV (1949), 502–9.

Williams, Penry and Harris, G. L. "A Revolution in Tudor History"? *Past and Present*, XXV (1963), 3–58.

Zeller, Gaston. *Les institutions de la France au xvie siècle.* Paris: Presses universitaires de France, 1948.

Works Dealing with International Developments

Most of the works listed above contain considerable information on this phase of the Renaissance history. But there are several useful works that deal with this subject more specifically:

Bowsky, William. *Henry VII in Italy. The Conflict of Empire and City-State, 1310–1313.* Lincoln, Nebraska: University of Nebraska Press, 1960.

Cuttino, G. P. "Historical Revision: The Causes of the Hundred Years' War," *Speculum*, XXX (1956), 463–77.

Dickinson, Joycelyne Gledhill. *The Congress of Arras, 1435: A Study in Medieval Diplomacy.* Oxford: Clarendon Press, 1955.

Fisher, S. N. *The Foreign Relations of Turkey, 1481–1512.* Urbana, Illinois: University of Illinois Press, 1948.

Halecki, Oscar. *Borderlands of Western Civilization. A History of East Central Europe.* New York: The Roland Press Company, 1952.

Lot, Ferdinand. *L'art militaire et les armies au moyen âge en Europe et dans le proche orient.* 2 vols. Paris: Payot, 1946.

Mattingly, Garret. *Renaissance Diplomacy.* London: Jonathan Cape, 1955.

Oman, Charles. *A History of the Art of War in the Middle Ages.* 2d ed. Vol. II. New York: Burt Franklin, no date.

Penrose, Boies. *Travel and Discovery in the Renaissance, 1420–1620.* Cambridge: Harvard University Press, 1955.

Perroy, Edouard. *The Hundred Years' War.* Translated by W. B. Wells. New York: Oxford University Press, 1951.

Petrie, Sir Charles. *Earlier Diplomatic History, 1492–1713.* New York: The Macmillan Co., 1949.

Works Dealing with Renaissance Political Theory

Allen, John William. *A History of Political Thought in the Sixteenth Century.* London: Methuen and Co., Ltd., 1928.

Baron, Hans, "Machiavelli: The Republican Citizen and the Author of 'The Prince,'" *The English Historical Review,* LXXVI (1961), 217–53.

Baron, Hans. *The Crisis of the Early Italian Renaissance.* Princeton: Princeton University Press, 1955.

Born, Lester K. (ed.). *The Education of a Christian Prince.* New York: Columbia University Press, 1936.

Carlyle, Alexander James and Robert Warrand. *Medieval Political Theory in the West.* 6 vols. Edinburgh: William Blackwood & Sons, Ltd., 1903–36.

Church, William Farr. *Constitutional Thought in Sixteenth-Century France.* Vol. XLVII of *Harvard Historical Studies.* Cambridge: Harvard University Press, 1941.

Cochrane, Eric W. "Machiavelli: 1940–1960." *The Journal of Modern History,* XXXIII (1961), 113–36.

Daly, L. J. *The Political Theory of John Wyclif.* Chicago: Loyola University Press, 1962.

Emerton, Ephraim. *Humanism and Tyranny, Studies in the Italian Trecento.* Cambridge: Harvard University Press, 1925.

Folz, Robert. *L'idée d'Empire en occident du ve au xive siècle.* Paris: Aubier, 1953.

Fortescue, Sir John. *De laudibus legum anglie.* Edited and translated by Stanley Bertram Chrimes. Cambridge: University Press, 1949.

Franklin, Julian H. *Jean Bodin and the Sixteenth-Century Revolution in the Methodology of Law and History.* New York: Columbia University Press, 1963.

Gewirth, Alan. *Marsilius of Padua, The Defender of Peace.* No. 46 of *Records of Civilization: Sources and Studies.* New York: Columbia University Press, 1951.

Gilbert, Allan H. (trans.). *Machiavelli, The Prince and Other Works.* New York: Hendricks House — Farrar, Straus, 1941.

Hexter, J. H. "Il Principe and lo stato," *Studies in the Renaissance,* IV (1957), 113–38.

Hinton, R. W. K. "English Constitutional Theories from Sir John Fortescue to Sir John Eliot," *English Historical Review,* LXXV (1960), 410–25.

Kantorowicz, Ernest H. "Mysteries of State: An Absolutist Concept and Its Late Mediaeval Origins," *The Harvard Theological Review,* XLVIII (1955), 65–91.

Lewis, Ewart. *Medieval Political Ideas.* New York: Alfred A. Knopf, 1954.

McIlwain, C. H. *Constitutionalism, Ancient and Modern.* Ithaca, New York: Cornell University Press, 1947.

Miller, S. J. T. "The Position of the King in Bracton and Beaumanoir," *Speculum,* XXXI (1956), 263–96.

Morris, Christopher. *Political Thought in England, Tyndale to Hooker.* London: Oxford University Press, 1963.

Mueller, William A. *Church and State in Luther and Calvin.* Nashville, Tennessee: Broadman Press, 1954.

Nicholl, Donald. *Dante: Monarchy and Three Political Letters.* "Library of Ideas"; New York: The Noonday Press, 1954.

Parker, Maynard Thomas. *Christianity and the State in the Light of History.* London: Adam and Charles Black, 1955.

Poujol, Jacques. "Jean Ferrault on the King's Privileges: A Study of the Medieval Sources of Renaissance Political Theory in France," *Studies in the Renaissance,* V (1958), 15–26.

Power, Eileen. *The Social and Political Ideas of Some Great Mediaeval Thinkers.* Edited by F. J. C. Hearnshaw. New York: Barnes and Noble, Inc., 1949.

St. Thomas Aquinas. *On Kingship: To the King of Cyprus.* Translated by Gerald B. Phelan and revised by Th. Eschmann. Toronto: The Pontifical Institute of Mediaeval Studies, 1949.

Tooley, M. J. "Bodin and the Mediaeval Theory of Climate," *Speculum,* XXVIII (1953), 64–83.

Tooley, M. J. (trans.). *Six Books of the Commonwealth of Jean Bodin.* Oxford: Basil Blackwell, 1955. (This is an abridged translation.)

Ullman, Walter. *The Growth of Papal Government in the Middle Ages.* New York: Barnes and Noble, Inc., 1953.

Walker, Leslie J., S. J. (trans. and commentator). *The Discourses of Niccolò Machiavelli.* New Haven: Yale University Press, 1950.

Index

ACKNOWLEDGMENTS

The author wishes to thank the following publishers for permission to quote from their publications listed below:

Clarendon Press
London, England

Byzantium, An Introduction to East Roman Civilization, edited by Norman H. Baynes and H. St. L. B. Moss

Edward Arnold & Co.
London, England

Renaissance and Reformation
by V. H. H. Green

The Macmillan Company
New York

Cambridge Modern History, II
(the 1904 edition)

Royal Historical Society
London, England

Transactions of the Royal Historical Society,
series 4, XIX (1936)